SOCIAL CHANGE AND HALAKHIC EVOLUTION IN AMERICAN ORTHODOXY

T0341889

THE LITTMAN LIBRARY OF
JEWISH CIVILIZATION

Dedicated to the memory of
LOUIS THOMAS SIDNEY LITTMAN
*who founded the Littman Library for the love of God
and as an act of charity in memory of his father*
JOSEPH AARON LITTMAN
and to the memory of
ROBERT JOSEPH LITTMAN
who continued what his father Louis had begun
יהא זכרם ברוך

*'Get wisdom, get understanding:
Forsake her not and she shall preserve thee'*
PROV. 4: 5

*The Littman Library of Jewish Civilization is a registered UK charity
Registered charity no. 1000784*

SOCIAL CHANGE AND HALAKHIC EVOLUTION IN AMERICAN ORTHODOXY

◆

CHAIM I. WAXMAN

London

The Littman Library of Jewish Civilization
in association with Liverpool University Press

The Littman Library of Jewish Civilization
Registered office: 4th floor, 7–10 Chandos Street, London WIG 9DQ

in association with Liverpool University Press
4 Cambridge Street, Liverpool L69 7ZU, UK
www.liverpooluniversitypress.co.uk/littman

Managing Editor: Connie Webber

Distributed in North America by
Oxford University Press Inc., 198 Madison Avenue
New York, NY 10016, USA

Catalogue records for this book are available from the
British Library and the Library of Congress

ISBN 978–1–786941–64–0

Publishing co-ordinator: Janet Moth
Proof-reading: Agi Erdos
Index: Meg Davies
Design and typesetting by Pete Russell, Faringdon, Oxon.

Printed and bound by CPI Group (UK)
Ltd, Croydon, CR0 4YY

PREFACE AND
ACKNOWLEDGEMENTS

I HAVE BEEN ROOTED in the disciplines of sociology and Jewish studies for most of my adult life. Early on I maintained a compartmentalized (schizophrenic?) stance, and kept the two apart. My early work was in the areas of the sociology of social welfare and political sociology, with almost no explicit reference to Jews or Judaism. This followed from the advice I received when I began thinking about a topic for my doctoral dissertation. My adviser, who was a committed Jew, suggested I choose a topic that was not specifically Jewish. This advice, which was given to me in the mid-1960s when cultural pluralism and ethnic pride were part of the American national cultural ideology, was nevertheless very appropriate and helpful. In fact, even today, despite the cultural changes in American society and the American scholarly world over the past half-century, the social scientific study of Jews and Judaism is still frequently seen as parochial. The merging of my scholarly and personal interests was spurred by the Six Day War of June 1967. I was personally affected, and was also intrigued by its initial impact on large segments of American Jewry. Thus began my academic studying of American Jewry.

In the mid-1970s I was invited to give a course on America's Jews at the University of Pittsburgh in its new Jewish studies programme, and shortly afterwards I was invited to give a similar course at Yeshiva University's Wurzweiler School of Social Work, in its new summer block programme. During the second half of the 1980s, Rabbi Dr Norman Lamm, who was then president of Yeshiva University, invited me to join with several colleagues, under the direction Rabbi Robert Hirt, to help establish the Orthodox Forum, an annual meeting of Jewish scholars, educators, and communal professionals who would serve as a think-tank for the Modern Orthodox community. At the first Orthodox Forum, in September 1989, I presented a paper which was sub-sequently published in the Orthodox journal *Tradition*, and in the first vol-ume of what became a series of conference volumes. That was the first of several articles that began as papers I delivered at meetings of the Forum. Several year later, the newly established Rutgers University Center for the Study of Jewish Life (now the Allen and Joan Bildner Center for the Study of Jewish Life) held a major conference on 'Modern Orthodox Judaism: Visions and Challenges', where my paper analysing the 'haredization' of American

Orthodoxy sparked considerable feedback. Since then, I have been studying American Orthodoxy, and especially its changing standards of religious practice.

It was as a Dorset Fellow at a seminar of the Oxford Centre for Hebrew and Jewish Studies that I began to see the unity in much of my writing and decided to rethink and rework the material within the framework of a new book. I thank the seminar convenors, Adam Ferziger and Miri Freud-Kandel, as well as my colleagues in that seminar for challenging and inspiring me.

When I discussed several possible publishers with Shaul Stampfer, he enthusiastically recommended the Littman Library of Jewish Civilization, with whose books I had long been familiar. Haym Soloveitchik reinforced that recommendation and sang the praises of the painstaking editing that it provides. I am very grateful for those recommendations, which were anything but exaggerations. Littman's managing editor, Connie Webber, and publishing co-ordinator, Janet Moth, are an amazingly knowledgeable and skilled team whose tireless devotion to this work I greatly appreciate.

A number of friends and colleagues read and commented on earlier drafts of sections of this book and/or assisted in other ways, and I am grateful to all of them, especially Kimmy Caplan, Yehuda Gellman, Jeffrey Gurock, Ranon Katzoff, Menachem Kellner, Marty Lockshin, Uzi Rebhun, and Gideon Sylvester.

I also thank the staffs of the Rutgers University Library, Hebrew University Library, and the National Library of Israel.

Finally, to Chaya, my lifetime partner, most wonderful critic, and strongest moral supporter, who keeps me laughing. I can never sufficiently express my love and deepest gratitude. It's been a fascinating ride, and I pray that we continue on it together in good health 'till 120'.

This book is dedicated to our children, grandchildren, and great-grandchildren, each of whom has and will, consciously or not, inevitably experience halakhic evolution.

CONTENTS

NOTE ON TRANSLITERATION

THE TRANSLITERATION of Hebrew in this book reflects consideration of the type of book it is, in terms of its content, purpose, and readership. The system adopted therefore reflects a broad approach to transcription, rather than the narrower approaches found in the *Encyclopaedia Judaica* or other systems developed for text-based or linguistic studies. The aim has been to reflect the pronunciation prescribed for modern Hebrew, rather than the spelling or Hebrew word structure, and to do so using conventions that are generally familiar to the English-speaking reader.

In accordance with this approach, no attempt is made to indicate the distinctions between *alef* and *ayin*, *tet* and *taf*, *kaf* and *kuf*, *sin* and *samekh*, since these are not relevant to pronunciation; likewise, the *dagesh* is not indicated except where it affects pronunciation. Following the principle of using conventions familiar to the majority of readers, however, transcriptions that are well established have been retained even when they are not fully consistent with the transliteration system adopted. On similar grounds, the *tsadi* is rendered by 'tz' in such familiar words as barmitzvah. Likewise, the distinction between *het* and *khaf* has been retained, using *h* for the former and *kh* for the latter; the associated forms are generally familiar to readers, even if the distinction is not actually borne out in pronunciation, and for the same reason the final *heh* is indicated too. As in Hebrew, no capital letters are used, except that an initial capital has been retained in transliterating titles of published works (for example, *Shulhan arukh*).

Since no distinction is made between *alef* and *ayin*, they are indicated by an apostrophe only in intervocalic positions where a failure to do so could lead an English-speaking reader to pronounce the vowel cluster as a diphthong— as, for example, in *ha'ir*—or otherwise mispronounce the word.

The *sheva na* is indicated by an *e*—*perikat ol, reshut*—except, again, when established convention dictates otherwise.

The *yod* is represented by *i* when it occurs as a vowel (*bereshit*), by *y* when it occurs as a consonant (*yesodot*), and by *yi* when it occurs as both (*yisra'el*).

Names have generally been left in their familiar forms, even when this is inconsistent with the overall system.

INTRODUCTION

O RTHODOX JUDAISM did not exist until the nineteenth century. Rather, what prevailed was traditional Judaism. 'Orthodoxy' as a term was introduced in the early nineteenth century with the emergence of Reform Judaism. As Samson Raphael Hirsch averred, 'It was the modern, "progressive" Jews who first applied the epithet "Orthodox" to their "old-style," backward brethren to distinguish them, in a derogatory sense. Initially, the old-style Jews resented this label, and rightly so.'[1] It was in response that the 'old-style Jews' transformed the disparaging epithet and adopted it as a badge of honour. Since then, Ashkenazi Orthodox Jewry in the United States, that is, Orthodox Jewry that stems from Europe, has divided into two basic sub-groups, broadly referred to as ultra-Orthodox and Modern Orthodox.[2] The ultra-Orthodox are further subdivided into the 'yeshivish', those who follow the Lithuanian yeshiva traditions, and the 'hasidish', the followers of hasidic sects. These groupings developed in central and eastern Europe, and did not exist in America until the second half of the nineteenth century. In America, as will be discussed, the Modern Orthodox are now subdivided between the 'Centrist' Orthodox, who have become more circumscribed in religious perspective, and the 'Open' Orthodox, who adopt a less restrictive religious perspective.

[1] Hirsch, *Collected Writings*, vi. 114.
[2] Although, as will be discussed, the Jews in what became the United States were predominantly of the Sephardi tradition, by the time of the American Revolution in 1776, the majority were Ashkenazim. In 1989 Daniel Elazar reported that 'the Sephardic community [in America] comprises approximately 2.89% of the general Jewish population' (Elazar, *The Other Jews*, 166). Analyses of data from the 1990 National Jewish Population Survey suggested that the number of Sephardim was probably higher but that Sephardim still comprised considerably less than 10 per cent of America's Jews (DellaPergola and Rebhun, 'Sociodemographic and Identification Aspects' (Heb.)). Analyses of data from the Pew Research Center, 'A Portrait of Jewish Americans' (2013), indicate that the percentage of Sephardim in the United States is actually lower than it was in 1990 (I thank Uzi Rebhun for these data analyses). There was a small wave of immigration of Iranian Jews following the revolution there, but that has been offset by the immigration of Russian and Israeli Jews; the former are almost exclusively Ashkenazim and the vast majority of the latter are as well (Rebhun and Lev Ari, *American Israelis*, 55). It may be presumed that the percentage of Ashkenazim among Orthodox American Jews is even higher than in the wider American Jewish population. Therefore, when we speak of Orthodox Jews in America, we are overwhelmingly speaking of Ashkenazim.

It should be emphasized that these divisions of Orthodoxy are what the sociologist Max Weber called 'ideal types': they are 'ideal' not in the sense of being best but in the sense that they are concepts. They are heuristic devices constructed for the purpose of understanding and analysing phenomena, including groups. As Weber put it, an ideal type 'is not a *description* of reality but it aims to give unambiguous means of expression to such a description'.[3] Ideal types do not actually exist in the pure form, and there is much overlap among them. Moreover, perhaps because of the variations within Orthodoxy, there are no precise and acceptable terms which adequately capture the basic nature of its streams or branches. For example, 'ultra-Orthodoxy' has an implicitly pejorative connotation, as does 'sectarian'. More recently, the term 'haredi' (pl. haredim) has been imported from Israel and applied to the more conservative wing of American Orthodoxy. Literally, it means one who trembles before God, and it has the advantage of being acceptable to many of those who identify with a version of Orthodoxy that emphasizes ritual punctiliousness. One of its disadvantages is that it obscures many differences between American ultra-Orthodox and their Israeli counterparts. For lack of a better term, 'ultra-Orthodoxy' will be used throughout this book to refer to that branch of American Orthodoxy that is variously known as 'right-wing', 'haredi', or 'sectarian'.[4] A similar difficulty exists with respect to the other branch, with some preferring Centrist Orthodoxy in place of Modern Orthodoxy rather than seeing it as one stream within a larger Modern Orthodoxy grouping. Because of its history and wide usage, I will use the term Modern Orthodoxy to refer to the larger grouping.

As indicated, these are 'ideal types', and not all ultra-Orthodox or Modern Orthodox Jews in America neatly exemplify these characteristics. To take but one example: as will be seen, American ultra-Orthodox Jews as a group have lower incomes than their Modern Orthodox counterparts. This, of course, does not mean that *all* American ultra-Orthodox Jews have lower incomes than all the Modern Orthodox. Indeed, there are many wealthy ultra-Orthodox Jews and there are many Modern Orthodox Jews who are barely getting by economically. We are dealing with *group* characteristics. This type of situation is invariably found when characterizing social groups. Sociologist Gerhard Lenski makes the point with respect to definitions of social classes, and points out that there may be overlap, with no firm lines of division between them:

[3] Weber, *The Methodology of the Social Sciences*, 90.
[4] See S. C. Heilman, *Defenders of the Faith*, 11–13. For an expression of opposition to the designation 'ultra-Orthodox' see Shafran, 'Swearing Off the "U" Word'. For a view favouring use of the term, see Waxman, 'Is It All in the Name?'.

Whether we like it or not, this kind of phrasing is forced on us by the nature of the reality we seek to analyze. In most cases human populations simply are not stratified into a limited number of clearly differentiated, highly discrete categories. Rather, they tend to be strung out along continua which lack breaks that can be utilized as class boundaries. Furthermore, if we were to insist that members of classes stand in *identical* positions with respect to the distribution of things of value, we should have thousands, possibly millions, of classes in many societies, most with but a handful of members, and some with only one.[5]

Broadly speaking, ultra-Orthodox Jews look askance upon and separate themselves as much as possible from the norms and values of modernity, which they view as antithetical to and threatening of what they view as 'authentic Judaism'. In contrast, Modern Orthodox Jews have an essentially positive view of modernity and see their role as being involved in society and improving it.

The framework of this book is sociological rather than ideological or religio-legal. Within that context, and borrowing from the pioneer French sociologist Émile Durkheim, Orthodox Judaism is viewed phenomenologically and defined broadly, recognizing variations in the systems of beliefs and practices maintained by those who define themselves and are defined by others as Orthodox Jews. The 'practices' part of the system is conceived as halakhah (Orthodox religious law). A specialist might object that not only are there different levels and views of halakhah but that there are also Orthodox Jewish practices which are not pursued to accord with halakhah, but which, rather, can be characterized as *minhag* (custom). Indeed, that is true. However, those differences are not highly significant for a sociological portrait and understanding of Orthodox Jews and Judaism. As Rabbi Nachum Rabinowitz points out, even the great halakhist Maimonides often used a single broad term, *mitsvah* (obligation), for different types and levels of halakhic requirement, some of which are biblical and others of which are rabbinic in origin.[6]

This book looks at Orthodox Judaism in America from the nineteenth century until today, examining a series of halakhic changes as well as changes in what is deemed to be proper Orthodox conduct, such as developments that have taken place with respect to the status of women. In some cases, the movement has been towards greater leniency and openness; in others, it has been towards rigidity and isolation; and in many cases we witness two diametrically opposed trends within different sectors of the American Orthodox community. I will attempt to explain the various directions in which 'acceptable' Orthodox behaviour is moving by studying these changes from a social

<hr>

[5] Lenski, *Power and Privilege*, 76–7.
[6] Rabinovitch, *Studies in Maimonides* (Heb.), 74.

and psychological perspective.[7] Where the historian Adam Ferziger provides a convincing institutional analysis of changes within Orthodoxy over the past half-century or so,[8] I will offer an explanation of those institutional changes from the perspective of the community they impact on, in terms of their effect on their members' religious outlook and ritual behaviour. But to understand how and why these changes are taking place, we need first to consider the beginnings of Orthodox Judaism in America and its development since the late nineteenth century.

Judaism in America until the End of the Nineteenth Century

The initial five Jewish communities in what became the United States—Shearith Israel (New York); Yeshuat Israel (Newport, Rhode Island); Mikveh Israel (Philadelphia, Pennsylvania); Beth Elohim (Charleston, South Carolina); and Mikveh Israel (Savannah, Georgia)—were established by Sephardim, Jews of the Spanish and Portuguese tradition. The leadership and liturgy of the congregations remained Sephardi even though, as in New York's Shearith Israel, by the time of the American Revolution the majority of the membership was Ashkenazi. In fact, few Sephardim arrived in America after 1760: from the beginning of the eighteenth century, more Ashkenazim—from England and central Europe—than Sephardim immigrated. The Ashkenazim seem to have integrated quite well into the Sephardi communities, so well in fact that the rate of intermarriage between the two groups grew considerably during the century.

A very important feature of these synagogue communities was the absence of rabbinic leadership. Rabbis did not begin to appear significantly on the American scene until well into the nineteenth century, and the traditional rabbinic scholarly elite did not exist until the twentieth century. The same individual, invariably the most Jewishly educated person in the community but without formal rabbinic qualifications or ordination, often served both as 'minister' (as synagogue rabbis were then called in America) and cantor (ḥazan), and also read from the Torah. Since few Jewish rituals require the presence of an ordained rabbi, according to traditional Jewish law the absence of rabbis did not present an insurmountable problem for these communities. Matters relating to divorce and some other issues, which did require an ordained rabbi, were referred to the rabbinates in Amsterdam and London.

---

[7] This is not a work in halakhic methodology and therefore does not deal with the halakhic process or with rabbinic jurisprudence. Among the major works on those, see Berkovitz, *Not in Heaven*; Broyde and Bedzow, *The Codification of Jewish Law*; Lewittes, *Principles and Development of Jewish Law*; Sperber, *The Path of Halakhah* (Heb.); and Urbach, *The Halakhah* (Heb.).

[8] Ferziger, *Beyond Sectarianism*.

While the absence of ordained rabbis did not severely impair the day-to-day routine of the Shearith Israel community in New York or the other communities, it did have a great impact upon the cultural life of American Jewry. Specifically, it meant the perpetuation of a rather low level of Jewish education which, in turn, affected the degree to which the community could retain its members within the fold. Instruction of children was the responsibility of the minister in each community, and usually consisted of three to five years of learning to read Hebrew and to understand basic passages from the Bible and prayer book, and becoming acquainted with the fundamentals of the synagogue service and the Jewish ceremonial calendar.

One of the earliest such schools was established by Shearith Israel in 1755. It was a day school; in addition to Hebrew, general education, including such subjects as Spanish, English writing, and arithmetic, was also provided. The school lasted until the late eighteenth century, when most of the city's Jews left New York.[9] Subsequently, several other attempts were made to establish Jewish day schools in New York during the nineteenth century, but they were short-lived. The Jewish day-school movement did not really take off in the United States until the twentieth century.

As Jonathan Sarna suggests, America was built on democracy, and that affected Judaism as well. America contained the full range of Jews, from the very devout to the most assimilated. Jews practised, or did not practise, their Judaism as they saw fit.[10] Although there were many who went to great lengths to remain observant, overall it is difficult to disagree with the assessment of the prominent American Jewish financier Haym Solomon, a Polish-born Ashkenazi Jew who, in a letter to family members still living in Europe, commented that there was 'vaynig Yiddishkeit' (very little Judaism) in America.

Increased immigration during the early nineteenth century led to the break-up of the single-synagogue community. Larger cities were now able to support more than one synagogue, and new communities began to develop along lines that reflected their members' places of origin or religious practice. In New York, for example, Shearith Israel was *the* synagogue until the 1820s, and its officials set the standards for acceptable behaviour. Although there had been a decline in traditional religious behaviour—such as increasingly public violations of the norms of sabbath observance and dietary laws, and even marriage to non-Jews—Shearith Israel was nevertheless the single New York Jewish community. In 1825, however, a group of Ashkenazi members seceded and formed their own synagogue, B'nai Jeshurun. By 1840 there were four more Ashkenazi synagogues in New York, and by 1860 there were

[9] Grinstein, *The Rise of the Jewish Community of New York*, 228–9.
[10] Sarna, *American Judaism*, 46–7.

about twenty-seven, the overwhelming majority of which were formed by a series of secessions from older synagogues.

This pattern continued across the country. There were secessions from older synagogues and, as Jews moved to new towns, there was a mushrooming of new synagogues. Since there was no structure or organization to maintain uniformity and overall control, Jewish communal service societies were formed independent of the synagogue, and men set themselves up as rabbis and performed marriages and divorces as they wished, without the sanction of any established synagogue.

In contrast to the denominational character of contemporary American Judaism, until the 1820s there was only one form of Judaism in the United States: traditional Judaism in the Sephardi ritual. In 1820, the Jewish population in the United States numbered fewer than 5,000. By 1880, it had grown to about a quarter of a million, most of whom had immigrated from Germany and other parts of central Europe.[11] During those years, American Judaism was dramatically transformed by the rapid growth and development of Reform Judaism. The first American attempt at religious reform of the synagogue service took place in Charleston, South Carolina, in 1824. Headed by Isaac Harby, an educator, journalist, and dramatist,[12] a group of forty-seven members of Congregation Beth Elohim who were unhappy with the synagogue service submitted a petition at a 'meeting of the Convention of Israelites', the community meeting, to implement a number of changes.[13] When their petition was rejected they organized themselves as the Reformed Society of Israelites and formed their own congregation. Although it lasted only a few years, it established a pattern for the following decades. With the determination and organizational skills of the Reverend Isaac Mayer Wise,[14] by 1880 American Judaism had a full-fledged Reform branch with a rabbinic seminary—Hebrew Union College (HUC); a rabbinic organization—the Central Conference of American Rabbis (CCAR); and a synagogue organization—the Union of American Hebrew Congregations (now the Union of Reform Judaism), which by then comprised more than

[11] The first few Jewish communities were founded by Sephardi Jews, but by the late eighteenth century most of the approximately 2,000 Jews in the country were Ashkenazim from central Europe.   [12] For a biography, see Zola, *Isaac Harby of Charleston, 1788–1828*.

[13] Their initial request to the *adjunta* of Beth Elohim included abbreviating the service, having some of its parts read in both Hebrew and English, eliminating the practice of auctioning synagogue honours, and having a weekly discourse, or sermon, in English. By the second half of the twentieth century, changes such as these, which were rejected by the board, were completely normative in American Orthodox congregations, but at the time they were major innovations.

[14] For a biography of Wise, the institution builder of American Reform Judaism, see Temkin, *Creating American Reform Judaism*.

half of all known synagogues in the country.[15] There is some disagreement as to whether the growth of American Reform Judaism was rooted primarily in theology or in sociology and social psychology—in other words, a desire for Americanization and respectability.[16] Certainly, the latter played a very significant role.

Traditional Judaism in America also underwent change, though not as radical as that of Reform. Under the leadership of the Reverend Isaac Leeser, there took place what Lance Sussman termed the 'Protestantization of American Judaism'.[17] For example, Leeser established the sermon as a part of the standard service. The tradition the world over was that sermons were delivered infrequently, usually twice a year, on the sabbath between Rosh Hashanah and Yom Kippur and on the sabbath before Pesach. The weekly synagogue service had consisted solely of prayer.[18] In 1843 Leeser persuaded Philadelphia's Congregation Mikveh Israel to adopt the practice of a weekly sermon in English. He also formally transformed the position of *ḥazan* into that of minister,[19] and he introduced his English-language translation of the Bible into the synagogue

---

[15] Silverstein, *Alternatives to Assimilation*, 48–9.

[16] Leon Jick views American Reform Judaism as a product of Americanization: see his *The Americanization of the Synagogue*. Naomi Cohen and Michael Meyer argue that theology was also in play: see N. W. Cohen, *Encounter with Emancipation*; Meyer, *Response to Modernity*.

[17] Sussman, 'Isaac Leeser and the Protestantization of American Judaism'. Leeser had no formal schooling in Judaism: he was self-taught and had an abiding reverence for Jewish tradition as he understood it. Born in Westphalia, Germany, he arrived in the United States at the age of 18, and spent his life in the Jewish community and in Jewish communal work. For twenty-one years, from 1829 to 1850, he served as *ḥazan*, reader, and preacher in Congregation Mikveh Israel in Philadelphia. It would not be much of an overstatement to suggest that he single-handedly stamped the basic character of American Judaism—certainly its traditionalist branch. Among his accomplishments are: advancing the professionalization of the rabbinate; the first English-language translation of the Bible (which can still be found in many older synagogues), as well as translations of the Ashkenazi and Sephardi prayer books, and of Moses Mendelssohn's *Jerusalem*; the establishment of a Jewish hospital in Philadelphia; the establishment of the Hebrew Sunday school, Hebrew high school, and the first American Jewish seminary, Maimonides College, in Philadelphia; the first American Jewish Publication Society; the writing and publishing of numerous Hebrew textbooks; the editorship of a national English-language Jewish weekly newspaper; and the organization of America's Jews to defend the rights and well-being of Jews in other parts of the world. There is some debate as to where to place him in terms of contemporary American Judaism. Some scholars, such as the late Moshe Davis, view him as the forerunner of Conservative Judaism (see Davis, *The Emergence of Conservative Judaism*). Sussman, *Isaac Leeser and the Making of American Judaism*, considers him more akin to Modern Orthodoxy than to Conservatism, neither of which existed at the time. Leeser did not receive rabbinic ordination, but because he functioned as a religious leader he adopted the American Protestant term 'Reverend'.

[18] Traditional Jewish communities in America at the time were small and it was not feasible to gather a quorum for a weekday prayer service.

[19] The terms *ḥazan* and minister applied to the position. A knowledgeable individual occupying that position was called Reverend.

service. When the first wave of east European Jewish immigrants arrived, they found a Judaism that was alien to them.[20]

East European Jews and Their Immigration to America

Prior to 1869 few Jewish immigrants arrived in America from the Pale of Settlement, the area within the Russian empire to which Jews were restricted,[21] but between 1869 and 1880 an estimated 30,000 emigrated from there to the United States.[22] The major cause of the increased Jewish emigration from Russia at this time was the severe economic situation faced by many Jews, accompanied by demographic growth and the rapid pace of industrialization, from which Jews were excluded.[23] In March 1881 Tsar Alexander II was assassinated, sparking anti-Jewish riots and massacres in scores of Jewish communities. Following these, laws that restricted the lives of Jews were passed. The combination of economic and political hardships and the fear of physical persecution generated a massive Jewish migration from eastern Europe, with the overwhelming majority making their way to the United States.[24] That dramatic influx of almost 3 million immigrant Jews from eastern Europe between 1881 and 1924 transformed American Jewry and American Judaism in fundamental ways.[25]

Most of the east European Jews who went to America, especially prior to 1881, did so in response to economic incentives.[26] The first to arrive were probably among the least rooted, both occupationally and religiously, in their native Jewish communities. As Liebman suggests, 'Willing as they were to take extended leave of family and home, they were no doubt less committed to tradition than their relatives and neighbors who came much later.'[27] To the

[20] There were several rabbis of east European background in the United States at midcentury, but they did not have much influence on the condition of American Judaism at the time. See Tabak, 'Rabbi Abraham Rice of Baltimore'; Sherman, 'Bernard Illowy and Nineteenth-Century American Orthodoxy'; Ellenson, *Tradition in Transition*, 101–22.

[21] The Pale of Settlement was an area of about 386,000 squares miles which spanned the territory from the Baltic to the Black Sea and comprised ten Polish and fifteen Russian provinces with 236 districts.   [22] Wischnitzer, *To Dwell in Safety*, 289 n. 1.

[23] Kuznets, 'Immigration of Russian Jews to the United States'; Stampfer, 'The Geographic Background of East European Jewish Migration', 223.

[24] Until recently, it was assumed that the pogroms were the major stimulus to the emigration of Jews from the Pale of Settlement, especially after 1881. More recent analyses of post-1881 emigration data indicate that 'The onset of Jewish mass migration was geographically unrelated to the 1881 pogroms; rather, post-1881 migration originated from areas not subject to pogroms and was a continuation of pre-1881 trends.' See Spitzer, 'Pogroms, Networks, and Migration', 4.

[25] Waxman, *America's Jews in Transition*.

[26] Kuznets, 'Immigration of Russian Jews to the United States', 94; Stampfer, 'The Geographic Background of East European Jewish Migration', 224.

[27] Liebman, 'Orthodoxy in American Jewish Life', 29.

extent that they had occupations, they were of the sort that were not dependent on a specific community. In addition, for many, traditional Judaism did not significantly shape their lives. When, however, they did wish to express their Judaism, they wanted to do it in a familiar religious environment. Whether they were personally observant or not, they came from an area in which traditional Judaism was the prevalent culture of the Jews. Whether they regularly went to synagogue or not, they knew what a synagogue was and, if they had reason to go, they knew where to go and what was expected, and that was very different from what confronted them in America. Much more than the differences between the Ashkenazi and Sephardi traditions, it was the Americanized synagogue service which was alien to them.

The east European immigrants tended to keep to themselves socially. One reason for this was that they were typically looked upon negatively by American Jews of central European, especially German, origin. As Hyman Grinstein put it, 'The German Jew considered the East European, whether he was a Lithuanian, a Pole, a Rumanian, or a Galician, a person of a lower status. He was an *Ostjude* to be kept at arm's length.'[28] In addition, Jews from different countries frequently have different synagogue customs. As mentioned above, this had been a major reason why, in several American cities in earlier decades, Jews from central Europe broke away from the parent congregations which followed the Sephardi tradition.[29] Not surprisingly, therefore, the east European immigrants established synagogues in their own traditions, such as the 'Suvalker shul', the 'Kalvarie (Kalvarija) shul', and the 'Bialystoker shul'. The desire to stay close to their fellow countrymen also manifested itself in the unique phenomenon of *landsmanshaftn*, fraternal societies of Jewish immigrants from the same locality which provided members with social networks and a range of social services, such as free loans, medical assistance, and burial rights.[30]

In an analysis of the membership lists of *landsmanshaftn* Shaul Stampfer found that the majority of Jews who emigrated to the United States from eastern Europe during the era of mass migration were from the north-western part of the Pale of Settlement.[31] Joel Perlmann, in his analysis of data on Jewish immigrants in the passenger lists of ships at the port of New York around 1900, came to a similar conclusion,[32] as did Yannay Spitzer, who suggests

---

[28] Grinstein, 'The Efforts of East European Jewry', 76.

[29] Waxman, *America's Jews in Transition*, 11.

[30] Soyer, *Jewish Immigrant Associations*; Weisser, *A Brotherhood of Memory*.

[31] Stampfer, 'The Geographic Background of East European Jewish Migration'; Spitzer, 'Pogroms, Networks, and Migration'.

[32] Perlmann, *The Local Geographic Origins of Russian-Jewish Immigrants*, 18.

that although the sources and patterns are complex, there was an over-representation of immigrants from the Polish and Lithuanian sectors.[33] In other words, there was within this wave of immigration a disproportionate representation of 'Litvaks', those from the area that Jews defined as 'Lita', Lithuania. As Dovid Katz points out, 'In the study of Lithuanian Jewish culture, the word *Lithuania* does not refer to the territory of the present Republic of Lithuania, nor to that of its predecessor in the period between the world wars. It refers to a land known in Jewish cultural history as *Lita*',[34] which is much larger than the contemporary country of Lithuania. Jewish Lita 'stretches from the Baltic Sea in the northwest (modern Lithuania and Latvia); Bialystok (now Poland) and Brisk (now Brest, Belarus) at its southwest; to somewhere near Smolensk (now in the Russian Federation) in the northeast; and, finally, defining an arc for its southern border, touching the Black Sea at a point just east of Odessa (now Ukraine)'.[35]

The evidence indicates that rabbis who immigrated from eastern Europe were also disproportionately Litvaks. For example, in 1902 the fifth volume of Ben-Zion Eisenstadt's six-volume encyclopedic Hebrew work, *Rabbis and Writers of the Generation*, which provided biographical sketches of prominent rabbis and authors of works in the Jewish world of the time, was published. Titled *Sages of Israel in America*, it is not definitive but does supply a useful source of information on rabbinic figures,[36] containing brief biographies of 198 rabbis and authors, the vast majority of whom were Orthodox. An analysis of their background reveals that 128 of the 198 subjects, or 65 per cent, were from Lita. Likewise, Kimmy Caplan, in his study of immigrant rabbis at the time, writes that the overwhelming majority were from Russia or Lita, and most were from towns and villages in the Kovno (Kaunas) or Vilna (Vilnius) districts.[37] It is thus fair to say that Jews from Lita and their culture played a significant role in the character of east European Jewry in America at the time. By the mid-twentieth century, the differences among American Jews who originated from Lita, Galicia (an area that straddles the borders of Poland and the Ukraine), and Poland had, to all intents and purposes, disappeared. By then they viewed themselves as American Jews of east European background, and were oblivious to cultural differences that a half-century earlier had been significant, at least among themselves. At the end of the nineteenth and beginning of the twentieth centuries, however, although to others, such as German Jews, they were all east Europeans, *Ostjuden*, and no more, each group of east European immigrants was convinced of its uniqueness.

[33] Spitzer, 'Pogroms, Networks, and Migration'.   [34] Katz, *Lithuanian Jewish Culture*, 14.
[35] Ibid. 15.   [36] Sherman, *Orthodox Judaism in America*, 57.
[37] Caplan, *Orthodoxy in the New World* (Heb.), 71.

Indeed, as Mordechai Zalkin indicates, careful 'examination of a wide variety of cultural and behavioral elements of these people, as well as of their own collective self-perception and self-determination, reveals a unique picture'.[38] He shows that among the most outstanding characteristics of Litvaks were their rationalism and realism. These manifested themselves most decidedly in the premium they placed on literacy and erudition. Lita had a long history of being the major supplier of communal rabbis and teachers, *melamdim*, to all of Europe.[39] For some, the values of literacy and realism contributed to the growth of traditional Jewish scholarship and the development of the famous Torah academies, higher yeshivas, of Lita, such as Slobodka, Telz, and Mir.[40] Those values also spurred the development of the Musar movement, the nineteenth-century movement among yeshivas in Lita which strove for ethical and spiritual self-discipline.[41] For others, the same values spurred the development of a strong Haskalah, the Jewish Enlightenment movement, which was a powerful presence in Lita for more than half a century.[42] Its unique character in Lita manifested itself in circles comprising rich and poor, writers and musicians, alongside businessmen and tradesmen, traditionalists and radicals. This social mix among the local supporters of the Haskalah (known as maskilim) developed as an attempt to integrate a traditional Jewish lifestyle with central European Haskalah values.[43] In sum, Litvaks were

largely non-hasidic people, who on the one hand preserved the old, traditional religious way of life, but were on the other hand open to the 'new winds' and tried, albeit to a limited extent, to take advantage of almost everything modernity could offer. They represented the old, maskilic, moderate integrative option which was already neglected by both the hasidim and the progressive elements.[44]

Another of the special characteristics and qualities of Lithuanian Jewish culture was manifested in the status of rabbis. Lita was a traditional Jewish society but its rabbis did not reign supreme.[45] Zalkin indicates that, in contrast to the position of rabbis in the hasidic world, rabbis in Lita were viewed almost exclusively as talmudic scholars and halakhic experts, particularly in the area of *isur veheter*, ritual law, which includes the laws of *kashrut*,

[38] Zalkin, 'Lithuanian Jewry and the Concept of "East European Jewry"', 61.   [39] Ibid. 62.
[40] Ibid. See also Stampfer, *Lithuanian Yeshivas of the Nineteenth Century*.
[41] Brown, *The Lithuanian Musar Movement* (Heb.); Etkes, *Rabbi Israel Salanter and the Mussar Movement*; Y. Mirsky, 'Musar Movement'.
[42] Zalkin, *A New Dawn* (Heb.), 62–75; id., *From Ḥeder to School* (Heb.). For a history of the Haskalah, see Wodziński, *Haskalah and Hasidism in the Kingdom of Poland*.
[43] Zalkin, *A New Dawn* (Heb.), 62.
[44] Zalkin, 'Lithuanian Jewry and the Concept of "East European Jewry"', 69.
[45] There were no branches or denominations of Judaism in Lita. Jewish religious tradition there meant what today is labelled Orthodoxy, and its rabbis were in the same sense Orthodox.

sexual conduct, sabbath observance, and so on. However, when it came to questions relating to broader matters, such as issues of communal policy, most people gave no special weight to the rabbis' opinions and did not consult with them. The limited authority of rabbis also stemmed from the fact that they were appointed by the local elite who, from the outset, restricted their power. This was not a phenomenon limited to the nineteenth century: there are many indications of this approach in earlier periods. Moreover, even as rabbis were viewed as the local authority in halakhic matters, it was not uncommon to find members of the community who challenged their halakhic rulings, and when rabbis were viewed as overstepping their authority they were even subjected to verbal and sometimes physical abuse. Throughout the nineteenth century, the laity steadily grew in stature, often at the expense of the power and authority of the rabbis.[46]

The vast majority of the immigrants to America were, of course, not rabbis. They were individuals who, in Lithuania as elsewhere, consulted their rabbi in a limited range of situations. The major motive for their emigration was economic, and they were ready to undertake the move despite exhortations from rabbinic leaders, who feared its religious consequences. How intense and widespread the opposition to emigrating to America was is questionable, but it was a factor to be reckoned with. As Stampfer has suggested,

The move to America might well have been motivated by economic considerations, but it was opposed not only by sentimental attachments to the home but by religious ones as well. It was generally felt that it was impossible to observe Jewish religious commandments in the United States, and this was, indeed, not far from the truth. Laws of sexual purity, the sabbath, and even kosher food laws were often hard to keep . . . Those who did immigrate were then, ipso facto, those who were least likely to heed the words of the rabbis and who thus had a decided bent toward rationalism and an openness to change.[47]

Nor was it only the masses who emigrated for economic purposes; rabbis did as well. Like others, they went to America to make a living and, in fact, many started in regular occupations—whatever work they could find—

---

[46] Zalkin, 'Leading Local Rabbi'? (Heb.).

[47] Stampfer, 'The Geographic Background of East European Jewish Migration', 228–9. Menahem Blondheim has surveyed scores of writings by rabbis who emigrated to the United States, and found that what stands out in virtually all of them is their use of an apologetic and defensive tone to justify their decision. It is variously described as a move imposed by heavy debts, health problems, entanglements with government in eastern Europe, or, more positively, to enable a family reunion. 'With just a single exception', he writes, 'I did not find in the scores of explanations in the prefaces even one rabbi who presented his immigration as a mission and as a response to a challenge, as a premeditated attempt "to heal the religious rupture" of his brethren in America.' Blondheim, 'The Orthodox Rabbinate Discovers America' (Heb.), 489.

before assuming rabbinical positions.[48] Earning a living was viewed by Litvaks as both a societal and a religious obligation. For many, rabbinic positions in large cities which had substantial Orthodox populations were preferred over those in remote parts of the country. Others were willing to serve as rabbis in communities where there wasn't even a quorum of religiously observant Jews. Those who had no offers in the rabbinate sought non-rabbinic positions in the Jewish community.

Facing the urgent need to secure a livelihood and feed their families, the vast majority of the immigrants were unable to be religiously observant in accordance with tradition. Indeed, it seems reasonable to assume that, even before setting foot in the country, they probably knew that they would have to work on a Saturday, the sabbath.[49] This did not mean that they rejected Judaism. There were those who did of course, but the stories of huge numbers of immigrants throwing their tefillin (phylacteries) into the ocean on their way to the United States as a symbol of their rejection of Judaism are highly exaggerated. Most tried to adapt their religious practice to the realities of American society and culture without abandoning religion entirely. Indeed, according to Marshall Sklare,[50] this was the underlying theme of Conservative Judaism, which can be said to have begun with the founding in 1886 of the Jewish Theological Seminary of America in New York by moderate traditionalists as a bulwark against Reform. He viewed Conservatism as a uniquely American religious movement that responded to the changing needs and values of American Jewry and reshaped Judaism accordingly. Those immigrants from eastern

[48] For example, Rabbi Eliezer Silver—who immigrated in 1907 and went on to become president of the Union of Orthodox Rabbis of the United States and Canada for several decades, president of Agudath Israel of America, and president of the Orthodox Holocaust rescue committee Vaad Hatzalah—began working in the United States for his wife's uncle as a salesman in the garment industry and later as an insurance salesman (Rakeffet-Rothkoff, *The Silver Era*, 52). As late as the 1950s, Rabbi Anshel Wainhaus, who had studied in the yeshiva of Mir, arrived in the United States via a circuitous route through the good fortune of having obtained a visa from the famous Japanese consul Chiune-Sempo Sugihara. On weekday mornings he was a Talmud teacher at Toras Emes Yeshiva, and in the afternoons and evenings he worked for the Star Drug Company, a pharmaceutical distributor in which he was a partner (Levine, *In Search of Sugihara*; Bachrach, Kassof, and Phillips (eds.), *Flight and Rescue*). At one point during the 1952/3 school year, he held a contest in his Talmud class with the prize of two tickets to the Jackie Gleason television show, one of whose sponsors was the maker of a product distributed by Star Drug. I was the fortunate winner. Such an episode is almost inconceivable today. There were, of course, many differences between the mass immigration era and the immigration that took place several decades later, but these examples show a consistent commitment on the part of Orthodox rabbis to secure a livelihood.

[49] Sarna points to 'the decline of Sabbath observance . . . as an indicator of the spiritual collapse within the Jewish immigrant community' (*American Judaism*, 162). The demand that employees work on Saturday must have been known to the majority of the immigrants while they were still in eastern Europe. [50] Sklare, *Conservative Judaism*.

Europe, and especially their children, who found Orthodoxy to be too con-
fining and inhibiting in their drive for economic and social mobility but
who strongly wished nevertheless to retain their Jewish ethnic and religious
identity embraced Conservative Judaism as the ideal option between the 'too
religious' Orthodox and the 'non-religious' Reform. The Conservative synagogue became the central institution of the new Jewish community, and the
community's religious and secular activities were centred within it. However,
the Conservative synagogue movement did not fully develop until 1913. Before
then, the immigrants founded Orthodox synagogues even if they attended
services infrequently, because that was the only synagogue service with which
they were familiar.[51]

The Beginnings of Ultra-Orthodoxy and Modern Orthodoxy in America

Among both Orthodox rabbis and laity there were different approaches to dealing with the challenges posed by American society and culture. Especially
among rabbis, there was a division between those whom Jeffrey Gurock termed
'resisters' and 'accommodators' of varying degrees,[52] that is, those who resisted Americanization and tried to establish barriers to integration and assimilation, and those who were ready to accept the advantages of American society
by adapting Orthodoxy to it. One major early effort of those who were more
overtly resistant came in the summer of 1902 with the establishment of Agudat
Harabanim, known in English as the Union of Orthodox Rabbis of the United
States and Canada, which delineated a range of matters of concern for the future
of Orthodoxy in the country.[53] For the first half of the twentieth century this was
the most prominent rabbinic organization representing the staunchly Orthodox rabbis. They viewed integration into American society as one step before
assimilation, so they were not prepared to compromise or modify any aspect of
the religious tradition. They represented what is currently referred to as ultra-
Orthodoxy, sectarian Orthodoxy, or haredism.

In the United States even more than in Lita, although the rabbi was considered the halakhic authority in each congregation, Orthodox synagogues and
other communal institutions were generally founded, headed, and operated by

[51] One indication of this is in the 1916 Census of Religious Bodies, which reported '450 more
synagogues than in 1906, an increase of 37.4 percent, which worshipped in foreign languages
only (Hebrew and Yiddish)'. These were surely Orthodox congregations, as, probably, were the
68.3 per cent of older congregations that introduced some English into their services. Engelman, 'Jewish Statistics in the US Census of Religious Bodies', 157.
[52] Gurock, *American Jewish Orthodoxy in Historical Perspective*, 1–62.
[53] Union of Orthodox Rabbis of the United States and Canada, *Jubilee Book* (Heb.), 19–36.

volunteers from the community who were not religious isolationists. Almost all of the Orthodox institutions founded in the late nineteenth and first half of the twentieth century, especially those which became prominent and continue to function today, were not led by rabbis, though they did have rabbis in honorary positions among the leadership. For the most part, the organizers and activists were committed laymen—businessmen and others—who wanted an Orthodoxy that would encourage both religious allegiance and integration into and advancement in American society. Although some of the east European Orthodox of the era of mass immigration were ambivalent about being American, most of their children saw it as a blessing, and they increasingly internalized modern American values and adjusted their Orthodoxy to conform with those values.

It was during this period that the first seeds of what is now Modern Orthodoxy—an Orthodoxy that views modernity in a positive light, and being part of and engaging with the broader American Jewish community as a religious value—began to sprout. Its values were in large measure legitimated religiously through the Rabbi Isaac Elchanan Theological Seminary, the rabbinical seminary of what was then Yeshiva College (now Yeshiva University), which incorporated and encouraged talmudic study accompanied by higher secular education,[54] and the Rabbinical Council of America, the movement's counterpart to the Union of Orthodox Rabbis. Precisely what 'modern' Orthodoxy'[55] meant was never spelled out, and in its initial stages there was not even any attempt to define it. Even afterwards, when it came to be seen as a movement, it was characterized by heterogeneity both philosophically and behaviourally.[56] Especially in the first half of the twentieth century, this approach to Orthodoxy was characterized by an accommodation, with varying degrees of enthusiasm, between Orthodox Judaism and modernity.

Rabbi Dr Joseph B. Soloveitchik and Modern Orthodoxy

Any analysis of the development of Modern Orthodoxy in the twentieth century must take as its focal point Rabbi Joseph B. Soloveitchik, who became the

[54] The institution's motto, which appears on its logo, is 'Torah Umadda'—Torah and secular knowledge. Today, Yeshiva University has four campuses in New York City housing male and female undergraduate schools that offer dual curricula comprising Jewish studies and liberal arts and sciences courses and a theological seminary, as well as graduate schools of Jewish studies, law, medicine, psychology, social work, and Jewish education and administration.

[55] Modern Orthodoxy as a formal movement was not established until after the Second World War; here the term 'modern' is descriptive and therefore not capitalized.

[56] See Liebman, 'Orthodoxy in American Jewish Life'; Bulka (ed.), *Dimensions of Orthodox Judaism*; S. C. Heilman and Cohen, *Cosmopolitans and Parochials*.

unparalleled religious and intellectual leader of the movement. His father, Rabbi Moshe Soloveitchik, had served at the Rabbi Isaac Elchanan Theological Seminary as a *rosh yeshivah* (principal) from 1929 until his death in January 1941. Shortly after he died, Agudat Harabanim proclaimed its right to determine who his successor should be, and asserted the halakhic right of his eldest son to serve in his father's position. The east European students at the seminary supported his appointment, though the American students opposed it as they objected to Agudat Harabanim's influence at the yeshiva.[57] However, the appointment went ahead.

Before taking up his father's role, Rabbi Soloveitchik had lived in Boston where, with his wife Tonya, he established the Maimonides School in 1937. The school inculcated a philosophy that incorporated both Orthodoxy and modernity through its curriculum and activities: it was co-educational throughout, from kindergarten to high school, in all subjects, secular and religious, including the study of Talmud.[58] Boston remained his home throughout his life, but his career and reputation developed from his position at the Theological Seminary. It was there that he forged his institutional base as, for nearly half a century, he was the teacher and mentor of thousands of students, many of whom went on to occupy pulpits and other important positions in the Jewish communal structure. In 1966 the *New York Times* described him as 'one of the world's leading talmudic scholars'.[59] In 1952, he was named chairman of the Halakhah Commission of the Rabbinical Council of America.

Until the mid-1960s his reputation spread primarily by word of mouth, through a range of lectures to a variety of audiences: within the yeshiva's Semicha Program, to the annual convention of the Rabbinical Council of America and Yeshiva University Rabbinic Alumni, and to the lay public through weekly lectures in Boston and at the Moriah Synagogue in Manhattan, which he began giving in the early 1950s. His annual public lecture given on the anniversary of his father's death (*yahrzeit*) was delivered in the packed auditorium of Yeshiva University and became a major public event within the Orthodox community. It was attended by thousands of men and women, and frequently lasted several hours. The lecture manifested rigorous preparation both conceptually and linguistically and, though formally divided into halakhah (law) and aggadah (lore), also invariably incorporated ideas and concepts from philosophy, history, and science. His lectures to his students at the yeshiva, while less formal, were always well prepared: for the students they were an intellectual experi-

---

[57] Rakeffet-Rothkoff, *The Silver Era*, 267–71.
[58] Farber, *An American Orthodox Dreamer*.
[59] Dugan, 'Orthodox Rabbis to Meet Upstate'.

ence, an opportunity to see a great mind at work, because he frequently worked out questions, problems, and issues with his students as he taught.

The lectures that he gave to the lay Jewish public enhanced his growing reputation among those familiar with him as a unique thinker and teacher. He taught classes not only in Talmud and rabbinics, but in the weekly Torah portion as well, and these always incorporated Midrash and Jewish philosophy on a wide range of subjects. In addition, both in his position at Yeshiva University and in his public lectures, he was a 'democratic elitist'—he believed in the authority of the masters of halakhah, but he also believed that everyone should learn, and that mastery of halakhah was not restricted to specific professions. He was unique in not necessarily encouraging his students to go into the rabbinate or become *rashei yeshivah*. This approach contributed to the development of a cadre of learned Modern Orthodox laypeople by enhancing their Jewish self-esteem and encouraging them to continue learning. In turn, they held him in great esteem and looked to him as their mentor. This became increasingly important towards the end of the century, when American society and culture in general witnessed a growing detachment from the formal organizational sphere. Soloveitchik's temperament came across as one that eschewed formal organizational activity and participation and focused on the individual, a very modern, if not postmodern, notion. This first became apparent in the mid-1960s with the publication of his seminal essay, 'The Lonely Man of Faith'.

It was during the 1960s that his reputation and the nature of his leadership underwent change. Until that time, his ideas had mostly been transmitted orally—by word of mouth or via tape recordings by individuals who were present at his talks. His few published writings were typically in Hebrew and Yiddish, in periodicals of limited circulation, with almost nothing in English. Indeed, as late as 1972 the journalist Edward Fiske, writing in the *New York Times*, observed that '"the Rav" is largely unknown outside Orthodox Jewish circles, and even within them, he remains a somewhat cryptic figure. The main reason for this is his reluctance to publish during his lifetime, a practice that is something of a family tradition.' At that time, as Fiske wrote, 'His published bibliography consist[ed] of less than half a dozen substantive articles.'[60]

The first of those substantive articles, 'Confrontation', appeared in 1964, in the relatively new scholarly journal of the Rabbinical Council of America,

---

[60] Fiske, 'Rabbi's Rabbi Keeps the Law Up to Date'. Fiske seems to have been unaware that only a few years earlier Eugene Borowitz, the prominent Reform Jewish theologian and founding editor of the highly regarded 'Journal of Jewish Responsibility', *Sh'ma*, had included him, along with the Jewish Theological Seminary's Abraham Joshua Heschel, as among the leading Jewish theologians and developers of a 'new Jewish theology' (Borowitz, *A New Jewish Theology in the Making*).

Tradition.[61] The article was first delivered as an address at the Rabbinical Council's 1964 midwinter conference, and was in response to overtures from the Vatican to engage in religious dialogue and bring about a reconciliation between Catholicism and Judaism.[62] Through an extensive philosophical analysis, rooted in halakhah and aggadah, of human existence, Soloveitchik rejected interfaith dialogue on theological matters. That part of his essay became policy for the Rabbinical Council and for most of the Orthodox community. There was, however, an important second part to his thesis, which resonated much more with the Modern Orthodox, namely, 'we are determined to participate in every civic, scientific, and political enterprise. We feel obligated to enrich society with our creative talents and to be constructive and useful citizens.'[63] This was not only authoritative legitimation but the assertion of a religious imperative to actively participate in the wider general society.

One year later, his essay 'The Lonely Man of Faith' appeared in the summer 1965 issue of *Tradition*. This essay, which subsequently appeared in book form, was based on a series of lectures in a project titled 'Marriage and Family', sponsored by the National Institute of Mental Health, which focused on the problem of religion in a secular world. This was a time when virtually every observer was predicting the unstoppable secularization and concomitant inevitable demise of religion in the modern and postmodern West. America was viewed as the epitome of 'the secular city', in which 'the death of God' had been proclaimed. How could a person of faith live in such a world? The details of his analysis aside, Soloveitchik's presentation of both the problem and the 'resolution'—which was not really a resolution but an affirmation of a condition—had great appeal to American Modern Orthodox Jews. As moderns living in American society they could not avoid the essential dilemma, and Soloveitchik's response to it was both intellectually and practically persuasive. Basing himself on the two accounts in Genesis of human creation, he proposed that human beings be seen as composed of two distinct parts, 'majestic man' (Adam I) and the 'man of faith' (Adam II). Adam I is commanded to conquer the universe, to be part of what sociologist of religion Peter Berger called the 'world-building process', by imposing '*nomos*', social and cultural order, upon the world.[64] The community of Adam I is pragmatic, 'forged by the indomitable desire for success and triumph and consisting . . . of two grammatical *personae*, the

---

[61] In 1958 the Rabbinical Council of America initiated *Tradition: A Journal of Orthodox Jewish Thought*, whose editors have typically been perceived as intellectuals, particularly among Jews who consider themselves to be Modern Orthodox. Especially in its early years, one of the latent functions of *Tradition* was to provide an air of sophistication to reinforce belief in the ultimate validation and triumph of Modern Orthodoxy over what was viewed as the archaic, exclusivist, and parochial 'ultra-Orthodoxy'.   [62] Korn, 'The Man of Faith and Religious Dialogue'.
[63] J. B. Soloveitchik, 'Confrontation', 27.   [64] P. L. Berger, *The Sacred Canopy*.

"I" and the "thou" who collaborate in order to further their interests'.[65] The man of faith, Adam II, by contrast, is lonely even as he is part of and committed to a community. It is a covenantal community, 'a community of commitments born in distress and defeat and comprises three participants: "I, thou [i.e. the community], and He", the He in whom all being is rooted and in whom everything finds its rehabilitation and, consequently, redemption'.[66]

The Modern Orthodox community was proud of the sophisticated manner in which the dilemma was presented. It gave both philosophical depth and prestige to Orthodoxy. Indeed, the essay's subsequent publication as a book by a world-renowned publishing house further enhanced its prestige. In addition, the reaffirmation of not only the right but the mandate to conquer the world through material and non-material culture, including science and technology, was precisely the legitimation Modern Orthodox Jews sought for their active participation in the larger society. They benefited from Soloveitchik's analyses and, in turn, he became not only the halakhic leader but 'the intellectual leader of an open and engaged Orthodoxy'. His first significant publications in English, 'The Lonely Man of Faith' and 'Confrontation' brought him far broader Orthodox attention. But he was still relatively unknown outside Orthodox circles. In 1968, the Israeli publishing house Mossad Harav Kook published a Hebrew version of *The Lonely Man of Faith*, and this brought his thought to a wider intellectual Israeli audience.

Soloveitchik's involvement with religious Zionism was a fundamental aspect of his being regarded as a leader of Modern Orthodoxy. Although reared in a non-Zionist, if not anti-Zionist, environment, he identified with religious Zionism, and in 1946 was named honorary president of the American Mizrachi movement. On Israel's Independence Day in 1956 he gave an address in which he reflected on the theological significance of the Holocaust and the rise of the State of Israel. He developed two typological approaches for dealing with the reality of evil in the world, the man of fate and the man of destiny, and the two respective covenants which bind the Jewish people together. The covenant of fate is national, based on kinship and ethnicity, while the covenant of destiny is religious, based on a common religious commitment. He then chastised those who, in the name of religious and spiritual goals, turn their backs on the covenant of fate and do not share in their fellow Jews' suffering. This was a slap at the ultra-Orthodox approach as well as a staunch vindication and affirmation of the religious Zionist approach. His provision of the intellectual foundations of religious Zionism was warmly welcomed by those whose allegiance to the movement had until then been largely intuitive.

---

[65] J. B. Soloveitchik, *The Lonely Man of Faith*, 43.   [66] Ibid.

Within the American Orthodox community, Joseph B. Soloveitchik was peerless: a renowned halakhic genius whose strong institutional base as *rosh yeshivah* for half a century gave him wide influence—not only in Orthodox circles in America, but also throughout the diaspora and in Israel.

Modern Orthodoxy and Israel

There was another Israel connection in the growth of Soloveitchik's reputation and his status as the intellectual leader of Modern Orthodoxy, and that relates to the centrality of Israel within Jewish Orthodoxy in general and especially within Modern Orthodoxy. As will be seen, American Orthodox Jews are intertwined with Israel in a myriad of ways and, as a result of these religio-ethnic bonds, each influences the other. Jewish attachment to Erets Yisra'el, the Holy Land, is embedded in daily religious rituals and prayers as well as in law and lore. Three days each year in the Jewish ritual calendar are set aside as fast-days commemorating a significant part of the destruction of the Temple and the loss of the Holy Land; the loss of Jerusalem is symbolized in the rituals of the Jewish marriage ceremony; the daily prayers are recited facing east, towards Jerusalem; and the domestic ritual at Pesach, the *seder*, concludes with the exclamation, 'Next year in Jerusalem!' These serve as constant reminders and sustain the persistent yearning both to be in Erets Yisra'el and for the ultimate messianic redemption. Talmudic lore is replete with statements affirming the superior status of the Holy Land, the obligation to live there, and the absolute faith in the ultimate collective return of the Jewish people to their rightful land. Each day, in the morning, afternoon, and evening prayers, as well as in the blessings recited after each meal, Jews pray for the return to Zion and the rebuilding of Jerusalem. And they remain confident of the ultimate return, which is guaranteed in a variety of authoritative passages. As the American Jewish theologian and philosopher Abraham Joshua Heschel eloquently put it,

Throughout the ages we said No to all the conquerors of Palestine. We said No before God and man emphatically, daily. We objected to the occupations, we rejected their claims, we deepened our attachment, knowing that the occupation by the conquerors was a passing adventure, while our attachment to the land was an eternal link.

The Jewish people has never ceased to assert its right, its title, to the land of Israel. This continuous, uninterrupted insistence, an intimate ingredient of Jewish consciousness, is at the core of Jewish history, a vital element of Jewish faith.

How did the Jews contest and call into question the occupation of the land by the mighty empires of the East and West? How did they assert their own title to the land?

Our protest was not heard in the public squares of the large cities. It was uttered in our homes, in our sanctuaries, in our books, in our prayers. Indeed, our very existence as a people was a proclamation of our link to the land, of our certainty of return.[67]

In addition to many of the prayers in the services and almost all of the festivals, which are rooted in and directed towards Israel, there have been, when feasible, empirical connections between Jews in the diaspora and in Israel which manifest the value of Israel as the highest religio-ethnic plane. As a result, although in the late nineteenth and early twentieth centuries east European Orthodoxy had largely opposed Zionism, in America, although both pro-Zionist and anti-Zionist factions were present, the pro-Zionists were a clear majority.[68] After the establishment of the State of Israel, and especially after the Six Day War of June 1967, American Jewry as a whole became strongly pro-Israel and American Orthodoxy became even more Zionist. Studies show that, by every criterion, the Orthodox in America have a stronger attachment to Israel than do non-Orthodox American Jews.[69] This is especially pronounced within American Modern Orthodoxy, for which Zionism is perhaps the strongest value distinguishing it from all other forms of American Judaism. One of the most significant ways through which that bond has been intensified is through the reinforcement of an ages-old religious value within a modern institutional framework: supporting the study of Torah in the Holy Land and, when feasible, going to study Torah there.

The special value placed on Torah and Jewish learning in Erets Yisra'el is based on a well-known biblical verse: 'For out of Zion shall go forth the Torah, and the word of God from Jerusalem' (Isa. 2: 3). Ancient Jerusalem was the first community to implement the notion of public Jewish education on the basis of this verse.[70] During much of the two thousand years since the destruction of Jerusalem and the Second Temple, the small Jewish communities in Erets Yisra'el sent out emissaries to diaspora Jewish communities: one of the major requirements of those emissaries was that they bring Torah to the diaspora.[71] One of the earliest recorded, Rabbi Moses Malki from Safed, visited New York's Congregation Shearith Israel for four months in late 1759, and then went to Newport, Rhode Island, for a brief stay. In 1761 another emissary from Safed, Haim Mudahy, arrived in New York to raise funds for the relief of those who

[67] Heschel, *Israel*, 54–5.

[68] N. W. Cohen, *American Jews and the Zionist Idea*, 6–7; Gurock, 'American Orthodox Organizations in Support of Zionism'; Caplan, 'The Beginning of "Hamizrahi" in America' (Heb.).

[69] S. M. Cohen, *Ties and Tensions*, 17. Subsequent studies have only reinforced Cohen's findings. See Chapter 1 below. [70] BT *BB* 21a.

[71] Yaari's *Emissaries from Erets Yisra'el* (Heb.) analyses and discusses this in detail.

had suffered in the earthquake in Safed on 30 October 1760. Perhaps the most notable among the early emissaries from the Holy Land to the New World was Rabbi Haim Isaac Karigal from Hebron, who in 1772 spent a month in Philadelphia, almost six months in New York, and then stayed in Newport from March to July 1773. One of his sermons, preached in Newport on the first day of Shavuot, became the first Jewish sermon to be published in America. During the course of his stay in Newport, Karigal developed a close relationship with the Reverend Ezra Stiles, a local Congregationalist minister who later became president of Yale University.[72]

Following the efforts of these emissaries, correspondence between Jews in Erets Yisra'el and traditional Jewish congregations in North America, in which the former solicited funds from the latter, became a fairly regular phenomenon, and the bonds between religiously observant Jews and the Holy Land were maintained. It is therefore not surprising that, even when the east European yeshivas were viewed as the most educationally prominent, there were young Jewish men who went from America to study in yeshivas in the Holy Land.[73]

The mid-1950s saw the start of a pattern of US high-school graduate boys going to Israel to spend a year studying in a yeshiva, where they received a strong religious Zionist orientation. This scheme was the brainchild of Rabbi Zevi Tabory, head of the Department for Torah Education and Culture of the Jewish Agency in New York. His first recruits were high-school seniors, who went to study at what was then the only *hesder* yeshiva, Yeshivat Kerem B'Yavneh.[74] Though it began modestly with only a handful of students, primarily from New York and Chicago, taking part, the scheme grew slowly but steadily until, after the Six Day War of 1967 and under the guidance of Tabory's successor, Rabbi Mallen Galinsky, it had more or less become the norm in the Modern Orthodox community. As Shalom Berger found in his study of the phenomenon, by the mid-1990s the scheme involved nearly 90 per cent of boys graduating from yeshiva high schools.[75] The effect was to intertwine American Modern Orthodoxy and Israeli Zionism, especially Religious Zionism, to the

---

[72] Waxman, *American Aliya*, 52.

[73] Jonathan Sarna, in 'How Matzah Became Square', relates that Behr Manischewitz—the founder of the well-known B. Manischewitz matzah company—had very close ties with Jerusalem, and sent two of his sons to study there. The first, Hirsch, went in 1901, at the age of 10, and remained for thirteen years, during which time he studied at three yeshivas: Etz Chaim (1901–7), Torat Chaim (1908–10), and Me'ah She'arim (1910–14). The elder son, Max, went when he was older and also studied for the rabbinate at Etz Chaim. It is estimated that one-third of the yeshiva students killed in the 1929 massacre in Hebron were Americans (Tikochinski, *Torah Scholarship, Musar, and Elitism* (Heb.), 269 n. 154.

[74] A religious Zionist yeshiva which combines Torah studies with military service.

[75] Berger, 'A Year of Study in an Israeli Yeshiva Program'.

point where they are now frequently viewed as synonymous;[76] it was also this programme that exposed students to much more Jewish philosophy than they had previously encountered and introduced many of them to the thought of Joseph B. Soloveitchik.[77] His growing influence in various spheres enhanced his status both as a prominent intellectual figure and as the spiritual leader, if not the founder, of American Modern Orthodoxy.[78]

The Yeshiva Movement

The approach of many Modern Orthodox Jews to halakhah and to its relationship with the surrounding society and culture is somewhat different from that generally taken by the ultra-Orthodox. On the one hand, Orthodoxy teaches the Torah is divine[79] and that halakhah, which consists of *mitsvot* (commandments) and *minhag* (custom), is also divinely decreed or inspired.[80] Traditional

---

[76] Waxman, 'If I Forget Thee, O Jerusalem . . .'.

[77] In 1973 (5734), the World Mizrachi Organization published *Ḥamesh derashot* (Five Lectures), a Hebrew translation of Soloveitchik's Yiddish lectures to the organization; in 1975 the World Zionist Organization's Department for Torah Education and Culture in the Diaspora published Pinchas Peli's translation of Soloveitchik's lectures to the Rabbinical Council of America, given during the High Holidays, entitled *Al hateshuvah* (On Repentance). Both of these became standard texts for those on the one-year programmes, and were subsequently published in Jerusalem in English translations. *Al hateshuvah* was first published in English in 1980, then in 1984 in a revised edition by Paulist Press, in its Classics of Western Spirituality series. A year earlier (1983), *Ḥamesh derashot* was published in English as *The Rav Speaks*. In 1976 Peli published a collection of Soloveitchik's articles entitled *Besod hayaḥid vehayaḥad: mivḥar ketavim ivriyim* (In Aloneness, in Togetherness). Since then, a series of works by Soloveitchik has been published in English by Ktav and the Toras Horav Foundation; and in Hebrew by Yediot Ahronot Books, and numerous books on his thought have also appeared.

[78] T. Lichtenstein, 'Reflections on the Influence of the Rov'. In addition to its debt to Soloveitchik himself, Modern Orthodoxy's growth and development owed much to a number of loyal students of his who, as well as being prominent synagogue rabbis, were active communal leaders and thinkers. Two of them are Norman Lamm, for many years rabbi of New York's Jewish Center and the founding editor of *Tradition*, who went on to beome president and then chancellor of Yeshiva University, and Walter Wurzburger, who succeeded Lamm as editor of *Tradition*; Wurzburger was president of the Rabbinical Council of America and the Synagogue Council of America, rabbi of Congregation Shaaray Tefila in Lawrence, New York, and a professor of philosophy at Yeshiva University. Emanuel Rackman was an early Modern Orthodox thinker and activist, whom Charles Liebman called 'the central figure in modern Orthodoxy' (Liebman, 'Emanuel Rackman and Modern Orthodoxy', 23). However, he cut his formal organizational ties with American Modern Orthodoxy, made *aliyah*, and became president and chancellor of Bar-Ilan University. See Singer, 'Emanuel Rackman'; L. Kaplan, 'From Cooperation to Conflict'.

[79] There are, however, different interpretations of precisely what that means, as I discuss in Chapter 7 below.

[80] On the approach to implementing halakhic change in almost all versions of Orthodoxy in recent times, see Tamar Ross, *Expanding the Palace of Torah*, 47–70.

Judaism is thus inherently resistant to change, and especially rapid change.[81] On the other hand, there have long been different approaches to the relation- ship between halakhah and the surrounding society as well as to the legitimacy of introducing halakhic change after the geonic period. Where most ultra- Orthodox Jews hold very conservative positions with respect to halakhah, Modern Orthodox rabbis tend to be somewhat more accommodating and are prepared to interpret the law in a flexible way. As will be seen in later chapters, this has generated debate between the ultra-Orthodox and Modern Orthodox, which in turn has had an impact on both denominations.

As a result of the growth of the yeshiva movement in eastern Europe in the second half of the nineteenth century,[82] increasing numbers of Orthodox Jews were exposed to the notion of studying in a yeshiva, though only a small min- ority actually did so. Among the immigrants who arrived in the United States on the eve of the Holocaust were rabbis who had been heads of yeshivas in eastern Europe, and almost immediately upon their arrival they set about reconstruct- ing those yeshivas on American soil. Some of these institutions expressed their founders' ambivalent attitude towards modernity, including suspicion of secular knowledge, and they discouraged their students from gaining a secu- lar education beyond that required by law. Others were more overtly tradition- alist and actually prohibited their students from attending secular institutions of higher education.[83] The latter also established in their yeshivas *kolels*, groups of married men who studied Talmud and related works, receiving a monthly stipend to enable them to devote themselves full-time to their studies. The *kolel* also had the effect of cultivating 'a large cadre of individuals who were com- mitted to Torah study and—unlike the "modernists", especially those from Yeshiva University, who dominated American Orthodoxy during the mid- twentieth century—did not idealize integration into the broader culture'.[84] Although the heads and students at the other newly established yeshivas may not have expressed it as overtly and explicitly as did the founder of Lakewood's Beth Medrash Govoha, Rabbi Aharon Kotler, who immigrated in 1941, they probably did agree with him that America's Jews 'must create an atmosphere of dedication to the Torah . . . without involvement in any external and tangential

---

[81] Yehuda Gellman has suggested to me that theological change has, at times, been a 'one-man show', as in the case of some of the rationalist-based changes introduced by Maimonides. See e.g. Kellner, *Maimonides' Confrontation with Mysticism*. Even theological change is, however, very rare.　　　　　[82] Stampfer, *Lithuanian Yeshivas of the Nineteenth Century*.

[83] Ner Israel Rabbinical College (Baltimore; 1933), Mesivta Chaim Berlin (Brooklyn; 1937), and Mesivta Torah Vodaath (Brooklyn) are among the former; Beth Medrash Govoha (Lake-wood; 1943), Telshe Yeshiva College (Cleveland; 1941), and Mirrer Yeshiva (Brooklyn; 1946) are among the latter. See Helmreich, *The World of the Yeshiva*, 32–51.

[84] Ferziger, *Centered on Study*, 15.

thing'.[85] His influence on Torah growth in America went far beyond Lakewood, which grew to be the biggest yeshiva in the country.[86] In addition, he was a driving force in Torah Umesorah, the National Society for Hebrew Day Schools, he was on the presidium of Agudat Harabanim, and he was a member of Agudath Israel's Council of Sages.

Approximately a year before Rabbi Kotler immigrated, Rabbi Yosef Yitzchak Schneersohn, the sixth *rebbe* of the Chabad-Lubavitch movement,[87] arrived in New York and settled in the Crown Heights section of Brooklyn. He, too, was to have significant impact on Orthodox Judaism and Judaism in general. A decade later, upon his death in 1950, his son-in-law Rabbi Menachem Mendel Schneersohn was designated the seventh *rebbe* and went on to transform Chabad from a small hasidic sect to a world-wide movement. With its emphasis on religious outreach and its creative use of media, Chabad has succeeded in becoming the largest and most dynamic movement within Judaism. It stands out for its ubiquitousness,[88] for its generosity in assisting those in need, and for a somewhat different attitude towards women than that of other hasidic groups.[89] At times it is also the object of severe criticism, particularly with respect to its messianism and the nature of its interactions with existing Jewish communal structures.[90]

In addition, a significant push for furthering Torah education among young American Jews was undertaken in 1944 with the founding of Torah Umesorah. Spearheaded by Rabbi Feivel Mendelowitz and Rabbi Kotler, its objective was to encourage and assist in the founding of Jewish day schools—elementary and high schools that would provide an intensive Jewish education along with a quality secular curriculum across the country.[91] This type of day school was in itself an adaptation to modernity. Many of the very same rabbinic leaders

[85] Kotler, 'On the Maintenance of Torah in Israel' (Heb.), 32. For an analysis of Rabbi Kotler's perspectives, see Finkelman, 'An Ideology for American Yeshiva Students'; id., 'Haredi Isolation in Changing Environments'.

[86] Landes, 'How Lakewood, N.J., is Redefining What It Means to be Orthodox in America'.

[87] Chabad is an acronym for the Hebrew words *ḥokhmah, binah, da'at* (wisdom, understanding, knowledge), the movement's motto; the movement is also known as Lubavitch from the town where the group's leaders were based in the nineteenth century.

[88] It sends emissaries to and has centres in the remotest parts of the world. A popular joke goes: 'What are the two things found everywhere in the world? Coke and Chabad.'

[89] Chabad maintains strict gender segregation, but women in Chabad play a much more active, public role than women in other hasidic and non-hasidic ultra-Orthodox groups.

[90] On the social/communal activity of Chabad, see Fishkoff, *The Rebbe's Army*. For biographies of the *rebbe* and analyses of his thought, see D. Berger, *The Rebbe, the Messiah, and the Scandal of Orthodox Indifference*; S. S. Deutsch, *Larger Than Life*; S. C. Heilman and Friedman, *The Rebbe*; Ch. Miller, *Turning Judaism Outwards*; Steinsaltz, *My Rebbe*; Telushkin, *Rebbe*.

[91] Unusually, the American day schools were frequently called 'yeshivas' or 'yeshivot', whereas elsewhere the term 'yeshiva' refers to higher-level talmudic academies.

who inspired the day-school movement in the United States had previously been adamantly opposed to schools that combined sacred and secular education.[92] Another significant aspect of the day schools was the fact that many of them encompassed both boys and girls, with co-educational classes except for Talmud, from which girls were excluded. As indicated above, Joseph Soloveitchik's Maimonides School in Boston had co-educational classes in all subjects, including Talmud.

Not all of the Orthodox who supported intensive Jewish education were satisfied with the options for girls. Boys could choose between co-education or day schools that were solely for boys, but the options for girls were much more limited. The American branch of the ultra-Orthodox organization Agudath Israel established a Bais Yaakov elementary school in Brooklyn in 1937. Subsequently, other Bais Yaakov schools, elementary as well as high schools and a teachers' seminary, were established. Most of these schools were in New York, although later more were established in other cities as well. Rather than viewing themselves as institutions designed to help Orthodox Jews integrate into American society and culture while maintaining their faith, Bais Yaakov schools 'struggled to hold on to a pure, traditional world, free of the assimilating influences of American society'.[93]

The notion of day-school education took hold rapidly. Within twenty-five years, between 1940 and 1965, the number of day schools grew from 35 to 323 and enrolments grew from 7,700 to 63,500. By 1975 there were 425 day schools and 138 high schools, with a total enrolment of 82,200 students. These schools were located not only in the New York metropolitan area but in thirty-three states across the country. By 1975, every city in the United States with a Jewish population of 7,500 or more had at least one day school, as did 80 per cent of cities with a Jewish population of between 5,000 and 7,500. Among cities with smaller Jewish populations, 25 per cent of those with a population of 1,000 Jews had a Jewish day school.[94] While the notion of day schools had long been anathema to non-Orthodox Jews, who viewed them as isolating the students from American society and thus inhibiting their future success, attitudes gradually changed. Such schools came to be prized by Conservative and even Reform communities as well as by some who did not iden-

---

[92] The closing of the yeshiva in Volozhin is frequently cited by opponents of secular education as a case of the heroism of the yeshiva's *rosh yeshivah*, who allegedly closed the yeshiva rather than bow to government orders requiring that the students have a secular education. See e.g. the story related by Shulamit Meiselman in *The Soloveitchik Heritage*, 226. This myth has been convincingly debunked by Jacob Schacter and Shaul Stampfer. See Stampfer, *Lithuanian Yeshivas of the Nineteenth Century*, 191–251, and Schacter, 'Haskalah, Secular Studies and the Closing of the Yeshiva in Volozhin'.   [93] Weissman and Granite, 'Bais Ya'akov Schools'.
[94] Schiff, *The Jewish Day School in America*; Waxman, *America's Jews in Transition*, 125–6.

tify with any particular denomination. The change among the non-Orthodox reflected a number of significant developments in the United States. Following the tumultuous years of the 1960s, there was increased concern about the racial situation and the quality of public schools. In addition, the increasing prominence of ethnicity and religion in the American public sphere rendered Jewish education much more palatable if not desirable, as did the growing concern of Jewish parents over the future of Jewish identity and identification in America. In the 2013/14 school year, about 255,000 students from nursery school to high school were enrolled in 861 day schools across the United States. The overwhelming majority of these schools are Orthodox, but 13 per cent are not.[95]

In the years following the Second World War, approximately 140,000 Jews arrived in the United States, with the largest number in a single year, about 41,200, arriving in 1949. The Jewish population in the United States at the time numbered about 5 million, which means that the number of immigrants in the post-war period amounted to about 2.8 per cent of the total Jewish population.[96] Although many Orthodox Jews had previously resisted leaving eastern Europe and travelling to the United States, they now made every effort to flee and were more than ready to gain sanctuary in the West. The available evidence suggests that Orthodox Jews were disproportionately represented among Holocaust refugees who arrived in the United States. As William Helmreich found in his study of Holocaust survivors, which entailed in-depth interviews with 170 individuals, approximately 41 per cent identified as Orthodox as compared to the 10 per cent or less in the American Jewish population as a whole.[97] Lest it be argued that Helmreich's interviewees may not be representative, my own analysis of data from the 1990 National Jewish Population Survey indicated similar patterns. Looking at respondents who stated their current religion as Jewish, I found that, among those who had been born elsewhere and arrived in the United States during the years 1937–48, 20 per cent identified as 'currently Orthodox' and 45 per cent identified as 'raised Orthodox'. Among those of comparable ages born in the United States, 6 per cent identified their current denomination as Orthodox and 19 per cent identified the denomination in which they were raised as Orthodox.

Among the post-war refugees were many who belonged to such hasidic sects as Belz, Bluzhov, Bobov, Chernobyl, Ger, Munkatch, Novominsk, Sanz, Satmar, Skver, Stolin, Talin, and Vizhnitz, to name some of the more prominent ones. These sects have their differences, but they nevertheless view

---

[95] Schick, *A Census of Jewish Day Schools in the United States 2013–2014*, 1–2.
[96] Rosenwaike, 'A Synthetic Estimate of American Jewish Population Movement'.
[97] Helmreich, *Against all Odds*, 78–9.

themselves as part of a common overarching community. The hasidim, per-haps even more than others, were determined to retain their traditional way of life even within the modern metropolis, and they were largely successful in achieving that goal.[98] They have also had a significant impact on the larger Orthodox community and on the broader population in the cities and in New York State in general, where they are concentrated. Their impact on the wider Orthodox community derives from their determination and their numbers; they have a higher birth rate than other Orthodox Jews and a much higher birth rate than the wider American Jewish community.

The largest of the post-war hasidic immigrant sects, Satmar, originated in Hungary. Its size may have been a result of the relatively late Nazi invasion of Hungary and thus the shorter period during which Hungarian Jews were subjected to the Nazi policy of genocide. The sect's founder, Rabbi Joel Teitel-baum, was a brilliant scholar and a staunch opponent of modernity and Zion-ism who created a highly insular community with a very powerful communal structure.[99] The Satmar hasidim retain a tradition which developed in Hun-garian ultra-Orthodoxy of acerbic hostility towards ideologically motivated non-believers, such as advocates of Reform or any other system which op-poses Orthodoxy.[100] The sect's size and organizational structure enable it to influence the zeal for insularity in most of the other hasidic sects who, in turn, influence the entire world of ultra-Orthodoxy.

Despite the increased numbers of ultra-Orthodox Jews, Modern Ortho-doxy was widely viewed as the wave of the future in American Orthodox Judaism. Its rabbinic organization, the Rabbinical Council of America, contin-ued to grow because many Orthodox rabbis had a much more positive attitude to modernity, to secular studies, and to co-operation with non-observant Jews than was deemed appropriate within the ultra-Orthodox Agudat Harabanim. Increasingly, the Rabbinical Council came to be perceived as the major Ortho-dox rabbinic association, especially after Soloveitchik became the 'guiding spirit and mentor to the Rabbinical Council' as well as chair of its Halakhah Commission.[101]

An important source of the popularity of Modern Orthodoxy at this time was the variety of perspectives within Modern Orthodox thought, there being a range of reasons why Jews identified as Modern Orthodox. Two clear types of Modern Orthodox can be distinguished: some Jews are philosophically or

[98] See the 1997 award-winning documentary film by Daum and Rudavsky, *A Life Apart*; see also J. Mintz, *Hasidic People*.

[99] J. Berger, *The Pious Ones*. For a biography of Rabbi Teitelbaum, see Keren-Kratz, 'Rabbi Joel Teitelbaum' (Heb.),

[100] For the roots of this approach, see Ferziger, *Exclusion and Hierarchy*, 61–89.

[101] Rakeffet-Rothkoff, *The Rav*, i. 46. See also http://www.rabbis.org/about_us.cfm.

ideologically modern, while others can more appropriately be characterized as behaviourally modern. The 'philosophically modern' Orthodox are those who have an integrated framework within which they are meticulously observant of halakhah and, at minimum, view general education and knowledge positively, as a *mitsvah*, a religious obligation to acquire as much knowledge as possible and to use it in the service of God and humanity. These adherents view themselves, from a religious perspective, as being part of and feeling a sense of solidarity with the larger Jewish community, the larger society, and all of humanity. They are committed to Israel and religious Zionism out of an understanding of the role these play within Jewish religious thought.

The 'behaviourally modern' Orthodox, by contrast, are not deeply concerned with philosophical ideas about Judaism, modernity, or religious Zionism. This should be no surprise. Most people are not philosophically inclined and behave as they do without giving it great intellectual reflection. Many of this group are both modern and Orthodox in the sense that they are observant, but not meticulously or rigidly so. They view themselves as 'normal', as religious as they can be in a modern world, but feel free to pick and choose in their observance of rituals. Their sense of 'freedom of choice', although never articulated in terms of dogma, is similar to that evident among non-Jewish Americans, who view themselves as religious but nevertheless are selective in their religiosity.[102] In many ways, their definition of themselves as Modern Orthodox has the same basis as that of those, in the mid-1950s, whom Marshall Sklare found to define themselves as Conservative. That is, when asked, 'What do you mean when you say you are Conservative?' the responses were, typically: 'Now—I'd guess you'd call it middle of the road, as far as (not) being as strict as the Orthodox, yet not quite as Reformed as the Reformed'; or: 'I don't like the old-fashioned type, or the Reform. I'm between the two of them.'[103] Similarly, most of those who define themselves as Modern Orthodox do so in reference to right-wing or 'sectarian' Orthodoxy. The 'philosophically modern' Orthodox are frequently viewed by the behaviourally modern

---

[102] Roof and McKinney, *American Mainline Religion*. These are different from those whom Sklare referred to as the 'non-observant Orthodox', who were very prevalent among the immigrant generation and their children, namely, those who are 'heterodox in personal behavior but who, when occasionally joining in public worship, do so in accordance with traditional patterns' (Sklare, *Conservative Judaism*, 46). The behavioural Modern Orthodox are much more observant. For example, they observe the sabbath completely in public, though they may take various degrees of halakhic liberties in their home. Likewise, they observe *kashrut* though they eat unsupervised food in a restaurant that serves vegetarian and dairy dishes. Or they may not always go to synagogue to pray; they may not even pray regularly. Blum, 'This Normal Life', takes it further and argues that today everyone chooses what they observe, but he sees no significant difference between those who choose to observe maximally and those who choose to do so minimally.   [103] Sklare, *Conservative Judaism*.

group as spiritual and intellectual legitimators, if not authenticators, of their selective religious behaviour. As the status of Modern Orthodox intellectuals grew, so did the number of their followers. Adherents of these two types of Modern Orthodoxy, as well as variations within each of the types, thus made for a significant sector within Orthodoxy.[104]

Much of this has changed dramatically over the last fifty years. Today the ultra-Orthodox comprise the majority of the American Orthodox population, with the Modern Orthodox being less than one-third.[105] This demographic and institutional rebalancing has resulted in changes in social networks, and helps explain changes to a variety of religious norms and values that have increasingly led to friction between and within the major factions comprising American Orthodoxy.

One outstanding issue over which the factions divide is the role and status of women in Judaism and in society. So significant are the attitudes, values, and policies concerning this question that a separate chapter on the subject might have been expected here. However, that would risk minimizing its centrality in the entire process of change. Precisely because the issue of women's role and status is so central, it is contextualized and dealt with throughout this book where appropriate. It is the broader norms and values of American Orthodoxy that I am concerned to address.

---

[104] There are intellectual and behavioural ultra-Orthodox Jews as well, among both the hasidic and the 'yeshivish' sectors, and among them there may well be variations in punctiliousness in the performance of religious rituals. However, it seems doubtful that among the ultra-Orthodox there are those who ideologically legitimate their less than complete compliance with halakhah: when challenged, they might respond that they know that they are behaving improperly but argue that they are weak.

[105] Pew Research Center, 'A Portrait of American Orthodox Jews', 4.

GROUP SIZE, SOCIAL CLASS, RELIGION, AND POLITICS

D ETERMINING the size of the Orthodox Jewish population in the United States is no easy task. Some of the difficulties are related to the problem of estimating the Jewish population there as a whole. The US Census does not include a religion question because it is deemed that this would be a violation of the First Amendment to the Constitution's guarantee of separation of church (religion) and state. Accordingly, a variety of other avenues have been taken, such as self-studies conducted by organized local Jewish communities, national surveys sponsored by agencies of the American Jewish community, and, more recently, a major national survey conducted by an independent survey organization, the Pew Research Center. All of these face what in Israel is a significant political question, namely, 'Who is a Jew?'[1] There is a fairly broad acceptance among social scientists and Jewish communal professionals of the notion of the 'core Jewish population': those who, in a survey, identify themselves as Jews by religion and/or ethnicity or who are so identified by the respondent in their household, and do not identify with any other religion. In addition, those who say they have no religion but that their parents are Jewish are counted as Jews. Leaving aside the fact that many included in this core may not meet a halakhic definition, there are still major debates with significantly different estimates of population size among those specializing in Jewish demography.[2]

With respect to the Orthodox Jewish population in the United States, the problem can be somewhat alleviated by assuming that the vast majority of those who identify as Orthodox Jews are in fact Jewish by religion. There remain questions as to whether belonging to an Orthodox synagogue makes one Orthodox, or whether being Orthodox entails matters of faith and behaviour

---

[1] For a variety of opinions in response to this question in relation to Israel's Law of Return, see Ben-Rafael, *Jewish Identities*, and Litvin and Hoenig, *Jewish Identity*. For an analysis of a variety of historical opinions as to whether Jewish immigrants should be uniquely classified by the immigration authorities and, if so, how, see N. Goldberg, Lestchinsky, and Weinreich, *The Classification of Jewish Immigrants*.   [2] See e.g. DellaPergola, 'World Jewish Population, 2015'.

and, if so, how one measures them. For a social scientist, the only approach is similar to that of defining the broader Jewish population, namely, self-definition.

According to the US Bureau of the Census, there were some 242.5 million (to be precise, 242,542,967) adults (defined as over the age of 18) in the United States in 2013. The Pew Center estimates that 1.5 per cent of these, or about 3,638,000, are Jews by religion.[3] Pew also estimates that 12 per cent of Jews by religion, about 437,000, are Orthodox. Of these, 66 per cent, or about 291,000, are ultra-Orthodox (this includes hasidic and 'yeshivish' Jews), and 33 per cent, or about 146,000, are Modern Orthodox.[4] This distribution is almost identical to that found in the 2011 study sponsored by the UJA-Federation of New York of the eight-county New York City area, the city with the largest Orthodox population in the country.[5] Curiously, that study's estimate of the total Orthodox population in New York City, 493,000, is significantly higher than that estimated in the Pew survey for the country as a whole.[6]

Throughout much of the twentieth century there was a significant attrition rate from Orthodoxy. But by the beginning of the current century it was evident that the tide had turned, and the American Orthodox population is now growing, because of both a lower attrition rate and a higher birth rate. As reported by Ukeles Associates, 'the findings from the local studies show that younger Jewish respondents are more likely to define themselves as Orthodox Jews than are older Jewish Americans'.[7] Moreover, according to Pew, the fact that American Orthodox Jews 'are much younger, on average, and tend to have much larger families than the overall Jewish population . . . suggests that their share of the Jewish population will grow'.[8]

The issue of family size will be discussed shortly. At this point, suffice it to say that if the Orthodox segment continues to be an increasing percentage of the American Jewish community its status and role in that community may have significant implications for the community's future direction.

Social Class

There is a history within the social sciences of different approaches to the relationship between religious orthodoxy and social class. As indicated by Charles Glock and Rodney Stark, there is 'a long tradition in Western thought [that]

---

[3] Pew Research Center, 'A Portrait of Jewish Americans', 28.   [4] Ibid. 48.
[5] S. M. Cohen, Ukeles, and Miller, *Jewish Community Study of New York*, 212.
[6] Ibid., 'Exhibit 7-1'.   [7] Ukeles Associates, *Young Jewish Adults in the United States Today*, 55.
[8] Pew Research Center, 'A Portrait of Jewish Americans', 10.

has viewed religion . . . as a haven for the dispossessed'.[9] This suggests that those in the lower classes are more religious. An analysis of Jews, and especially Orthodox Jews, in America seems to support this. At least since the beginning of the mass immigration from eastern Europe in the late nineteenth century, Orthodox Jews as a group have had lower incomes than non-Orthodox Jews. This should not be surprising; surveys indicate that such patterns are typical. For example, a 2009 Gallup poll found that there was a 'strong relationship between a country's socioeconomic status and the religiosity of its residents. In the world's poorest countries—those with average per-capita incomes of $2,000 or lower—the median proportion who say religion is important in their daily lives is 95%. In contrast, the median for the richest countries—those with average per-capita incomes higher than $25,000—is 47%.'[10] These figures would appear to support the thesis of religion as a haven for the dispossessed, and it would seem to follow that this explains the religious commitment of the Orthodox in the United States. However, the Gallup data also indicated that the United States does not conform to the pattern equating poverty with religiosity. Despite America being one of the world's wealthiest countries, almost two-thirds of Americans (65%) say religion is important in their daily lives. In other words, the 'haven for the dispossessed' thesis is not applicable to the United States, and there is therefore no reason to believe that the religious commitment of Orthodox Jews is a response to their economic status; in fact, it can be argued that the generally lower income levels of this community are a *result* of their religious commitment.

Although there is a paucity of data on the income patterns of American Jews before the second half of the twentieth century, the evidence available suggests that the Orthodox have consistently been the poorest. W. Lloyd Warner and Leo Srole found this to be the case in their study of 'Yankee City', for which the research was conducted between 1930 and 1935, and they attributed it to Judaism's restrictive religious requirements, to which the Orthodox adhere more closely than other Jews. As they saw it, 'the progressive defection of successive generations of Jews from their religious system in a process apparently nearly completed among the children of the immigrants themselves' was much more obvious among the Orthodox than among other groups. They commented: 'The religious subsystem of [the 'Yankee City' Jewish] community is apparently in a state of disintegration',[11] primarily because of the economic factor. If Jews were to successfully compete in the economic

---

[9] Glock and Stark, *Religion and Society in Tension*, 185.

[10] Crabtree, 'Religiosity Highest in World's Poorest Nations'.

[11] Warner and Srole, *The Social Systems of American Ethnic Groups*, 199–200. 'Yankee City' is the name given by socio-anthropologist W. Lloyd Warner to a community he studied in Newburyport, Massachusetts.

sphere, they had to break with the traditional religious patterns that restricted them. The sabbath was a case in point:

The Jewish Sabbath falls on Saturday. In Russia the Jews, comprising an important part of the merchant class, maintained their own work rhythm in the week, and non-Jews had to adapt themselves to it. On Saturday their shops were closed, whereas on Sunday they were 'open for business.' The work rhythm of the American week, however, is Christian. Sunday is the Sabbath, and Saturday is a work day, the most important day in the week. This rhythm the Jews are powerless to resist. They must accept it or lose out in the competitive race.[12]

Whereas Warner and Srole pointed to denomination as influencing social class, Liston Pope emphasized how social class influences denomination. As he put it, 'Differentiation within Judaism corresponds to a combination of ethnic and class pressures, with the latter probably stronger in the large. Higher-class and better-educated Jews tend to leave Orthodox synagogues and to join Conservative or Reform congregations, or to become secularized.'[13] Falling between these two approaches, political scientist Charles Liebman, in a study based on data from synagogues in New York, showed that by the mid-twentieth century Orthodoxy was not composed solely of lower-class Jews. The data clearly showed that by then Orthodox synagogues had been established even in the highest-income neighbourhoods. To Liebman the data suggested a more complex relationship between religiosity and social status, and he argued that the increasing social distance between the Orthodox right and left was not due to an improvement in social status causing a shift to religious liberalism.[14]

However, the 1990 National Jewish Population Survey (NJPS) indicates that the basic pattern remained. The Orthodox had the highest proportion of individuals in the group earning less than $30,000 a year, and no members at the highest income levels. Indeed, there was a gap of more than $10,000 between the mean family incomes of Orthodox and Conservative Jews, and a similar gap between the mean family incomes of Conservative and Reform baby boomers (those born between 1946 and 1964). Almost two-thirds of the Orthodox baby boomers reported a combined annual family income of less than $45,000, whereas only half of the Conservatives and 42.5 per cent of the Reform Jews did.[15]

The picture is actually more complex. Data from the 2013 Pew Center survey of American Jews indicate that the Orthodox still have the highest number

[12]   Warner and Srole, *The Social Systems of American Ethnic Groups*, 200.
[13]   Pope, 'Religion and the Class Structure', 90.
[14]   Liebman, 'Changing Social Characteristics of Orthodox, Conservative and Reform Jews'.
[15]   Waxman, *Jewish Baby Boomers*, 35.

of members with an annual family income of under $30,000. However, a higher percentage of Orthodox (28.1%) than Conservatives (24.6%) have an annual income of $150,000 or more. The percentage of Modern Orthodox with an annual income of $150,000 or more (37.6%) is even higher than that of Reform Jews (31.8%). Also, the median annual family incomes of the Orthodox and Conservative wings are almost identical.[16]

Liebman's hypothesis that the differences between the religious right and left in Orthodoxy are not primarily related to social status gained support from studies by Bernard Lazerwitz, which suggested that, in the United States, social class plays much less of a role in influencing religio-ethnic identification than do age or generation. He found a significant overlap between generation and age to the point that 'in today's Jewish community either can be used as the equivalent of the other'. The significance of generation lies in the fact that the members of each successive generation 'differ from the past generations in having substantial lessening of their religious and pietistic behavior, their lack of traditional Jewish beliefs, and in the greatly reduced Jewishness of their childhood homes'.[17]

Lazerwitz may have been correct for Conservative and Reform Jews but there is no evidence that there is a generational decrease among Orthodox Jews in religious and pietistic behaviour, traditional Jewish beliefs, or 'Jewishness', whatever that may mean. As Table 1.1 indicates, in 2013 a higher percentage of parents of American Orthodox (including Modern Orthodox) Jews had been born outside America than the parents of Conservative and Reform Jews. It seems fair to assume that, in most cases, the parents of both variations of Orthodox were also Orthodox. Yet, as will be discussed, current evidence indicates that both the numbers of American Orthodox variations and the religiosity at least of the American ultra-Orthodox are increasing. Moreover, it is interesting to note in the table that the ultra-Orthodox, who are often viewed as being more punctilious in religious observance than the Modern Orthodox, have a higher percentage of American-born members than the Modern Orthodox. Perhaps that is because a higher percentage of the ultra-Orthodox were raised Orthodox (see Table 1.2). Also, across both types of Orthodox Jews a lower percentage had American-born parents than did Jews of other denominations. Nevertheless, there is no evidence that there has been a generational decline among the Orthodox in the United States.

---

[16] My own analysis of Pew data; the analyses in this chapter were done before Pew published its report 'A Portrait of American Orthodox Jews', but, aside from slight variations, the results are basically the same.

[17] Lazerwitz, 'Contrasting the Effects of Generation, Class, Sex, and Age', 55. 'Generation' here refers to immigration, the immigrant being first-generation, the immigrant's children second-generation, and so on.

Table 1.1 American-born Jews by denomination, 2013 (%)

	Ultra-Orthodox	Modern Orthodox	Conservative	Reform
Respondent	80.8	71.5	88.3	93.0
Father	63.0	72.1	74.1	84.7
Mother	61.3	74.8	79.1	88.7

Table 1.2 Current denomination of respondents, by upbringing (%)

	Current denomination			
	Ultra-Orthodox	Modern Orthodox	Conservative	Reform
Raised as:				
Orthodox	74.1	58.1	14.6	5.2
Conservative	12.6	12.4	65.9	28.9
Reform	4.6	12.1	11.2	59.0
No particular denomination	7.5	15.0	5.9	5.6
Other Jewish denomination/identity	0.8	1.3	1.6	1.0
Not raised Jewish	0.3	1.1	0.7	0.3
Total	99.9	100	99.9	100

As Table 1.1 indicates, almost two-thirds of the ultra-Orthodox and almost three-quarters of the Modern Orthodox who were American-born have parents who were also American-born. Even assuming that some of the parents of the Orthodox were not Orthodox themselves, current evidence indicates that both the numbers and the religiosity of the contemporary American Orthodox are increasing.[18] Moreover, it is interesting to note in the table that the ultra-Orthodox, who are often viewed as being more punctilious in religious observance than the Modern Orthodox, have a higher percentage of American-born members than the Modern Orthodox. Perhaps that is because a higher percentage of the ultra-Orthodox were raised Orthodox (see Table 1.2).

[18] Statistics in Tables 1.1–1.17 are my own analysis based on the data in Pew Research Center, 'A Portrait of Jewish Americans' (2013); Pew's definition of 'Orthodox' aligns with my own use of the term 'ultra-Orthodox'.

Table 1.3 Highest educational level attained by respondents, by denomination (%)

	Ultra-Orthodox	Modern Orthodox	Conservative	Reform
Master's, Ph.D., JD (Doctor of Jurisprudence), MD (medical doctorate), rabbinic ordination*	16.8	28.8	30.7	32.4
Some postgraduate study	2.0	1.4	2.4	3.6
Bachelor's degree	20.2	35.6	30.5	27.0
Two-year degree	11.6	6.2	8.5	11.1
Some college education, no degree	16.8	7.9	10.2	16.6
High school	29.8	19.0	16.7	8.2
Did not complete high school	3.0	1.1	1.1	1.0
Total	100	100	100	100

* A much higher percentage of Orthodox are ordained. If ordination were not counted, the differences between the Orthodox, especially the ultra-Orthodox, and the non-Orthodox would be much greater.

Having been born in the United States or not is clearly only one of many variables which influence income. Another significant one is education, and when levels of education by denomination are examined we find that the Orthodox have significantly lower levels than the others (see Table 1.3). In their analysis of the 2001 NJPS data, Hartman and Hartman found that 'the Orthodox have the lowest proportion with college degrees, slightly more than half, followed by the unaffiliated, with slightly more than 60%, whereas more than 70% of Conservatives and Reform/Reconstructionists have college degrees'.[19]

The Pew 2013 data indicate that, compared to the non-Orthodox, three times as many Orthodox Jews have not completed high school. When we look at the percentage having achieved a bachelor's degree or higher (Table 1.4), the data indicate that less than 40 per cent of the Orthodox have done so as compared to more than 60 per cent of each of the other groups. It is interesting to note that the percentage of those who achieved a bachelor's degree or higher is greatest among the Modern Orthodox.

It should be emphasized that these figures concerning educational level refer to secular education and/or institutionally conferred degrees, including ordination. Many ultra-Orthodox men spend long years in yeshiva studying religious texts without necessarily obtaining a formal degree. For them, the

[19]   Hartman and Hartman, *Gender and American Jews*, 175.

Table 1.4 Respondents with a bachelor's degree or higher (%)

Ultra-Orthodox	39.0
Modern Orthodox	65.8
Conservative	63.6
Reform	63.0

objective is learning for its own sake, as a religious obligation, rather than for any pragmatic end. Although they are clearly not illiterate or uneducated, they are underrepresented in the tables above because of their lower levels of *secular* education.[20] Most of them are aware that secular education is important for economic advancement in the United States, and many readily accept their lower income status. Some have been quite successful in business or other occupations without a higher degree but, as a group, the ultra-Orthodox have lower incomes, which in the United States are frequently associated with lower educational status.

There is an additional significant reason for lower incomes in some Orthodox households, namely, that far fewer ultra-Orthodox married women have paid work. For example, in the study of Jewish baby boomers based on the 1990 NJPS, it was found that the wives of one-third of ultra-Orthodox respondents did not have a job outside the home, as compared to less than one-quarter of the wives of Conservative and Reform respondents. The gap has since decreased but apparently still exists. A 2011 study of the New York Jewish community found that a significantly lower percentage of ultra-Orthodox ('hasidic' and 'yeshivish') female respondents and spouses than Modern Orthodox and non-Orthodox respondents and spouses were either self-employed or employed full-time.[21]

[20] It is frequently taken for granted that there was a high rate of literacy among Jews in eastern Europe. However, Shaul Stampfer has analysed census data and other records that indicate high levels of illiteracy and functional illiteracy in this population. East European Jewish society was, he suggests, an oral society. Most of those who went to the United States during the era of mass immigration quickly realized that to succeed one needed literacy and an education, and they were successful in achieving those. See Stampfer, *Families, Rabbis, and Education,* 190–210. The Orthodox, however, continue to have much more of an oral than a book-based tradition, and even the latter is geared to religious texts rather than secular books: see H. Soloveitchik, 'Rupture and Reconstruction'. At the same time, it should be noted that a 2010 study found that Orthodox Jews are disproportionately represented on Jewish Internet sites. Ari Kelman reports that 'Orthodox Jews are actively involved in Jewish life online, and as such play a disproportionately large role in the overall shape of the network of Jewish websites': see Kelman, *The Reality of the Virtual: Looking for Jewish Leadership Online.*

[21] Waxman, *Jewish Baby Boomers,* 35, table 2-13. S. M. Cohen, Ukeles, and Miller, *Jewish Community Study of New York,* 219, table 7-6.

Economic status involves more than family income. Family size is another important variable, and all the evidence indicates that the Orthodox have larger families than the non-Orthodox. On the basis of analyses of NJPS 2001 data, DellaPergola, Gilboa, and Tal suggested that, 'For U.S. Jewish women aged 40 to 44, at the end of their reproductive stage, the number of births is 1.86, compared to 1.93 births in the total U.S. population, while the replacement level is 2.1. The exception is the Orthodox population, with 3 to 4 children per family.'[22] As will be seen below, that estimate of the Orthodox birth rate is more appropriate for the Modern Orthodox. The birth rate among the Orthodox when more broadly defined, i.e. including the ultra-Orthodox, is even higher.

Even if our focus is on the Modern Orthodox segment, the reality is more complex than is indicated by income level alone. Even in households with a high income, many struggle economically because of the high cost of Modern Orthodox Jewish living. For example, in the major Modern Orthodox day schools in New York, Boston, and Los Angeles, tuition and other costs per child in primary school are approximately $20,000 per year. Synagogue membership is between $1,200 and $1,900 per family annually. Summer camp is another $3,500 to $8,000 per child, depending on the length of stay. That is just to start. There are also, of course, a variety of annual institutional fund-raising dinners which one is expected to attend, to say nothing of the regular costs of maintaining Jewish religious dietary laws, and the expenses incurred during Jewish festivals, even when one doesn't go to a luxury hotel for Pesach and Sukkot. The high cost of Jewish living is, of course, not unique to Modern Orthodox Jews, but it does appear to have a greater impact on them. With the ultra-Orthodox, they have the highest cost of living, especially if the value of time is factored in to what Carmel Chiswick has called 'the full price of religious observance'.[23] But they are also 'modern', which means that, in contrast to the ultra-Orthodox, their communities are less intensely focused on intra-communal relations and their members are less intensely involved with others in the community. As a result, the needy in modern communities have a greater chance of going unnoticed by others than is the case in ultra-Orthodox communities.[24]

The 2011 study of the Jewish population of New York, which has the largest concentration of Orthodox Jews of any city in the United States, subdivided the Orthodox sector into hasidic, yeshivish, and Modern Orthodox. Until recently it was estimated that the Modern Orthodox comprise as much as two-thirds of American Orthodox Jewry. The New York study found that they

[22] DellaPergola, Gilboa, and Tal (eds.), *The Jewish People Policy Planning Institute Planning Assessment, 2004–2005: The Jewish People between Thriving and Decline*, 201.

[23] Chiswick, *Judaism in Transition*, 70–1.

[24] See e.g. Oppenheimer, 'Beggarville', and J. Berger, *The Pious Ones*.

are now a minority, comprising only 43 per cent of the city's Orthodox population. The majority, 57 per cent, are hasidic and yeshivish. As for family size,

By any measure, Hasidic households are the largest in the New York-area Jewish population. In terms of number of Jews, Hasidic homes are far more than twice as large as non-Orthodox households (4.8 for Hasidic versus 1.8 for non-Orthodox), while Yeshivish households, with 4.1 Jews, are nearly as large as Hasidic families. Modern Orthodox homes are somewhat smaller (2.8), but still much larger than non-Orthodox households. . . . Hasidic households are home to 12 times the number of children as non-Orthodox homes. Even Modern Orthodox households are home to four times the number of children as the non-Orthodox.[25]

The 2013 Pew survey, which sampled American Jews across the country, found that 'Jews by religion average more children (2.1) than Jews of no religion (1.5), and the average number of children born to Orthodox Jews (4.1) is about twice the overall Jewish average. By contrast, Reform Jews have 1.7 children and Conservative Jews have 1.8 children, on average.'[26]

The lower socio-economic status of American Orthodox Jews, both hasidic and yeshivish, is putting pressure on their communities. As the Orthodox birth rate rises, there is a growing need for housing, schooling, social services, and employment which the communities themselves find it hard to meet.[27] This affects the broader American Jewish community in a variety of ways. In some cities, notably New York, it creates severe challenges for such central communal organizations as the United Jewish Appeal (UJA) and the Jewish Federation. In addition, the evidence indicates that as the proportion of Jews identifying as Orthodox grows, they may drain resources from other parts of the community. This, in turn, may affect the position of the Jewish community on the American socio-political scene, as increased internal Jewish needs leave less resources for activities in the broader sphere that would enhance the community's status.

---

[25] S. M. Cohen, Ukeles, and Miller, *Jewish Community Study of New York*, 213–14.

[26] Pew Research Center, 'A Portrait of Jewish Americans', 40.

[27] There are many differences between the condition of haredim in the United States and in Israel, but there are also many similarities, especially high birth rates and low levels of education. For at least thirty years I have had a disagreement with a colleague and good friend who predicts the collapse of haredi society as a result of economic pressures. Although I cannot explain why it has not happened, I see no evidence of such a collapse. Eli Berman, an economist who has studied the economic condition of haredim, has indicated that 'such groups show no sign of disappearing, and those with the most demanding practices seem to be growing fastest. UltraOrthodox Jewry, the modern Anabaptist traditions (such as the Amish, Mennonites, and Hutterites), and radical Islam are thriving, despite a multitude of time-intensive requirements': Berman, 'Sect, Subsidy, and Sacrifice', 908.

Religious Beliefs

Sociologists of religion studying American Judaism have usually focused on such issues as how American Jews feel about their religion; the extent to which they observe both personal and family rituals; the extent to which they engage in other types of Jewish religious behaviour; and the extent to which their core religious beliefs flow from their religious socialization, especially education. Social scientific studies of American Jewry measure affiliation, ritual, and other types of religion-related behaviour, but they rarely ask questions concerning religious belief.[28] Thus, although the 1990 NJPS had more than two dozen questions about religious affiliation and behaviour, it had but one or two questions about religious belief, perhaps the most explicit of which concerned the authorship of the Bible. The 2013 Pew survey did include a number of belief questions, which will now be examined denominationally.

More than 90 per cent of Americans respond affirmatively when asked, 'Do you believe in God?'[29] It is thus not surprising that more than 90 per cent of American ultra-Orthodox (98.7%), Modern Orthodox (97.5%), and Conservative (86.9%) Jews likewise affirm that belief. Among Reform Jews, the percentage is somewhat lower (79.5%). When the issue was probed further and respondents were asked to indicate the firmness of that belief, analysis indicates significant denominational variation. As indicated in Table 1.5, the ultra-Orthodox are more absolutely certain than the Modern Orthodox, and both are much more absolutely certain than the non-Orthodox.

When respondents were asked whether they believe that God gave Israel to the Jewish people, Modern Orthodox replied affirmatively in greater numbers (94.9%) than did ultra-Orthodox (88.9%). This is apparently a reflection of the centrality of Israel in Modern Orthodoxy, which manifested itself in responses to other questions as well. Once again, significantly higher percentages of both ultra-Orthodox and Modern Orthodox believe that Israel was divinely ordained for the Jewish people than do Conservative (68.6%) and Reform (49.7%) Jews (see Table 1.6).

Nor is the finding surprising that the importance of religion in one's life varies denominationally, with the ultra-Orthodox attributing greatest importance to it and Reform the least (Table 1.7). When the respondent is asked how important being Jewish is in his or her life (Table 1.8), we find that slightly more Modern Orthodox (89.6%) than ultra-Orthodox (87.1%) say it is 'very important'. Also, much higher percentages of Conservative (71.6%) and Reform (47.2%) Jews say that being Jewish is 'very important' than say that

---

[28] Waxman, 'What We Don't Know about the Judaism of America's Jews'.
[29] Newport, 'More than 9 in 10 Americans Continue to Believe in God'.

Table 1.5 Responses to 'How certain are you about your belief in God?' (%)

	Ultra-Orthodox	Modern Orthodox	Conservative	Reform
Absolutely certain	91.9	80.4	47.5	39.6
Fairly certain	6.8	17.1	39.4	39.9
Not too certain	0.7	1.2	10.7	16.4
Not at all certain	0.5	1.3	2.4	4.1
Total	99.9	100	99.9	100

Table 1.6 Responses to 'Do you literally believe that God gave the land that is now Israel to the Jewish people?' (%)

	Ultra-Orthodox	Modern Orthodox	Conservative	Reform
Yes	88.9	94.9	68.6	49.7
No	11.1	5.1	31.4	50.3
Total	100	100	100	100

religion is very important in their lives. This is apparently a reflection of the various dimensions Jews attribute to Jewishness and Jewish identity, in its ethnic and cultural as well as its religious aspects.

American Jews pray much less frequently than do non-Jewish Americans. Indeed, they are half as likely to pray. More than half of Americans (55%) say that they pray every day, but only about a quarter of America's Jews (26%) say they do.[30] Data on denominational variation in frequency of prayer among American Jews are unavailable, but there are data on attendance at synagogue services. In the non-Jewish American population, about 37 per cent say they attend worship services at least once a week.[31] That figure includes both males

[30] Pew Research Center, 'Prayer in America'; Lipka, '5 Facts about Prayer'. There may be some differences between Jews and others in the definition of prayer: Jews may be more likely to understand it to mean attending a prayer service rather than praying in private. On the other hand, the data in Table 1.8 on synagogue attendance by American Jews suggest that the 26 per cent who stated that they prayed daily meant it in the same way as other Americans, i.e. praying in private. Also, in the 2001 National Jewish Population Survey, when American Jews who identified as 'Jewish by religion' were asked if they ever prayed privately using their own words, 26 per cent replied that they did not. It seems reasonable to assume that if they were asked whether they prayed daily, the percentage of those saying they do not would be much higher than this.

[31] Lipka, 'What Surveys Say about Worship Attendance'. As with all surveys, these data indicate only what people say they do, not what they actually do. With reference to attendance at

Table 1.7 Responses to 'How important is religion in your life?' (%)

	Ultra-Orthodox	Modern Orthodox	Conservative	Reform
Very important	82.8	77.4	44.3	17.2
Somewhat important	14.7	18.1	41.1	44.9
Not too important	1.4	1.3	11.7	30.9
Not at all important	1.1	3.2	2.9	7.1
Total	100	100	100	100.1

Table 1.8 Responses to 'How important is being Jewish in your life?' (%)

	Ultra-Orthodox	Modern Orthodox	Conservative	Reform
Very important	87.1	89.6	71.6	47.2
Somewhat important	12.6	10.4	22.7	42.9
Not too important	0.3	—	2.9	9.0
Not at all important	0.1	—	2.8	0.8
Total	100.1	100	100	99.9

and females. However, studies indicate that attendance at services is significantly higher for women than for men.[32] With regard to Orthodox Jews, the rate of synagogue attendance for women is much lower than for men, for a variety of religious and cultural reasons. The data in Table 1.9 indicate a dramatic difference in rates of attendance between Orthodox and non-Orthodox males, with more than half of the former and less than 5 per cent of the latter attending synagogue more than once a week. Also, almost three-quarters of both ultra-Orthodox and Modern Orthodox attend at least once a week, while only 15 per cent of Conservative and only about 3 per cent of Reform Jews do.

There is further evidence to suggest that Orthodox and non-Orthodox Jews have basically different conceptions of Jewishness, with the Orthodox placing primacy on its religious aspects and the non-Orthodox placing primacy on its ethnic and cultural aspects. As seen in Table 1.10, about 80 per cent of the Orthodox, as compared to 26 per cent of Conservative and 11 per cent

religious services, Lipka points out that there is evidence that people tend to exaggerate their frequency of attendance.

[32] See e.g. Newport, 'Americans' Church Attendance Inches Up in 2010'.

Table 1.9 Responses to 'How often do you attend synagogue services?' (males) (%)

	Ultra-Orthodox	Modern Orthodox	Conservative	Reform
More than once a week	62.1	51.5	4.7	0.9
Once a week	10.8	22.3	10.3	2.4
Once or twice a month	5.5	7.1	28.0	12.8
A few times a year/High Holidays	15.2	1.0	41.6	49.6
Seldom	4.3	12.2	10.4	22.8
Never	2.2	5.8	5.0	11.6
Total	100.1	99.9	100	100.1

Table 1.10 Factors perceived as essential to being Jewish (%)

	Ultra-Orthodox	Modern Orthodox	Conservative	Reform
Observing Jewish law	80.1	79.2	26.0	10.9
Being ethical	81.3	90.1	71.3	76.8
Working for justice	52.9	66.1	60.2	63.7
Caring about Israel	55.2	78.8	60.2	44.2
Being part of a Jewish community	69.5	72.1	42.5	26.1

of Reform Jews, consider observing Jewish law essential to being Jewish. Even with respect to being ethical, which more than 70 per cent of the non-Orthodox view as essential, there is apparently an additional halakhic element which results in even higher percentages among the Orthodox viewing it as essential. That fully 90 per cent of the Modern Orthodox so believe may well be a reflection of a basic difference between them and both most of the non-Orthodox and the ultra-Orthodox. The Modern Orthodox differ from the non-Orthodox in that they view observing Jewish law as essential, and they view interpersonal relations as an essential part of Jewish law. The non-Orthodox view interpersonal relations as being within the ethnic and cultural arena but not as obligatory under Jewish law. The Modern Orthodox also differ from the ultra-Orthodox with respect to two categories of *mitsvah* (religious obligations): those focusing on one's connection with God (*bein adam lamakom*) and those focusing on relations with other people (*bein adam leḥavero*). The former are often viewed as 'purely religious' while the latter are often thought of as 'socio-religious'. Although there is no basis in Jewish thought for according higher status or greater holiness to one or other of these categories, the empirical evidence suggests that ultra-Orthodox Jews tend to accord greater significance to *mitsvot bein adam lamakom* and the Modern Orthodox place greater emphasis on those involving interpersonal relations. Similarly, more Modern Orthodox than ultra-Orthodox also see working for justice, caring about Israel, and being part of a Jewish community as essential for being a Jew.

Political Behaviour

America's Jews, the overwhelming majority of whom are not Orthodox, have long defied a general pattern that the higher one's socio-economic status, the more one is likely to be politically conservative. The presidential voting pattern of America's Jews since the Great Depression, which began with the collapse of the stock market in 1929 and reached its peak in 1932–3 when a quarter of the country's workforce was unemployed, has been for them to support and vote for liberal candidates. Decades ago, the late Milton Himmelfarb, long-time editor of the *American Jewish Year Book* and a keen observer of American Jewry, suggested that although Jews most resemble Episcopalians, 'the most prosperous of all white groups, their voting behavior continued to be most like the voting behavior of one of the least prosperous of all groups, the Puerto Ricans'.[33] In other words, though many American Jews earn as much as those at the highest levels of society, they vote like those at the bottom.

There have been numerous attempts to explain the political liberalism of America's Jews, but none is completely satisfactory. One approach, most fully developed by Lawrence Fuchs,[34] averred that Jewish liberalism derives from such Jewish values as charity and philanthropy, learning and a respect for scholarship, and the imperative to improve the world. Charles Liebman argued that, if that were the case, we would expect that those who are closer to Jewish tradition would be more liberal. However, various local studies, including one by Liebman himself, as well as more current national data from the 2013 Pew survey of American Jews, indicate that just the opposite is the case. In contrast to Fuchs, Liebman argued that America's Jews are liberal

---

[33] Himmelfarb, 'The Jewish Vote (Again)', 81. Herbert Weisberg and Rafael Medoff have raised serious questions as to the extent to which America's Jews voted for the Democrat candidate in a number of twentieth-century presidential elections. See Weisberg, 'Reconsidering Jewish Presidential Voting Statistics', and Medoff, *Did the Jewish Vote Cost Truman New York?* Weisberg's analyses do not, however, challenge the broader trends, nor do they challenge the present findings and argument with respect to the voting patterns of Orthodox Jews.

[34] Fuchs, *The Political Behavior of American Jews.*

Table 1.11 Views on how Barack Obama is handling the economy (%)

	Ultra-Orthodox	Modern Orthodox	Conservative	Reform
Approve	23.7	36.3	59.4	65.6
Disapprove	76.3	63.7	40.6	34.4
Total	100	100	100	100

Table 1.12 Views on how Barack Obama is handling US policy towards Israel (%)

	Ultra-Orthodox	Modern Orthodox	Conservative	Reform
Approve	38.2	41.2	64.4	70.9
Disapprove	61.8	58.8	35.6	29.1
Total	100	100	100	100

Table 1.13 Views on how Barack Obama has dealt with Iran (%)

	Ultra-Orthodox	Modern Orthodox	Conservative	Reform
Approve	31.6	25.5	54.3	65.5
Disapprove	68.4	74.5	45.7	34.5
Total	100	100	100	100

because they are Jewishly ignorant and/or want to escape from their Jewish heritage.[35]

Orthodox Jews identify politically very differently than the non-Orthodox. When asked to evaluate President Obama's handling of the economy, his policies towards Israel, and how he has dealt with Iran, a significant majority of both ultra-Orthodox and Modern Orthodox disapproved, as compared to significant majorities of Conservative and Reform who approved (see Tables 1.11, 1.12, and 1.13).

Moreover, almost the same percentages of Modern Orthodox and ultra-Orthodox identify as Republicans, and there is a large gap between these two groups and the Conservative and Reform denominations (Table 1.14). The only differences between the ultra-Orthodox and Modern Orthodox in terms

[35] Liebman, *The Ambivalent American Jew*, esp. 53–159.

Table 1.14 Do you consider yourself a Republican, Democrat, or Independent?

	Ultra-Orthodox	Modern Orthodox	Conservative	Reform
Republican	42.0	41.0	15.7	11.3
Democrat	22.1	27.8	56.0	63.0
Independent	35.9	31.2	28.4	25.7
Total	100	100	100.1	100

Table 1.15 Responses to 'Do you lean more to the Republican Party or more to the Democratic Party?' (%)

	Ultra-Orthodox	Modern Orthodox	Conservative	Reform
Republican	53.2	61.3	55.2	31.5
Democrat	46.8	38.7	44.8	68.5
Total	100	100	100	100

of political party identification is in the percentages identifying as Democrat and Independent, with more of the Modern Orthodox identifying as Democrat and fewer as Independent.

However, the significance of that difference may be offset by the tendencies of the Independents. When those who did not identify as either Republican or Democrat were asked whether they lean more to the Republican Party or to the Democratic Party, significantly more of the Modern Orthodox than the ultra-Orthodox indicated that they leant towards the Republican Party (Table 1.15).

The significant differences between Orthodox and non-Orthodox political identification are in large measure manifestations of significant differences in socio-cultural ideology, i.e. whether one is conservative or liberal, with the Orthodox being significantly more conservative ideologically and the non-Orthodox much more liberal. As seen in Table 1.16, most ultra-Orthodox (58.7%) describe their political views as conservative or very conservative. Almost the same percentage of Modern Orthodox (57%) describe their political views as moderate to very liberal, while 42.9 per cent describe them as conservative or very conservative. Not surprisingly, both groups of Orthodox are significantly more politically conservative than both Conservative (27.9%) and Reform (14.1%).

Table 1.16 How respondents describe their political views (%)

	Ultra-Orthodox	Modern Orthodox	Conservative	Reform
Very conservative	13.5	15.9	4.3	1.8
Conservative	45.2	27.0	23.6	12.3
Moderate	28.8	35.2	36.1	30.4
Liberal	10.3	17.7	27.2	37.8
Very liberal	2.2	4.1	8.8	17.7
Total	100	99.9	100	100

Data on the greater political conservatism among the Orthodox have been documented since at least the mid-1980s. In a survey conducted for the American Jewish Congress, Martin Hochbaum found that among Jewish voters the Orthodox vote was the highest for the Republican Ronald Reagan and the lowest for the Democrat Walter Mondale, and that Orthodox Jews are much more likely than others to identify as politically conservative.[36] Although there do not seem to be any earlier survey data showing a higher rate of political conservatism, Liebman cited various indicators dating back to at least the 1960s to show that the Orthodox tend to be conservative.[37] This pattern is not at all unique to America's Jews, but is generally found in Western societies, with the more religiously traditional being more socio-politically traditional and the more religiously liberal being more socio-politically liberal. Moreover, as will be indicated below, many ultra-Orthodox and Modern Orthodox who do not explicitly identify as politically conservative hold conservative positions on a number of key political issues. Indeed, as Pew has found, 'Orthodox Jews more closely resemble white evangelical Protestants than they resemble other U.S. Jews.'[38] Perhaps this is related to different perspectives on life in general; conservatives are much less trusting and optimistic than are liberals and radicals.[39] In the religious realm, the ultra-Orthodox are suspicious and assume

[36] Hochbaum, *The Jewish Vote in the 1984 Presidential Election*.

[37] Liebman, *The Ambivalent American Jew*, 143–4. In fact, Werner Cohn has shown that, from 1886 until the end of the 1920s, while American Jews as a whole were 'famous for their radical voting habits', the Orthodox Yiddish press 'was generally Republican in its political preferences'. See Cohn, 'The Politics of American Jews', 621. During the 1930s the Orthodox favoured Roosevelt and the Democrats, where they remained solidly until the 1960s.

[38] Pew Research Center, 'A Portrait of American Orthodox Jews', 3.

[39] As Gerhard Lenski points out, conservatives have historically been distrustful of man's basic nature. For a summary of the basic philosophical, political, and social issues over which conservatives and radicals are divided, see Lenski, *Power and Privilege*, 22–3.

something is not kosher unless they are guaranteed that it is, even in Israel. Moreover, they do not trust the supervision of anyone who is not himself ultra-Orthodox—or even that of many who are.

An interesting aspect of this, however, is that the Orthodox are conservative on issues that Christian religious conservatives are not: they tend to be conservative on socio-cultural issues such as those involving sexuality, childrearing, and family life, but they are not necessarily conservative on socio-economic issues.[40] The correlation between religious conservatism and socio-political conservatism may be, as James Davison Hunter has argued, a reflection of the emergence of the 'culture wars' in American society with the 'orthodoxy' of religious and cultural-political conservatives on one side and the 'progressivism' of religious and cultural-political liberals on the other.[41] It is nevertheless puzzling that American Orthodox Jews are conservative on socio-economic as well as socio-cultural issues. When respondents were asked whether they would rather have a smaller government providing fewer services, or a bigger government providing more services, a majority of both ultra-Orthodox (57.5%) and Modern Orthodox (58.5%) said they would prefer a smaller government providing fewer services. In fact, on this question the Modern Orthodox were even slightly more conservative than the ultra-Orthodox. This is somewhat surprising, especially in light of what was suggested earlier about the Modern Orthodox placing greater emphasis on *mitsvot* involving interpersonal relations and the ultra-Orthodox placing greater emphasis on those involving relations between humans and God. On that basis, it might be expected that more of the Modern Orthodox would support such services as a reflection of a sense of society's collective responsibility for its needy,[42] which Jewish religious tradition supports. As Isadore Twersky pointed out,

the Halakhah has assigned an indispensable, all inclusive role to the community. The community acts not only as a supervisory, enforcing agency but occupies the center of the stage as an entity possessed of initiative and charged with responsibility. One may persuasively argue that the Halakhah makes of philanthropy a collective project; philanthropic endeavor, long-term aid (*kupah*) as well as immediate, emergency relief (*tamḥuy*), is thoroughly institutionalized.[43]

The Pew data indicating that Orthodox Jews would prefer fewer government-provided services are from 2013. We have no data from previous years. It may

[40] N. J. Davis and Robinson, 'Religious Orthodoxy in American Society'; Ellis and Stimson, *Ideology in America*, 115–48.

[41] Hunter, *Culture Wars*; Pew Research Center, 'Is There a Culture War?'

[42] Waxman, *The Stigma of Poverty*.

[43] Twersky, 'Some Aspects of the Jewish Attitude toward the Welfare State', 145.

Table 1.17 Views on whether homosexuality should be accepted or discouraged by society (%)

	Ultra-Orthodox	Modern Orthodox	Conservative	Reform
Encouraged	35.6	56.9	86.7	95.3
Discouraged	64.4	43.1	13.3	4.7
Total	100	100	100	100

Table 1.18 Agree/disagree with accepting homosexuals in the community (%; self-definition)

	Absolutely agree	Agree	Disagree	Absolutely oppose	Don't know/ refused to answer	Total
Haredim (ultra-Orthodox)	7	4	14	60	15	100
Ḥardalim /toraniyim (ultra-Orthodox Zionists)	5	14	8.5	64	8.5	100
National religious	16	23.5	19	34	7.5	100
Liberal/Modern Orthodox	36	21	16	25	2	100
Traditional religious	24	30	15	25	6	100
Traditional not religious	41	28	9	17	5	100
Secular	57	25	7	7	4	100

Source: Hermann et al., *The National-Religious Sector in Israel 2014* (Heb.), table 4.8 (p. 124). Categories are somewhat different in Israel but can nevertheless be used for comparison on certain issues, such as homosexuality.

be speculated, therefore, that Orthodox attitudes on government size and spending are related to their perceptions of President Obama's position regarding Israel. The Orthodox may have become increasingly disillusioned with the American government because of what many of them view as its less than warm relationship with Israel. Systematic study will be required to determine whether this suggestion has any validity.

The interpersonal focus of the Modern Orthodox is evident with respect to the question of whether homosexuality should be accepted or discouraged by society. Although less accepting than Conservative (86.7%) and Reform (95.3%), the Modern Orthodox (56.9%) are considerably more accepting than are the ultra-Orthodox (35.6%) (Table 1.17). The suggestion that the ultra-Orthodox and Modern Orthodox attitudes towards homosexuals in the community derive from the different categories of *mitsvot* which they emphasize appears to be supported by their similarity to those of their counterparts in Israel. A survey by the Israel Democracy Institute's Guttman Center for Surveys found similar percentages of Orthodox responding positively to the question whether homosexuals should be accepted in the community (Table 1.18). In recent years the divide between the Modern and ultra-Orthodox in Israel has apparently grown. Indications are that the rate of Modern Orthodox acceptance of homosexuality there has accelerated significantly.[44] For reasons discussed in the following chapters, it is more than reasonable to predict that there will soon be a similar growing divide in American Orthodoxy.

[44] Rosner, 'How Israel's Modern-Orthodox Jews Came Out of the Closet'.

TWO

THE CONTEMPORARY
ORTHODOX JEWISH FAMILY
IN AMERICA

ALL TOO FREQUENTLY, discussions of 'the Jewish family' are based on the assumption that there is one single model, and that is a stereotypical Jewish family in eastern Europe. But this is a misconception; from as early as 597 BCE, Jews have been 'a nation spread out and separated among the nations'. In every society that they have dwelt in, they have acculturated to some degree and internalized that society's cultural patterns. This is a major source of the differences between the traditions of Ashkenazim and Sephardim, of Jews from North Africa and those from Asia, and so on, and also a cause of variation within these groups. Hence, the Polish Jewish family differed from the German Jewish family, the German from the Turkish, and the Turkish from the Moroccan.[1]

There is also a tendency towards nostalgia, romanticizing 'good old days' that in many ways, as the late Professor Nathan Goldberg would consistently remind his students at Yeshiva College, were actually not so good at all. Nor were most Jewish families like the stereotypical large, multi-generational, extended family in which people married young, were cared for by parents and in-laws while they had many children, and where all the family members lived near each other and shared warmth and bliss.

Shaul Stampfer, for example, rejects the notion that the east European family was patriarchal. As he convincingly demonstrates, multi-generational families were to be found among farmers, but not among merchants and craftsmen, and since Jews were predominantly the latter, multi-generational families were rare among them. Also, physical abuse of women was roundly condemned; women had an active and independent role in economic matters; very many if not most wives worked to help support their families; and wives made the most important daily decisions for the family, including what

---

[1] This raises an interesting and important question, which cannot be discussed here, as to whether one can speak of 'Jewish culture' or even 'Jewish identity' as if there are such things when, perhaps, there is actually only a range of individual Jewish cultures and identities.

household items should be purchased, disciplining children, and finding spouses for their children.[2] He likewise shows that the age of marriage among east European Jews rose during the nineteenth century and even more significantly during the inter-war years of the twentieth century.[3] If that is not enough, the evidence also indicates that there was a high level of divorce in east European traditional Jewish society.[4]

With that understanding, the analysis now turns to the American Jewish family in general, and the American Orthodox Jewish family in particular.

Marriage

The evidence indicates that, until recently, although Jewish men and women in the United States married somewhat later than non-Jews, this was not a reflection of a decline in the significance of marriage and family for them. They were still more likely than non-Jews to marry eventually, and they were less likely to divorce and remain divorced.[5] Most recent evidence, however, leads us to question whether the values of the larger American Jewish community with respect to marriage and family remain as strong as they once were. According to the 2008 Pew Religious Landscape Survey, the gap between Jewish and Christian Americans has narrowed and, in some cases, is non-existent. The survey showed that rates of marriage for Jews and mainline Protestants[6] were identical, and only very slightly lower than that of Catholics.[7] Evidence also indicated that Jews have a high rate of cohabitation before marriage, and it has been suggested that this might be attributed to their high levels of education as well as to their liberal attitude towards premarital sex and cohabitation.[8] At least for the past decade, however, the percentage of American adults aged 25 and older who have never married has been rapidly increasing, and a growing number of Americans say that 'society is just as well off if people have priorities other than marriage and children'. That was

---

[2] Stampfer, *Families, Rabbis, and Education*, 121–41; id., 'How Jewish Society Adapted to Change in Male/Female Relationships'.   [3] Stampfer, 'Marital Patterns in Interwar Poland'.

[4] Stampfer, *Families, Rabbis, and Education*, 45–9; Freeze, *Jewish Marriage and Divorce in Imperial Russia*.   [5] Waite, 'The American Jewish Family', 38.

[6] 'Mainline Protestants' describes a group of Protestant churches in the United States that primarily includes the Methodists, Lutherans, Presbyterians, Episcopalians, Baptists, and Congregationalists. Until the mid-twentieth century, mainline Protestants were the majority of American Christians and, as George Marsden indicates, their 'leaders were part of the liberal-moderate cultural mainstream, and their leading spokespersons were respected participants in the national conversation' (Marsden, *The Twilight of the American Enlightenment*, 99). Since then, their numbers and prestige have declined.

[7] Pew Forum on Religion & Public Life, 'U.S. Religious Landscape Survey', 67.

[8] Ibid. 39–40.

the attitude of 50 per cent of those surveyed, while only 46 per cent believed that 'society is better off if people make marriage and having children a priority'.[9] Whether Jews follow these patterns is not evident from the national data.

The limited data available from previous research found a strong correlation between religious traditionalism and family traditionalism; that is, the more religiously traditional had a higher rate of marriage and an average number of children, and a lower rate of intermarriage.[10] The Pew 2013 survey dramatically confirms those earlier findings. Orthodox Jews have a much higher rate of marriage than other Jews. As compared to the 69 per cent of Orthodox Jews above the age of 18 who are married, 55 per cent of Conservative, 52 per cent of Reform, and only 44 per cent of Jews with no denominational affiliation are married. Perhaps the most surprising finding in this part of the survey is that, while 79 per cent of ultra-Orthodox adults are married, only 52 per cent of Modern Orthodox are. That is a slightly lower rate of marriage than that of Conservative Jews.

Taken as a whole, Orthodox Jews are more likely to marry than the non-Orthodox and they also marry younger. Of the married Orthodox Jews surveyed, 68 per cent were married by the age of 24, as compared to 32 per cent of Conservatives, 26 per cent of Reform, and 27 per cent of non-denominationally affiliated Jews. Once again, there are differences between ultra-Orthodox and Modern Orthodox Jews, with 75 per cent of the ultra-Orthodox but only 48 per cent of the Modern Orthodox married by the age of 24.[11]

Given both the higher rates and younger age of marriage among the Orthodox, it is somewhat puzzling that there is a fairly widespread sense in the American Orthodox community that it is becoming increasingly difficult for young, single Orthodox Jews to find a mate, and that there is a 'shidduch crisis'.[12] Orthodox magazines and newspapers have been discussing it during the past decade,[13] at least one book has been written on it,[14] and it has recently been featured on *Time* magazine's website.[15] If the Pew data are accurate, it would seem that, in fact, there is no such crisis, certainly not in the ultra-Orthodox community, on which most of the writing focuses.

The later age of marriage in the Modern Orthodox community is probably largely related to educational and occupational patterns. As will be discussed,

[9] Wang and Parker, 'Record Share of Americans Have Never Married', 4–5.
[10] Brodbar-Nemzer, 'Divorce and the Jewish Community'; Goldscheider, 'Childlessness and Religiosity'; Lehrer and Chiswick, 'Religion as a Determinant of Marital Stability'.
[11] Pew Research Center, 'Portrait of American Orthodox Jews', 8–9.
[12] 'Shidduch' is the Anglicized form of a Hebrew term meaning 'match', especially a match between a young man and woman for the purpose of marriage.
[13] A Google search turns up dozens of writings on the subject.
[14] Salamon, *The Shidduch Crisis*.
[15] Birger, 'What Two Religions Tell Us about the Dating Crisis'.

Modern Orthodox men and women have high educational and status aspirations, and one price of achieving those is to leave one's family and community and go to places where there are probably fewer Orthodox Jews who might serve as potential spouses. Whether there has been a general decline in the value of marriage in the Modern Orthodox community as there has been in American society as a whole is a question which requires further research.

Divorce

The 2008 Pew survey also found that the percentage of divorced or separated Jews (9%) was lower than that of Mainline Protestants (12%), Evangelical Protestants (13%), and Catholics (10%).[16] The data from that survey were not broken down by Jewish denomination, but the Pew 2013 data were. Interestingly, they show that, among Jews, the percentage of those who are divorced is virtually the same across denominational lines.[17] This contrasts sharply with the situation in the 1960s when, in their study of the Jewish population in Providence, Rhode Island, Sidney Goldstein and Calvin Goldscheider found the divorce rate to be higher among Reform than among Conservative and Orthodox Jews.[18] A decade later, there were indications that the Orthodox divorce rate had risen. For example, the guidance counsellor in a large Bais Yaakov girls' high school in Boro Park, Brooklyn, the largest Orthodox Jewish neighbourhood in the United States, estimated that about 8 per cent of the school's approximately 1,000 girls came from homes in which the parents were divorced. Given that this is an ultra-Orthodox school in an intensely Orthodox neighbourhood, this figure was a surprise, especially to those who were unfamiliar with the high rate of divorce among Jews in eastern Europe in the nineteenth and early twentieth centuries. Additionally, the reported figures relate to divorce in the families of high-school-age girls, where one might think that parents would be more hesitant to divorce out of concern for the impact on their children. If younger or childless divorced Orthodox Jews had been included in the sample, the percentage of divorcees might have been even higher. Even with the increase, however, the Orthodox divorce rate remained lower than that of the non-Orthodox up to 1990, as indicated in that year's National Jewish Population Survey, which found a significantly lower divorce rate among those baby boomers identifying as Orthodox than among those identifying as Conservative and Reform.[19] The finding in the 2013 Pew

---

[16] Pew Forum on Religion & Public Life, 'U.S. Religious Landscape Survey', 119.

[17] Pew Research Center, 'A Portrait of American Orthodox Jews', 3 n. 2.

[18] Goldstein and Goldscheider, *Jewish Americans*, 113.

[19] Waxman, *Jewish Baby Boomers*, 51.

survey that 'The share of divorced respondents is comparable across all Jewish denominations' is indicative of a dramatic change in the Orthodox community. Without more extensive research we can only speculate as to whether this suggests that Orthodox family life in the past was less perfect than it has frequently been portrayed as being, or whether it may be the result of increased social mobility. As outlined above, although the Orthodox generally have a lower educational and economic status than other denominations, with the exception of the hasidic community their position has improved. If the rise in the Orthodox divorce rate has its roots in increased social mobility, is that because of greater financial pressures on husbands, wives, or both? Is it because both partners have more contact with others outside the immediate environs of the Jewish world, which sometimes leads to personal relationships that jeopardize the marital bond? Has social mobility afforded wives a greater degree of economic independence, enabling some to escape what had previously been a marital trap? Has the rise in the educational status of Orthodox women led wives to be unhappy with what they increasingly view as their unequal status in both their marriage and the Orthodox community? These and many other possibilities need to be examined very carefully. Until they are, we can point to the change, but we cannot explain it.

Agunot

A related issue, particularly within the Orthodox community, is that of *agunot* (from *agunah*, anchored, in the sense of not being free to move on). In Jewish law, a woman is considered legally married until she receives a *get* (a bill of religious divorce) or until her husband dies. Historically, the term *agunah* brought to mind a woman whose husband was missing, his fate unknown. Currently, the term more typically refers to the wife of a recalcitrant husband who refuses to give his wife a *get*, either because he has not come to terms with the finality of divorce, out of a desire for vengeance, to extort a large sum of money from his wife, or as a bargaining chip because his wife is withholding access to the couple's children. The consequences of not having a *get* are much more severe for wives than husbands because the prohibition on men having multiple spouses is much milder and much more recent than the law regarding women. A woman who remarries during the lifetime of her husband without a *get* is deemed an adulteress, and a child from the new union is deemed a *mamzer*, a status which historically has severely restricted their ability to marry and be part of the Jewish community. In Jewish law, a husband can issue a *get* to his wife, but she can't give one to her husband; also, except in rare cases, a husband cannot be forced to issue a *get* against his will. He therefore has significant power over his wife. Moreover, while Israeli rabbinic courts have the authority to punish recalcitrant husbands and thus encourage them to issue the *get*, American rabbinic courts have no such authority. The document has no legal standing in the United States, and its administration is not centralized, so husbands are much freer and less subject to social controls.

There are no data indicating an increase in the percentage of *agunot*, but in recent years much more attention has been given to the phenomenon both by the media and in halakhic deliberations. Throughout the second half of the twentieth century there were various rabbinic proposals for ameliorating, if not solving, the *agunah* problem. The most famous of these proposals came from Rabbi Dr Eliezer Berkovitz and Rabbi Dr Emanuel Rackman,[20] but both were rejected by the leading halakhic authorities. In 1992, the Orthodox community succeeded in having the 'New York State *Get* Law' passed, which stated that the giving of a *get* would be calculated as one of a variety of factors that the courts weigh in determining the equitable distribution of marital property in divorce proceedings. This provided a legal incentive to husbands to co-operate. However, the law met with some opposition on both legal and halakhic grounds.[21] A more acceptable means of reducing, if not eliminating, the problem of *agunot* is through a prenuptial contract. One approach, approved in 1979 by Rabbi Moshe Feinstein in response to a query from Rabbi Yechiel Perr, is for the engagement contract (*tena'im*) to include a condition whereby if a married couple should separate, the husband will not resist giving a *get* and the wife will not refuse to accept it if a *beit din* (rabbinic court) so orders. By means of this condition, the secular courts can force both spouses to adhere to the *beit din*'s orders.[22] Several years later, in response to a question by his son-in-law Rabbi Dr Moshe D. Tendler, Rabbi Feinstein stated that it is permissible to attach to the standard *ketubah* (marriage contract), which is written in Aramaic, an English translation, so that both spouses will understand all of the conditions of the contract. They will be enforceable in civil courts, and in some cases may prevent the wife from becoming an *agunah*.[23] There are no data indicating how widely these suggestions of Rabbis Perr, Tendler, and Feinstein were implemented.

The most wide-ranging attempt thus far to encourage the use of a prenuptial agreement in the Orthodox community was undertaken by the Orthodox

[20] Berkovitz, *Stipulation in Marriage and Divorce (Heb.)*. Rackman's proposal, initially submitted in 1975, was strongly rejected by Rabbi Soloveitchik. In 1996 Rackman established his own *beit din* (rabbinic court) and used the technique of annulment, which had previously been rejected. See Singer, 'Emanuel Rackman', 139–40.

[21] Breitowitz, *Between Civil and Religious Law*; Broyde, 'The 1992 New York Get Law'; Malinowitz and Broyde, 'The 1992 New York Get Law: An Exchange'.

[22] Feinstein, *Igerot mosheh*, *Even ha'ezer*, pt. 4, no. 107.   [23] Ibid., no. 90.

Caucus, a short-lived Modern Orthodox venture in the early 1990s which, according to its mission statement, sought 'to promote and support community events and programs concerning ethical and rabbinical matters'. Its biggest success was in sponsoring and promoting a prenuptial agreement designed by Rabbi Mordechai Willig, a senior faculty member at Yeshiva University's Rabbi Isaac Elchanan Theological Seminary. The document was officially adopted in a 1993 resolution of the Rabbinical Council of America, which urged its members to use it. It was also widely endorsed by pulpit rabbis, and in 1994 the Rabbinical Council reaffirmed its endorsement and committed itself to making its importance known to as wide a public as possible.[24] In addition to virtually unanimous endorsement by Modern Orthodox rabbis, it has also been endorsed by many prominent ultra-Orthodox rabbis. Nevertheless, Agudath Israel of America refuses to endorse it. According to its director of public affairs, 'There is a concern that introducing and focusing on the possible dissolution of a marriage when it is just beginning is not conducive to the health of the marriage . . . I don't think it is really possible to gauge [the efficacy of prenuptial agreements] without data, and in any event, it would be impossible to know when the existence of a prenup might have eased the way toward a divorce when a marriage might, with effort and determination, have been saved.'[25] In sum, the agreement is recommended but not required by the Rabbinical Council, is not recommended by Agudath Israel nor, presumably, by most ultra-Orthodox rabbis, and is used much less frequently among the ultra-Orthodox than among Modern Orthodox Jews.

Singles and Sexual Activity

There has not only been a growing awareness of singles in the Modern Orthodox community, but also a noticeable growth of singles communities, such as the one in Manhattan's West Side. These communities present certain challenges even as they resolve others.[26] As early as the mid-1980s, Calvin Goldscheider pointed to the rising Orthodox divorce rate and suggested that the primary challenge was the potential religious alienation of the divorced as a result of their not being in a family. Likewise, he pointed to the growing pattern of later marriage as challenging in that it resulted in increasing numbers of Jews feeling rejected due to their unmarried status and becoming reli-

---

[24] The text of the prenuptial agreement as well as its rabbinic endorsements are in Herring and Auman (eds.), *The Prenuptial Agreement*.

[25] Quoted in Lavin, 'For Many Agunot, Halachic Prenups Won't Break Their Chains'.

[26] The Modern Orthodox singles community in the Katamon neighbourhood of Jerusalem was the subject of the popular Israeli television series, *Srugim*, created by Hava Divon and Eliezer Shapiro.

giously alienated.[27] The new Orthodox singles communities undoubtedly serve as a buffer against this alienation, but they may also be making it increasingly acceptable and less inconvenient to remain single longer. They also potentially challenge Orthodoxy in a number of ways, threatening a reduction in the birth rate and reduced observance of Jewish law with respect to sexual matters, such as the taboo on masturbation, the prohibition on sexual relations outside marriage, and the laws of *mikveh* (ritual bathing) and sexual purity.

The requirement of abstinence from all sexual activity prior to marriage has been a Jewish religious norm for at least 2,000 years and, presumably, it was always difficult to adhere to. Not only late marriage, but also the religious challenges it presents, are not new.[28] What has changed is the frequency, intimacy, and openness of interaction between men and women and, perhaps even more significant, their religious, ethnic, and sexual status. Their increased social and cultural equality in the wider society often removes the social and psychological barriers that once prevented the development of intimacy. As a result, there appear to have been changes in behaviour in this realm even among the Orthodox.

In the 1960s Rabbi Dr Irving ('Yitz') Greenberg, a prominent Modern Orthodox rabbi, historian, and theologian, was a highly regarded professor at Yeshiva University.[29] In an interview that appeared in the college newspaper, he made remarks about 'a new value system and corresponding new *halachot* about sex' which were interpreted by some as his advocating new halakhic approaches to sex for unmarried as well as married men and women.[30] This caused an uproar at Yeshiva University as well as within the Modern Orthodox community, and Greenberg wrote a lengthy letter to the editor of that newspaper in which he disavowed the permissibility of sex outside marriage, clarified his views regarding sex *within* marriage, and apologized for being insufficiently clear and precise in the interview.[31] Despite his clarification, he was roundly criticized by Rabbi Dr Aharon Lichtenstein, a more conservative Modern Orthodox intellectual.[32] Ultimately, the debate between these two leading intellectuals

[27] Goldscheider, 'Family Changes and the Challenge to American Orthodoxy'.

[28] Stampfer, *Families, Rabbis, and Education*, 7–25. For a study of the challenges and how they are dealt with, see Frances, 'A Qualitative Study of Sexual-Religious Conflict in Single Orthodox Jewish Men'. For studies of many of the same conflicts among Israeli Modern Orthodox singles, but with a somewhat different perspective, see Engelberg, 'Religious Zionist Singles', and id., 'Seeking a "Pure Relationship"?'

[29] On his subsequent contributions to Jewish theology and Jewish communal life, see S. T. Katz and Bayme (eds.), *Continuity and Change*.

[30] Harold Goldberg, 'Dr. Greenberg Discusses Orthodoxy, YU, Viet Nam & Sex', 11.

[31] I. Greenberg, 'Greenberg Clarifies and Defends His Views', 8.

[32] Lichtenstein (1933–2015), a son-in-law of Rabbi Joseph B. Soloveitchik, was then a *rosh*

was not about sexuality or the family but, rather, about the meaning and halakhic limits of Modern Orthodoxy, with Greenberg representing the more radical and Lichtenstein the more conservative approach.[33]

Despite the unanimous rejection by the Orthodox rabbinic leadership of the permissibility of sexual relations outside marriage, the phenomenon itself was apparently accelerating and the attitude towards it was becoming more accepting within the Orthodox population. In their mid-1980s study of varieties of Orthodox Jews, Samuel Heilman and Steven Cohen found, across the range of Orthodox types they studied, that 'younger respondents consistently reported more indulgent attitudes toward the practice of premarital sex than their older counterparts'.[34] According to Heilman and Cohen, almost a quarter of those they labelled 'centrists' did not disapprove of sexual relations between couples who were dating seriously; as many as 40 per cent did not disapprove of sex between couples engaged to be married; among younger centrists, only about half disapproved of sex between those dating seriously, and less than half disapproved of it for engaged couples. Although these figures reflect attitudes, it is hard to imagine that there was a highly significant gap between attitudes and behaviour.[35] The popularity of the expression 'tefillin date' also apparently reflected a reality of otherwise observant Orthodox Jews who slept with their date but took their tefillin with them, indicating that they were fairly certain they would stay overnight and that they would pray, wearing their tefillin, the following morning.

These attitudes and the corresponding behaviour are typically rationalized by those young Orthodox Jews who have sexual relations on dates, but they are not actually legitimated by the Orthodox establishment. One attempt to legitimate them halakhically came from Zvi Zohar.[36] Basing his argument on the opinions of such figures as Nahmanides, Abraham ben David (Rabad), Solomon ben Adret (Rashba), and Jacob Emden, he said that there is no prohibition against sexual relations outside marriage so long as the relationship

yeshivah at Yeshiva University. He subsequently emigrated to Israel, was *rosh yeshivah* at Yeshivat Har Etzion, and continued to be a leading intellectual figure within Modern Orthodoxy. See Hallamish and Schwartz, 'Edut le'aharon: Jubilee Volume' (Heb.); Yitzchak Blau, Jotkowitz, and Ziegler (eds.), 'Studies in the Thought and Scholarship of Rabbi Aharon Lichtenstein *zt"l*'. I thank Menachem Butler for providing me with copies of the letters from *The Commentator*.

[33] The much broader Greenberg–Lichtenstein debates are astutely recounted and analysed in Singer, 'Debating Modern Orthodoxy at Yeshiva College'.

[34] Heilman and Cohen, *Cosmopolitans and Parochials*, 173–9.

[35] Heilman and Cohen's designation of 'centrist' is very different from the way it is conceived at Yeshiva University, and this largely reflects the differences between behavioural and ideological Modern Orthodoxy discussed above. See David Berger's highly critical review of Heilman and Cohen's book.   [36] Zohar, 'Intimacy within Halakhah' (Heb.).

is not illicit, that is, it is consensual and monogamous, and the woman observes the laws governing abstinence and separation during and immediately after her menstrual period followed by immersion in a ritual bath. Zohar's thesis was strongly rejected by a range of prominent figures in the religious Zionist/Modern Orthodox community.[37] Despite their rejection of its halakhic legitimacy, the Israeli Orthodox and traditional communities perceived the phenomenon of sexual relations among the unmarried to be significant enough for Yonah Metzger, who was then Ashkenazi chief rabbi, to issue a ban on allowing unmarried women to use the *mikveh*.[38] Since women do not normally have to prove that they are married to do this, the effectiveness of the ban is anyone's guess.[39]

Intermarriage

One of the most striking differences between the Orthodox and non-Orthodox populations in the United States is in the area of intermarriage. The 2013 Pew survey found that, among married Jews with no denominational affiliation, less than a third (31%) have a Jewish spouse; among married Reform Jews, 50 per cent have a Jewish spouse; and among married Conservative Jews, almost 75 per cent are married to Jews. By contrast, virtually all Orthodox respondents who are married—98 per cent—have a Jewish spouse.[40]

These findings are interpreted by some as proof that Orthodoxy is the best, if not the only, safeguard against intermarriage and assimilation. Although the minuscule intermarriage rate and other characteristics of the Orthodox discussed in this study give cause for optimism about their survival and growth in American society, the findings on intermarriage should be taken with a measure of caution. It is well known that intermarriage is condemned in Orthodox communities, and it is reasonable to assume that someone raised as Orthodox who does intermarry will not want to experience the stigma of intermarriage, and will leave Orthodoxy. That person would not therefore be included in the Orthodox sample.

[37] Critiques by Ariel, Henkin, and Tikochinsky and Frankel appear in *Akdamot*, 17 (2007).

[38] His rationale apparently being that if they could not comply with the law of immersion after their menstrual period, they would refrain from sexual relations.

[39] It may have an impact on some single women known as such within their community, who may be forced to use a *mikveh* elsewhere.

[40] Pew Research Center, 'A Portrait of Jewish Americans', 37. Alan Cooperman and Gregory A. Smith, director and associate director of religion research at the Pew Forum, indicated in personal communications (7 Jan. 2015) that the sample was below the minimally acceptable size for analysis of differences between ultra-Orthodox and Modern Orthodox.

Abuse in the Family

As indicated by the data on divorce discussed above, not all Orthodox Jews have strong marriages or family values, nor do they all manifest those values in the same way. We do not have hard data on spouse abuse for either the broader American Jewish community or for the Orthodox community, Modern or ultra-Orthodox. In her study of responses to spouse abuse in ultra-Orthodox communities, Roberta Farber reported that professionals believe that spouse abuse is as common among Jews as it is in the general population.[41] Likewise, with respect to sexual abuse within families, Michelle Friedman studied more than 400 observant Orthodox women in the United States and Israel and reported that, 'Sadly, we found the same statistics for sexual molestation and abuse of girls and teens as in the secular population.'[42] Neither Farber and Friedman nor any other studies suggest that there has been an *increase* in either spousal or sexual abuse of minors within Orthodox families. What is significant here is that there is likewise no evidence of any *decrease* in either of these crimes. What has changed is the reaction to abuse. Until recently, abuse within the Orthodox community was, at best, dealt with within the community; but all too often it was simply ignored. Recently, there has been a growing awareness of the problem and calls for it to be handled by the authorities as required by law.[43]

Developments Influencing Sexual Behaviour

Be that as it may, there have clearly been social and cultural changes, including technological changes, in the United States that have affected the Orthodox Jewish approach to family and family behaviour. To begin with, sex is much more public than it was just a few decades ago. Not only are words and scenes that were previously taboo on television now normal prime-time fare; the Internet has broken all barriers. There are no longer any taboos, and it is increasingly difficult not to be bombarded with pornography. Whatever one thinks of the freedom of the press, the airwaves, and the Web, they impact on religious behaviour, especially among young adults. Some parents refuse to allow television and some refuse to allow the Internet into the home, while others implement various net filters, but none of these is foolproof and no one is immune. Of course, none of us was ever totally immune, and the Orthodox community is struggling to adapt as best as it can. It appears that the only ones who are talking publicly about the problem are those who have decided

---

[41] Farber, 'The Programmatic Response of the Ultra-Orthodox American Jewish Community to Wife Abuse'.   [42] Friedman, 'On Intimacy, Love, *Kedushah* and Sexuality', 187.
[43] On spouse abuse, see Twerski, *The Shame Borne in Silence*. On child abuse, see Eidensohn, *Child and Domestic Abuse*, and id., 'Child and Domestic Abuse: Compact Practical Guide'.

to completely ban the new technologies, but not too many appear to be following their lead.

Infertility and Artificial Insemination

Relatively recent scientific developments have also had a significant impact on Jewish family life in that for the first time in history human beings can conveniently and effectively control reproduction. This has had a major impact on attitudes towards sexual behaviour, making it less risky for those, both married and unmarried, who do not presently want children. New medical techniques have also been developed which enable previously infertile couples to have children. With all of that, however, come a myriad of halakhic issues. One of the first and most controversial of these is artificial insemination.

Beginning in the late 1950s, Rabbi Moshe Feinstein issued lenient rulings concerning different types of artificial insemination: where the donor was Jewish, where he was not, and where he was the husband. Feinstein was fiercely attacked by numerous opponents, including Joel Teitelbaum, the Satmar Rebbe. Since then, a large body of literature has emerged on matters of fertility and halakhah.[44] With respect to the specific issue at hand, Baruch Finkelstein analysed Rabbi Feinstein's method of ruling in a series of questions related to childbearing. He concluded that Rabbi Feinstein's lenient rulings 'were motivated by his compassion for the infertile woman'.[45] In an address to a conference in Jerusalem on the occasion of the publication in Hebrew of Richard Grazi's book on infertility, Rabbi Dr Benny Lau emphasized the impact of *hashkafah* (religious perspective) on halakhah and lauded the declarations by the rabbinic head of a leading fertility institute that 'There is no halakhic infertility' and that 'We will go the entire route with this couple in order to resolve the problem.' By contrast, Rabbi Gideon Weitzman rejected the notion that compassion motivated Rabbi Feinstein's decisions. He asserted that, for Rabbi Feinstein 'and all other *poskim*' it is halakhah that determines the approach to ethical problems, and decisions are based on a careful analysis of the halakhic sources; the law is not adjusted to accommodate the problem.[46]

Single Motherhood

An issue related to artificial insemination also addresses an aspect of the singles phenomenon, namely voluntary single motherhood. One of the earliest socio-

[44]   See e.g. Grazi, *Overcoming Infertility*, and all of the sources to which he refers.

[45]   Finkelstein, 'Characteristics and Patterns in Rabbi Moshe Feinstein's Rulings' (Heb.), 2. On Feinstein's decision, see Chapter 6 below.

[46]   Weitzman, 'Technology in the Service of the First Mitzvah'. The broad question of the role of the *posek* (decisor) in *pesikah* (halakhic decision-making), including the extent to which his own perspectives and sentiments, as well as social and psychological forces, have a place in the process of halakhic determination, is discussed in Chapter 6 below.

logical studies of this phenomenon focused only on the Reform branch of Judaism and found it to be basically accepting.[47] Since then, Conservative Judaism has likewise become increasingly accepting. Mainstream Orthodox Judaism opposes voluntary single motherhood, as a social policy if not on 'pure' halakhic grounds, but in Israel it is gaining acceptance among some Modern Orthodox rabbis. Dvora Ross, a computer engineer and mathematician, founder of an organization that aims to provide support for religious single mothers by choice, and herself a single mother by choice, has staunchly defended single motherhood in an article on artificial insemination.[48] Most of the Orthodox criticism of this article is not on purely halakhic grounds but focuses instead on the negative consequences for the Jewish family unit.[49] To many, as Rabbi Aharon Lichtenstein points out in his seminal essay on the role of social factors in halakhah,[50] such concerns are within the purview of the halakhist. Others, such as Rabbi David Stav, chief rabbi of the city of Shoham and a founder and chairman of Tzohar, an organization of religious Zionist rabbis that strives to bridge the gap between religious and secular Jews in Israel, argue that the only halakhic issue is that the father's identity is unknown, as that might present a problem of potential incest when the child wishes to marry. Other than that, 'on the halakhic level, there is no argument between the *posekim* that there is no prohibition on a woman becoming pregnant through artificial insemination . . . This is not a halakhic question but one that is in the realm of social policy.'[51] Weighing the anguish of single women who yearn to have children against the fear that the option of artificial insemination might encourage women to remain unmarried, and including the admittedly remote halakhic complications that might arise from not knowing the identity of the father, Stav was unable to give a firm ruling. However, his colleague Rabbi Yuval Cherlow allows, in certain circumstances, artificial insemination for single women aged 37 and over who have unsuccessfully sought to marry.[52]

The issue of voluntary single motherhood is one that is also controversial and emotionally charged in the wider American society. Some family experts and sociologists view it as very harmful to the children involved and, ultimately, to society as a whole,[53] while others present evidence indicating that, although such women became mothers in a 'radical' way, they were motivated

[47] Bock, 'Doing the Right Thing?'
[48] D. Ross, 'Artificial Insemination in Single Women' (Heb.).
[49] See e.g. Feldman's critical review essay, 'Halakhic Feminism or Feminist Halakha?' The reference to Ross's article is on p. 74.   [50] Lichtenstein, *Leaves of Faith*, i. 158–88.
[51] Rotem, 'That's How They Want It' (Heb.).
[52] Cherlow, 'Birth Without Marriage' (Heb.), pts. 1 and 2.
[53] See e.g. Popenoe, *Life Without Father*.

by normative family values and aspirations, and their family lifestyles are actually very conventional.[54] In terms of Orthodox voluntary single mothers, while the rabbis and others may debate the halakhic and meta-halakhic issues involved, the meagre evidence available suggests that some women are making their choice individually, without careful consideration of these issues.

Abortion

Abortion is another issue where the question of whether the personal predilections of the *posek* have any influence on his decision comes to the fore. To support his argument that a *pesak* (halakhic decision) is immune to the perspectives of the *posek*, Gideon Weitzman cites Rabbi Feinstein's ruling[55] in which he rejected a more lenient ruling by Rabbi Eliezer Waldenberg[56] and prohibited an abortion for a woman carrying a foetus with Tay-Sachs disease. 'Can we possibly claim that Rav Feinstein did not have compassion on those unfortunate couples who are both carriers of Tay-Sachs?', Weitzman asks.[57] To him, it is obvious that compassion had nothing to do with Rabbi Feinstein's rulings on abortion, artificial insemination, or any other issue. Interestingly, in his address to the conference mentioned above, Rabbi Binyamin Lau cited these halakhic decisions of Rabbi Feinstein as well as that of Rabbi Waldenberg and their respective arguments as proof that the perspective of the *posek* does influence his halakhic decisions. Rabbi Lau argued that Rabbi Feinstein took such a strict stance on abortion in order to counter what he perceived as the larger social and cultural patterns in which abortion was becoming too commonplace. Indeed, in the final paragraph of his responsum, Rabbi Feinstein explicitly states that he wrote the entire ruling in light of 'the huge breach in the world that the governments of many countries, including Israeli heads of state, have allowed the killing of foetuses, and countless foetuses have already been killed, such that at this time there is a need to make a fence [safeguard] for the Torah'. In other words, under other social conditions he might have ruled differently.

In line with Rabbi Feinstein's wishes, though more as a result of greatly improved and much more widely used methods of contraception, the number of abortions worldwide has declined since around 1990.[58] We have no data on the rate of abortion among the Orthodox in the United States. However, abortion is readily available and used in Israel and it has become more common in the religious community there as awareness of it has increased. According to estimates by several medical professionals, religious

[54]   See e.g. R. Hertz, *Single by Chance*.   [55]   Feinstein, *Igerot mosheh*, *Ḥoshen mishpat*, 2, 69.
[56]   Waldenberg, *She'elot uteshuvot tsits eli'ezer*, 51: 3, 239–40.
[57]   Weitzman, 'Technology in the Service of the First Mitzvah', 266.
[58]   Johnston, 'Worldwide Abortions'.

women don't speak of it publicly, but at least 70 per cent have an ultrasound test to detect Down's syndrome and, if it is detected, at least 90 per cent have an abortion. For more serious defects, where the foetus will not survive, even ultra-Orthodox women will abort. Not all religious women, ultra-Orthodox or otherwise, seek rabbinic advice; some decide on their own, as has always been the case. However, according to the head of the Division of Obstetrics and Gynecology at the Hadassah Medical Center in Jerusalem, there has been a revolution in the medical knowledge of rabbis. Many now understand the complexities better, are more sensitive to all of the issues, and are better able to help the pregnant woman make her decision. Professor Simcha Yagel claims that religious women cope better with that difficult decision because they have religious authority assisting them with it.[59]

Internet Responsa and Orthodox Jewish Family Life

The Internet was discussed above in the context of its negative effect on traditional Jewish values. It has also had an impact on the entire area of halakhah with the introduction, especially in Israel, of Internet responsa. Why this phenomenon is more marked in Israel than elsewhere is an interesting question: perhaps it has to do with the distinctive nature of the role of rabbi there; or perhaps it is because the wider ethnic mix in Israel and the non-denominational character of Judaism there have made Orthodoxy more pluralistic and open to wider interpretation.

Whatever the reason, the Internet has dramatically altered the role of the rabbi in a number of crucial ways. The anonymity of those engaged in the discussion allows people to ask very intimate and demanding questions which they might not have asked had their identity been known. In addition, the limits of the community which a rabbi serves have been expanded from finite physical boundaries to almost infinite virtual ones. Finally, for our purposes, the Internet provides for greater public awareness of a particular rabbi's decisions, which makes him more vulnerable to criticism but may also enhance his stature.

An examination of topics covered in Internet responsa reveals that family and sexual issues play a major role among the questions raised. Thus, of the four published volumes of such responsa by Rabbi Yuval Cherlow, the most prolific of the Internet rabbis, the largest volume, *The Private Sphere* (*Reshut hayahid*), is devoted to issues concerning modesty, couples, and family.[60] In published Internet responsa as well as on the leading Internet site for the

---

[59] Ehrlich, 'A Full Stomach' (Heb.).   [60] Cherlow, *The Private Sphere* (Heb.).

religious Zionist (*dati le'umi*) community (www.kipa.co.il),[61] as well as on a range of other Jewish religious Internet sites and blogs, family issues are central. Among the issues discussed there are early marriage—a concern especially for students in *hesder* yeshivas; singles; premarital sex; *agunot* whose spouses refuse to give them a *get*; and gays and lesbians in the Orthodox community.

Homosexuality

Perhaps the most emotionally charged family and sexual issue of our time is homosexuality. The empirical evidence suggests that there has not been any significant increase in homosexuality in the past half-century. However, this is difficult to determine reliably: there are no studies of the issue before the 1940s, and people are often reluctant to offer information on their sexual behaviour. Shaul Stampfer found hardly any references to it among east European Jews during the nineteenth and twentieth centuries,[62] but lack of written evidence is not conclusive. Today of course homosexuality is much more openly discussed, primarily because of the rise in identity politics in Western society and culture during the 1960s and 1970s. This new freedom might suggest that the number of those identifying as homosexual has increased as there is a greater tolerance towards it in society.[63]

Judaism across the spectrum incorporates the biblical condemnation of homosexuality as an abomination (*to'evah*) (Lev. 18: 22), and until recently it not only vehemently censured homosexual acts but ostracized the offenders as well. With the growing acceptance of homosexuality in the broader society, Reform Judaism was the first branch of American Judaism to alter its stance when, on 29 March 2000, the Central Conference of American Rabbis overwhelmingly approved a resolution giving rabbis the option to preside at gay and lesbian commitment ceremonies.[64] Not long afterwards, the movement's temple and synagogue organization, the Union for Reform Judaism, called for full legal equality for homosexual couples, including legal recognition of their relationships.

Eight years earlier, on 25 March 1992, Conservative Judaism's Committee on Jewish Law and Standards voted in favour of a lengthy responsum written by Rabbi Joel Roth which reiterated Judaism's traditional stance on homo-

---

[61] *Dati le'umi* translates as 'national religious', as in the NRP—National Religious Party. Outside Israel, the term 'religious Zionist' is used, as in the RZA—Religious Zionists of America.

[62] Stampfer, 'How Jewish Society Adapted to Change', 81.

[63] I thank Martin Lockshin for this suggestion.

[64] Central Conference of American Rabbis, 'Resolution on Same Gender Officiation'.

sexuality as an abomination.[65] It also rejected the criticisms of some social activists, who accused the decisors of being callous, and proclaimed, 'It is possible for a decisor to be understanding, empathic, sensitive, caring and without irrational fears and yet conclude that the halakhic precedents are defensible, warranted and compelling.' In a postscript, Roth went on to distinguish between halakhah and civil law, and stated that he saw 'no justification for civil legislation proscribing such acts'. Thus, while the organization of Conservative rabbis, the Rabbinical Assembly, reaffirmed its traditional prescription for heterosexuality, it supported complete civil equality for homosexuals; deplored violence against them; reiterated that they were welcome as members in their congregations; and called upon the entire movement to increase 'awareness, understanding and concern for our fellow Jews who are gay and lesbian'.

Awareness of homosexuality in the Orthodox community was increased by the award-winning documentary *Trembling Before G-d*,[66] which portrayed the conflict experienced by Jewish gays and lesbians, especially in relations with their families and communities, between their strong bond with God and Orthodox Jewish tradition, on the one hand, and Judaism's condemnation of homosexuality on the other.

A number of Orthodox rabbis, ultra-Orthodox as well as Modern Orthodox, have expressed compassion for homosexuals while at the same time affirming Jewish law's condemnation of prohibited homosexual activity, and have urged that those who transgress not be shunned any more than are other sinners, such as sabbath desecrators. Among the more strictly observant of those who profess compassion, one senses an outreach approach which aspires to enlist homosexual individuals in 'reorientation' programmes.[67] There is much debate in society at large as to the acceptability of such an approach, based on the question of whether homosexuality is hereditary or learned behaviour.[68]

For the Orthodox community in particular, the publication of a book titled *Wrestling with God and Men: Homosexuality in the Jewish Tradition* had the potential to create a real stir and perhaps even change some attitudes. Its

[65] J. Roth, 'Homosexuality'.

[66] Directed by Sandi Simcha DuBowski (2001).

[67] See e.g. Shafran, 'Dissembling Before G-d'.

[68] Jewish and Christian religious conservatives are highly prone to assert that homosexuality is learned and can be changed. Most of them feel compelled to affirm this because they would otherwise have difficulty with the biblical position on homosexual behaviour. Most scientific studies indicate a genetic basis for sexual orientation; see e.g. Sanders et al., 'Genome-Wide Scan Demonstrates Significant Linkage'. Some religious conservatives concede that sexual orientation may be genetically based, but argue that whether an individual acts on the basis of that orientation is nevertheless a choice.

author, Steven Greenberg, has ordination from the Rabbi Isaac Elchanan Theological Seminary of Yeshiva University and considers himself part of the Orthodox community. However, as Rabbi Asher Lopatin elucidates in his extensive, sympathetic, yet forthright critique,[69] the book is not and will not be seen as an Orthodox work because the author is by his own admission not fully committed to Orthodoxy; because its methodology and style are not those of Orthodox works; and because it is insufficiently creative halakhically. This and the fact that it was published by a university press with limited distribution and, even more, that it has an erotically suggestive image on the cover,[70] have made it a non-event in the public Orthodox community. How widely it was read under wraps in that community is anyone's guess. Not surprisingly, Greenberg replied to Lopatin's critique, stating that his intent

was not to settle the thorny halakhic issues, but to set the stage for richer halakhic engagements that in time will follow. It is my view that a full-fledged halakhic 'solution' to the problem of homosexual relations is premature . . . There is still too little understanding, let alone empathy, in the Orthodox community for the gay religious person and too much entrenched fear about the consequences of any partial, let alone full-fledged acceptance, of embarking on such a project.[71]

If one were to assume from this that there has been little change in the Orthodox community, one would be very mistaken. In the same year that Greenberg's book appeared, another book on Judaism and homosexuality was published by an Orthodox rabbi in the UK.[72] In this book, which is much more firmly rooted in halakhah, Chaim Rapoport reaffirmed traditional Jewish laws concerning homosexual behaviour, but also called for understanding and compassion for homosexuals and their struggles. He opposed calls for many of the therapy treatments which claim to 'cure' homosexuality, and advocated Jewish communal inclusiveness as well as increased halakhic observance by all. Several years later, speaking at a Limmud conference in the UK, Shlomo Riskin, founding rabbi of New York's Lincoln Square Synagogue who went to live in Israel in 1983 and is the rabbi of Efrat, declared that 'rabbis must not judge, but accept', and that he would not 'object to gay-lesbian parents or single mothers bringing a child into the world, as long as they do so responsibly'.[73]

Until relatively recently, homosexuality was not publicly discussed within the Orthodox community and homosexuals were shunned almost to the point of excommunication. There are now a number of openly gay Orthodox

---

[69] Lopatin, 'What Makes a Book Orthodox?'

[70] The cover image is from *Jacob Wrestling With the Angel*, by Eugène Delacroix, a painting based on the story in Genesis 32.   [71] Greenberg, 'The Orthodox Bookshelf'.

[72] Rapoport, *Judaism and Homosexuality*.   [73] Tene, 'Efrat's Rabbi'.

groups in the United States and in Israel. One, Havruta, held its first anniversary event in Jerusalem, and the guest of honour was Rabbi Yaakov Medan, who is one of the heads of a major religious Zionist yeshiva, Yeshivat Har Etzion. A number of other prominent Orthodox religious personalities participated as well.[74] In May 2014, a conference on the subject, 'Family in Formation', sponsored by Bat Kol, the organization of religious lesbians, was held at the Shalom Hartman Institute in Jerusalem, in which the opening panel included Rabbi Avi Gisser and Rabbanit Esti Rosenberg, both of whom are prominent Modern Orthodox figures.[75] There are also a number of gay ultra-Orthodox websites in Israel and in the United States.[76]

Once again Israeli Modern Orthodoxy appeared to be more progressive than its American counterpart. In December 2009 a panel on 'Being Gay in the Modern Orthodox World', co-sponsored by Yeshiva University's Wurzweiler School of Social Work, was moderated by the *mashgiaḥ ruḥani* (spiritual counsellor) of Yeshiva University's Theological Seminary. He opened by stating unequivocally that there would be no discussion of halakhah and that the focus would be on the challenges and sufferings of being gay in the Orthodox community. The panellists, consisting of three alumni and one current Yeshiva University student, recounted their experiences, and the discussion by and large stayed on track. Nevertheless, within days there was a variety of negative responses from within the Theological Seminary. A letter signed by the university's president, the dean of the seminary, and five of its senior faculty members stated, 'Homosexual activity constitutes an abomination . . . As such, publicizing or seeking legitimization even for the homosexual orientation one feels runs contrary to Torah. In any forum or on any occasion when appropriate sympathy for such discreet individuals is being discussed, these basic truths regarding homosexual feelings and activity must be emphatically reaffirmed.'[77] The strongest negative reaction came several days later, from Rabbi Mayer Twersky, who occupies the Leib Merkin Distinguished Professorial Chair in Talmud and Jewish Philosophy at Yeshiva University. He labelled the panel a *ḥilul hashem* (desecration of God's name) and a 'travesty', and asserted that 'Appropriate sympathy is correct and warranted but it's a travesty when that sympathy is cynically manipulated and exploited to create a legitimization, to create a new category of a Jew who should be able to come out of the closet and identify himself as oriented towards Toeva [an abomination].'[78] He went on to assert that because the panel was subtitled 'Being Gay in YU', all of Yeshiva University was implicated.

[74] Ettinger, 'Of Pride and Prayer'.   [75] Bendel, 'Rabbi Avi Gisser' (Heb.).
[76] See e.g. the site of the Gay and Lesbian Yeshiva Day School Alumni Association: http://www.orthogays.org/.   [77] Lipman, 'Gay YU Panel Broadens Discussion, Debate'.
[78] Orbach, 'Homosexuality Panel Draws Hundreds'.

Within approximately six months, more than a hundred Modern Orthodox rabbis and educators signed a Statement of Principles on 'the place
of Jews with a homosexual orientation in our community' which affirmed,
among other things, the basic dignity of human beings as having been created in God's image; that the question of whether sexual orientation is genetic
or learned is irrelevant to treating homosexuals with dignity and respect; that
heterosexual marriage is the ideal halakhic model and the only framework
for sexual expression; that all same-sex relations are halakhically prohibited;
and that the painful struggles and challenges experienced by halakhically
observant Jews must be recognized and that they 'should be welcomed as full
members of the synagogue and school community'.[79]

In the spring of 2015 a conference reminiscent of the 2009 Yeshiva University Wurzweiler panel but with a very different approach took place at
Columbia University. The conference, which included discussions between
four Orthodox rabbis and mental health researchers about homosexuality
and Orthodoxy, included participants and attendees from a variety of Orthodox perspectives: Nathaniel Helfgot, the former chair of the departments
of Tanakh and Jewish Thought at Yeshivat Chovevei Torah Rabbinical School
and the initiator of the draft of the Statement of Principles; Rabbi Mark
Dratch, executive vice president of the Rabbinical Council of America; Rabbi
Shmuel Goldin, a former president of the Rabbinical Council; and Shaul
Robinson, rabbi of the Lincoln Square Synagogue. Also attending, though
not as a speaker, was Rabbi Dr Tzvi Hersh Weinreb, the former executive vice
president of the Orthodox Union.

Do the developments documented here lend support to Blu Greenberg's
famous assertion that 'Where there's a rabbinic will there's a halakhic way'?
As a historical statement it may be accurate. Orthodox Judaism is, by definition, conservative, and all conservative religious groups manifest stronger
'traditional' values than the liberals do. On the other hand, no group is immune to the broader social and cultural patterns of its time, and Orthodox
believers today are not quite what they were half a century ago. However, if
the assertion is taken to be a political call to action, none of what has been discussed should necessarily be taken as supporting that assertion. All too frequently, such calls backfire and lead to a reactionary impulse, because they
are seen as undermining halakhic authority, and serve to make it even more
difficult to achieve the very objective intended by the call. As several of the
issues discussed above suggest, working with halakhic authorities, rather
than attacking them, is much more productive.

---

[79] Helfgot, 'Statement of Principles'. Although the statement made no reference to the
Theological Seminary responses, its timing suggests that it was in reaction them.

As the world shrinks—and technological innovations ensure that it does—broader social and cultural patterns will change even more rapidly, and they will increasingly impinge on Jewish life, including the Orthodox. Nor is there anything novel about it. As Rabbi Judah Hehasid, the author of *Sefer hahasidim*, recognized centuries ago, 'As is the custom of the gentiles, so are the customs of the Jews in most places.'[80]

[80] *Sefer hahasidim*, no. 1101. Judah Hehasid was a major figure among the Pietists of Germany in the twelfth and thirteenth centuries, and *Sefer hahasidim* is the most important work in ethical literature that the Pietists produced.

THREE

IT'S KOSHER TO BE
ORTHODOX IN AMERICA

A NUMBER OF WORKS on American Jewry written during the 1950s and 1960s begin with the contrast between the pessimistic evaluations of the state of American Judaism at the end of the nineteenth century and the authors' more optimistic current prognoses.[1] An even starker contrast can be made between the state of American Orthodox Jewry at the time of the Second World War and at the start of the twenty-first century.

The New York area has always been home to the majority of Orthodox Jews in the United States. According to the 2001 National Jewish Population Survey, 73 per cent of those who identify as Orthodox live in the Mid-Atlantic states of New York, New Jersey, and Pennsylvania. In the 1920s and 1930s, the overwhelming majority were in New York City proper and, as a result of immigration from eastern Europe between 1881 and 1923–26, this period was the 'heyday of American Orthodoxy'.[2] The sense of elation and self-confidence dissipated rather quickly. Indeed, as Jeffrey Gurock's detailed analysis demonstrates, the first half of the twentieth century was the 'era of non-observance' for American Orthodoxy,[3] and Orthodoxy was increasingly viewed as doomed in American society.

By the 1940s the English-speaking Orthodox rabbinate had suffered somewhat of a reversal and was forced to take stock of its future. Now muted, its characteristic buoyancy and optimism were succeeded by a barely disguised sense of thwarted expectations, especially pronounced among the second and third generation of students at the Rabbi Isaac Elchanan Theological Seminary, as the interwar years gave way to wartime and the 1950s. To the modernized Orthodox Jews, once confident that their form of Judaism would become the dominant religious expression of second-generation Americanized Jews, it now seemed as if a true modernized Orthodoxy could be found only in isolated instances, in 'pockets', and that the anticipated Orthodoxization of middle-class

---

[1] For example, M. Davis, *The Emergence of Conservative Judaism*.
[2] Joselit, *New York's Jewish Jews*, 2.
[3] Gurock, 'Twentieth-Century American Orthodoxy's Era of Non-Observance'.

American Jewry would not materialize. 'A lost cause', reflected a seminary grad-uate of 1942, 'Orthodoxy was not going anywhere.'[4]

One of the problems was that the most traditional and Jewishly educated members of east European Orthodox Jewry, and especially its rabbinic intel-lectual elite, were the most resistant to migration to the United States, for sev-eral reasons. First, the more traditionally religious are usually the most resistant to geographical mobility, in part perhaps because of its negative consequences for religious participation.[5] Second, east European Orthodox Jewry was further discouraged from migrating to the United States by negative reports about reli-gious life there. For example, New York's Rabbi Moses Weinberger, who had immigrated from Hungary, wrote a sharply critical portrait of Judaism in New York in the 1880s. He viewed American society as totally materialistic and bemoaned the low levels of Jewish education and observance of dietary rituals in the country. His book was, in large measure, a warning to his fellows in eastern Europe that the United States was a spiritual threat to religiously tradi-tional Jews.[6]

In the early 1890s, Rabbi Israel Meir Hacohen (Kagan) of Radun (Belarus), one of the most revered rabbinic authorities of his generation, widely known by the title of one of his works, *Ḥafets ḥayim*, published his own warning to east European Jewry about the dangers of emigrating to America. In the conclusion to *Nidḥei yisra'el* (The Dispersed of Israel), a work that clarifies some of the basics of traditional religious law for those living in 'distant countries', espe-cially America, he warned of the risks of leaving eastern Europe and asserted that the economic opportunities were not worth the price of losing one's Judaism or that of one's children.[7] In another work he devoted nine chapters to an in-depth consideration of reasons in favour of emigrating to distant coun-tries, and rejected each and every one.[8]

Another rabbinic influence was Rabbi Jacob David Wilowsky (Ridvaz), an outstanding talmudic scholar and community rabbi, founder of a prominent yeshiva in Slutsk, Belarus, and the author of several commentaries on the Jerusalem Talmud. He first travelled to the United States to raise money to complete his works on the Jerusalem Talmud. During his visit, which lasted about six months, he addressed a meeting of the Union of Orthodox Congre-gations in New York City, and was quoted as having condemned anyone

    [4] Joselit, *New York's Jewish Jews*, 80.
    [5] Finke, 'Demographics of Religious Participation'; Irwin, Tolbert, and Lyson, 'There's No Place Like Home'; Stump, 'Regional Migration and Religious Commitment'; Welch and Baltzell, 'Geographic Mobility, Social Integration, and Church Attendance'; Wuthnow and Christiano, 'The Effects of Residential Migration on Church Attendance'.
    [6] Weinberger, *People Walk on Their Heads*.   [7] Hacohen, *Nidḥei yisra'el*, 129–30.
    [8] Hacohen, 'Kuntres nefutsot yisra'el'.

who had emigrated to America, 'for here, Judaism . . . is trodden under foot. It was not only home that the Jews left behind them in Europe; it was their Torah, their Talmud, their Yeshebahs, their Chocomim [i.e. *ḥakhamim*, Torah scholars].'[9]

Reading back from the words and actions of many of the Orthodox elite in a later period, on the eve of the Holocaust, we can infer that there was at least one further reason that the majority remained in eastern Europe in the peak years of emigration to the United States, 1881–1923. They stayed then, as they did later, because they felt that they had an obligation as leaders to look after the members of the Jewish community.[10]

Not all prominent east European rabbis opposed emigration to America; there were some who saw it in a somewhat more favourable light. For example, Rabbi Chaim Soloveitchik said,

I know that the conditions [in America] are defective, but there are greater possibilities there, complete freedom, which is absent in Russia, and if people who are diligent in their practice of Judaism go there, they can achieve a great deal; and I am perplexed as to how it is possible for our rabbis and leaders to remain where they are and to see how holiness is destroyed among millions of Jews . . . If we wish to fulfil our obligations, the obligation of the hour, we should go to America to improve Judaism there and to build a secure haven there for our people and our Torah, until we return to Zion.[11]

A number of prominent rabbis did emigrate to America despite the warnings of the Hafets Hayim, Wilowsky, and others. In fact, somewhat ironically, Wilowsky himself immigrated shortly after the trip mentioned above, and at a rabbinical convention in Philadelphia was recognized as the *zaken harabanim*, the senior rabbi in the United States. He served as rabbi in Chicago for just one year, but became disillusioned and in 1905 left for Safed in the Holy Land, where he remained for the rest of his life.[12] Despite his own brief stay

---

[9] Reported in *American Hebrew* under the heading 'Union of Orthodox Congregations'. Interestingly, the newspaper report states that Wilowsky labelled anyone who had emigrated to America a 'Poshe Yisrael', a Jewish sinner. Hertzberg, '"Treifene Medina"', 25, cites Karp, 'The Ridwas', but incorrectly gives his source as p. 233; it is actually on p. 223. Moreover, Hertzberg quotes Wilowsky as saying that 'whoever comes to America is a heretic because Judaism is trodden here underfoot'. A heretic and a sinner are very different categories in Jewish law.

[10] Bobker, 'To Flee or to Stay?' Sara Reguer (*My Father's Journey*, 248) relates that her father had secured a visa for his father, Rabbi Simhah Zelig Reguer, the head of the rabbinic court in Brisk (Brest-Litovsk, Belarus), but he refused to leave his community. Shmuel Avidor Hacohen relates that when the chief rabbi of Palestine, Isaac Halevi Herzog, was about to return to Jerusalem following his trip to the United States to enlist support to save Jews in Europe, many American rabbis and others pleaded with him not to go because of fear of an invasion of Palestine by Rommel, but Herzog would not be dissuaded (Hacohen, *Unique in His Generation* (Heb.), 161–4).   [11] Quoted in Caplan, *Orthodoxy in the New World* (Heb.), 85.

[12] Anon., 'Brief Biography of the Author' (Heb.).

and eventual emigration, and although he was highly critical of the condition of Judaism in America, Wilowsky saw the Jewish experience there as having ultimate religious significance. He concludes the introduction to his Torah commentary by exhorting his readers to establish yeshivas for their children and their children's children. This is hardly the advice of an individual who believed that Judaism was doomed in the United States.

Even if they were not opposed to migration to America, almost all Orthodox rabbis were concerned about the future of Orthodoxy there, and with good cause. The empirical evidence suggests that some basic Jewish religious obligations, such as sabbath observance, especially given the economic limitations often associated with this, were coming under strong attack and were rapidly being abandoned by acculturating Jews. As I have indicated, most Jews readily dropped those religious traditions that inhibited their successful participation in American society. Thus, although Jews did not opt for mass assimilation and their actions did not result in the disintegration of the Jewish community, the nature of that community underwent a fundamental change. As Warner and Srole put it in their study of what they termed 'Yankee City':

In all other aspects of the Jewish community, the process of change is one of a replacement of traditionally Jewish elements by American elements. In the religious system of the Jews there is no such replacement. The Jews are not dropping their religious behaviors, relations, and representations under the influence of the American religious system. There are no indications that they are becoming Christian. Even the F[1] [native-born] generation can only be said to be irreligious.[13]

In other words the Jewish community was culturally assimilating without disappearing. Although the class system in 'Yankee City' was open and 'the Russian Jews climb its strata faster than any other ethnic group in the city',[14] there were certain requirements nevertheless. Clear standards of behaviour were expected of those moving up through the class system that were at odds with the norms of traditional Judaism, and almost all except those who had immigrated as adults adopted the American norms.

The leadership of Orthodox Jewry was apparently not equipped to overcome the challenges of the open American society. As Marshall Sklare put it at mid-century, 'Orthodox adherents have succeeded in achieving the goal of institutional perpetuation only to a limited extent; the history of their movement in this country can be written in terms of a case study of institutional decay.'[15] Nor was it solely institutional decline. Even into the 1970s, the

---

[13] Warner and Srole, *The Social Systems of American Ethnic Groups*, 202. On 'Yankee City', see Chapter 1 n. 11 above. [14] Ibid. 203.

[15] Sklare, *Conservative Judaism*, 43; see also Gurock, 'Twentieth-Century American Orthodoxy's Era of Non-Observance'.

available evidence suggests that the Orthodox were declining in numbers as well and that they would continue to do so.[16] The impact of the pre- and post-Holocaust immigrations was not yet evident.

The second half of the twentieth century also witnessed a significant shift within Orthodoxy itself. Although, in terms of numbers, Orthodoxy is the smallest of the major American Jewish denominations or branches, as Jonathan Sarna still prefers to refer to them,[17] it is also the most diverse. American Orthodoxy has neither a single seminary nor a single rabbinic organization, and is made up of a variety of philosophies and movements, including hasidic, 'yeshivish', and Modern Orthodox, all of which have their own seminaries and rabbinic organizations. The changes that Orthodoxy's two major groupings —ultra-Orthodoxy and Modern Orthodoxy—underwent during the second half of the twentieth century are the most significant.[18]

In their European antecedents as well as in their confrontation in the United States for much of the past century, these two perspectives are clearly distinguishable on the basis of three major characteristics: in their stance towards society in general and the non-Orthodox Jewish community, the ultra-Orthodox are isolationist and the Modern Orthodox inclusive; in their attitude to modernity, science, and technology, the ultra-Orthodox are antagonistic and the Modern Orthodox accommodating; and in their attitude to Israel and Zionism, the Modern Orthodox are supportive and the ultra-Orthodox generally less so, attributing no religious significance to the State of Israel and rejecting co-operation with secular Zionism.

During the first half of the century, American Orthodoxy tended much more towards the Modern variant. Although there were both pro- and anti-Zionist factions within American Orthodoxy at the beginning of the century, the pro-Zionists were the clear majority;[19] as Sarna indicates, many of the leaders of the Union of Orthodox Rabbis were ardently sympathetic to Zionism.[20] Indeed, many of those who sent their children to Jewish day schools rather than public schools did so in the hope that they would produce and

---

[16] Mayer and Waxman, 'Modern Jewish Orthodoxy in America', 101.

[17] Sarna, *American Judaism*, pp. xix–xx. I agree with him regarding American Judaism until the early twentieth century, but by mid-century it had denominationalized. The *Oxford English Dictionary* defines a denomination as 'a religious sect or body having a common faith and organization, and designated by a distinctive name', and that is what has happened to American Judaism over the past sixty or seventy years. So, although earlier it was proper to speak only of wings or branches of American Judaism, it has now become increasingly appropriate to speak of denominations.   [18] Friesel, 'The Meaning of Zionism'.

[19] N. W. Cohen, *American Jews and the Zionist Idea*, 6–7; Gurock, 'American Orthodox Organizations in Support of Zionism'; Caplan, 'The Beginning of "Hamizrahi" in America' (Heb.).   [20] Sarna, *American Judaism*, 202.

reinforce in the students a love for the Jewish people and their cultural heritage, as well as a strong connection with and commitment to Zionism.[21]

Likewise, the majority of American Orthodox Jews in the early twentieth century had an accommodating stance towards modernity, general scholarship, and science. When, in 1915, Yeshiva Etz Chaim (founded in 1886) merged with Yeshiva University's Theological Seminary (1897), the new institution's head, Rabbi Dr Bernard Revel, introduced a secular high-school curriculum. Such a mixture of sacred and secular programmes was taboo in the world of east European Orthodoxy. Most Orthodox Jews, however, did not wish to remain isolationist: they wanted to take advantage of the opportunities America offered, and sent their children to public schools. The more committed, who nevertheless took a positive view of modern scholarship and culture, wanted their children to be have both a quality Jewish education and a good general education. In addition to the more traditionalist day schools, which were for boys only and which kept Judaic and secular studies completely separated, such as the Rabbi Jacob Joseph School (1900), Yeshiva Rabbi Chaim Berlin (1906), the Talmudical Institute of Harlem (1908), and Baltimore's Yeshiva Torah Ve-Emuna Hebrew Parochial School (later renamed Yeshiva Chofetz Chaim—Talmudical Academy, 1917), the committed Orthodox also founded more accommodating day schools for both boys and girls which strove to integrate Judaic and secular studies, such as the Yeshiva of Flatbush (1927). Perhaps the most progressive Orthodox day school was the Ramaz School, founded on New York City's Upper East Side in 1937. Catering to an affluent clientele, this school saw its goal as providing students with a solid Jewish education together with academic preparation for acceptance into Ivy League universities.[22]

In 1928 Revel established Yeshiva College, and in 1946 Rabbi Dr Samuel Belkin transformed it into Yeshiva University, an institution which combines advanced Jewish religious studies, taught by some of the most renowned rabbinic scholars, with a full range of higher secular education. Such an institution was unthinkable in eastern Europe. In the United States, however, although there was opposition from rabbis who were products of east European yeshivas, including some who were on the faculty of the parent institution, the university was widely hailed among American Orthodox Jews. Revel proudly referred to the original college as 'The House of God on the Hilltop', and the European-born and -trained Rabbi Moses Zevulun Margolies, who served as the chief rabbi of Boston's Orthodox Jewry and after whom the Ramaz School was named, referred to it as 'the great Yeshiva College, the pride

---

[21]   Nardi, 'A Survey of Jewish Day Schools in America'.
[22]   Moore, *At Home in America*; Gurock (ed.), *Ramaz*.

of American Jewry'. It was viewed as Orthodoxy's crowning achievement and proof of its ability to adapt to the modern world.[23]

Much of this changed dramatically with the immigration of east European Jews precipitated by the Holocaust. As indicated above, a disproportionate number of these immigrants were ideologically committed Orthodox Jews from the Lithuanian-type yeshiva world, as well as leaders and followers of a variety of hasidic groups. They provided the numbers and the manpower for the renaissance in Orthodoxy which was to manifest itself almost a quarter of a century later. They also played a role in the intensification of religious belief and practice among the Orthodox, as well as in the increasing rift between them and the non-Orthodox.[24]

During the second half of the twentieth century, a series of vibrant Orthodox Jewish suburban communities developed across North America. According to Etan Diamond, the key to their success was a combination of the socio-economic affluence of their constituents and their religious commitment, which required them to live within a single neighbourhood—Orthodox religious law prohibits driving on the sabbath, setting the framework for a communal structure in which its members need to live in close physical proximity to each other.[25] The issue of driving on the sabbath was one of the major dividing lines between Conservative and Orthodox Judaism.[26] In 1950, the majority of members of the Committee on Jewish Law and Standards of Conservative Judaism in America permitted those who lived far away to drive to and from synagogue on the sabbath.[27] The ruling was intended to strengthen Conservative Judaism by fostering increased synagogue attendance. However, in 2003 Rabbi Dr Ismar Schorsch, chancellor of the Jewish Theological Seminary of America, Conservative Judaism's rabbinical seminary, asserted that the ruling had been a mistake as it meant that Conservative Judaism 'gave up on the desirability of living close to the synagogue and creating a Shabbos community'.[28]

Whether the Conservative movement could have prevented the decline of community is a moot question. While having to live within walking distance of a synagogue may limit the opportunities that come with geographical mobility, it also prevents many of the problems which mobility frequently entails for the rest of society. Orthodox observance of the rule fosters community: they

[23] Rakeffet-Rothkoff, *Bernard Revel*; Klaperman, *The Story of Yeshiva University*; Gurock, *The Men and Women of Yeshiva*.   [24] These issues are discussed in detail in Chapter 4.

[25] Diamond, *And I Will Dwell in Their Midst*.

[26] The issues of mixed seating in the synagogue sanctuary and the text of the *ketubah*, the religious marriage contract, were the first to mark off Conservative Judaism as a separate denomination or movement.   [27] *Proceedings of the Rabbinical Assembly*, 112–88.

[28] Cattan, 'Conservative Head Calls Sabbath-Driving Rule a "Mistake"'.

do not face the struggle to develop roots when they move to a new area because the sabbath restrictions on travel ensure that they will have a community; they do not have to worry about where they will meet people in their new neighbourhood—they know that they will meet them in synagogue. They also know that there will be children with whom their own children will socialize and, in many cases, go to school.[29] Some Orthodox Jews who were sufficiently modern to achieve relatively high educational and economic status and who internalized modern conceptions of social organization moved to the suburbs and built small communities that, once the communal foundations were laid, gradually attracted more Orthodox members. In contrast to the stereotype of Orthodox Jews as being concentrated in the lower socio-economic strata, by then many of them were fairly affluent. Although it is true that, as discussed in Chapter 1 above, the Orthodox as a group continued to have lower annual household incomes than Conservative and Reform Jews, when compared to the broader American population their incomes were above average.[30]

By the 1970s, there had emerged a pattern, discussed and analysed below in Chapter 4, that I have elsewhere called a 'haredization' of American Orthodox Jewry.[31] For a variety of reasons, American Orthodox Jewry became more punctilious in its ritual observance and turned inward in the sense of reducing its co-operation with the Conservative and Reform denominations. As Etan Diamond has observed, many of the new communities which had been developed by Modern Orthodox Jews started to become much more religiously conservative, parochial, and isolationist.[32] In part, this was a result of the growth of these communities: as increasing numbers of ultra-Orthodox moved in, many of the Modern Orthodox moved out, leaving a more inward-looking community. This pattern can be seen, for example, in the New York communities of Boro Park and Flatbush, the Five Towns in Nassua County, Monsey in Rockland County, and in Baltimore, as well as further afield in Toronto, and, most recently, in the Upper West Side in Manhattan.[33] This 'haredization' was also due to a number of sociological, ideological, and institutional factors both within American Jewry and within the wider American society and culture. Among these are the higher birth rate among the ultra-Orthodox; the more organized character of their communities, which have clear lines of authority and a high degree of social control; their tendency to respond to deviations from tradition by becoming ever more conservative;

---

[29] Waxman, 'The Sabbath as Dialectic', 41.
[30] Waxman, *Jewish Baby Boomers*.
[31] Waxman, 'The Haredization of American Orthodox Jewry'.
[32] Diamond, *And I Will Dwell in Their Midst*; and see Chapter 4 below.
[33] Leibovitz, 'Orthodox Boom Reshaping West Side'.

their dominance over day schools by virtue of their staunch commitment to intensive traditional Jewish education; and the weaker institutional base of Modern Orthodoxy. The ultra-Orthodox also have a strong sense of ideological certainty: they have no doubts about the correctness of their approach.

In addition, two important societal developments during the late 1970s and the 1980s significantly affected the character of American Orthodoxy. The first was a socio-cultural change in the United States as a whole. As is almost universally the case, the patterns of Jewish life are a reflection of the surrounding society and culture.[34] The 'turn to the right' in American Orthodoxy was, in large measure, a reflection of the broader turn to the right and the rise of fundamentalism in a variety of different countries and continents. If, in mid-century America, secularization appeared to be the wave of the future, an inevitable consequence of modernity—so much so that sociologist Peter Berger predicted that by the year 2000 'religious believers are likely to be found only in small sects, huddled together to resist a worldwide secular culture'[35]—by the closing decades of the century, Berger had recanted and averred that the world had become 'as furiously religious as it ever was'. Moreover, 'On the international religious scene, it is conservative or orthodox or traditionalist movements that are on the rise almost everywhere.'[36] The forces of moderation were viewed as having been widely replaced by fundamentalism, and it became fashionable to reject the culture—although not the technology—of modernity in favour of 'strong religion'.[37] It should therefore be no surprise that American Orthodoxy moved to the right: it was reflecting a pattern in the wider world.

With these developments, the ultra-Orthodox apparently gained a self-confidence that manifested itself in newer, more open patterns.[38] For example, whereas at mid-century religious outreach was the province of the Modern Orthodox, and later of Chabad, with the ultra-Orthodox largely being somewhat suspicious of *ba'alei teshuvah*, the newly religious,[39] by the end of the century the ultra-Orthodox were heavily engaged in religious outreach. They were by then actively involved, and in some cases had leadership roles, in the National Jewish Outreach Program and the Association for Jewish Outreach Programs, with which hundreds of Orthodox outreach organizations are affiliated, and the Orthodox Union's National Conference of Synagogue Youth.[40]

---

[34] See p. 72 above.

[35] See his 1968 article in the *New York Times*: 'A Bleak Outlook Is Seen for Religion'.

[36] Berger, *The Desecularization of the World*, 2, 6.

[37] See Almond, Appleby, and Sivan, *Strong Religion*.

[38] The developments within ultra-Orthodoxy indicated here refer to the 'yeshivish' component and are very different from those of the 'hasidish' Orthodox.

[39] Pelcovitz, 'The Teshuva Phenomenon'.   [40] Shafran, 'I Have a Dream'.

Ironically, the Modern Orthodox, who pioneered religious outreach, turned inward and, institutionally, hardly took any part in such activities. For the most part, they became defensive and were much more likely to engage in intellectual discussions among themselves than to actively reach out beyond their borders. Likewise, as Adam Ferziger has demonstrated, the Modern Orthodox rabbinical seminaries also turned inward and placed increasing emphasis on halakhic expertise, while the more right-wing institutions began programmes to train rabbis in religious outreach.[41] Much of this continues to the present day.

Chabad, the most prominent hasidic movement in the United States, is the outstanding exception to this pattern.[42] Its major focus has consistently been on religious outreach to all Jews, and it utilizes cutting-edge technology in its outreach and public relations activities.[43] Much of the Chabad approach was developed by the movement's leader for most of the second half of the twentieth century, Rabbi Menachem Mendel Schneersohn. Chabad as a movement in America began with the arrival in New York, in 1940, of his father-in-law, the previous *rebbe*, Yosef Yitshak Schneersohn.[44] Menachem Mendel and his wife arrived in 1941, and almost immediately he was appointed by Yosef Yitshak to head the educational arm of Chabad, Merkos L'Inyonei Chinuch. In that capacity he devised a series of programmes and activities for children which he actively oversaw. Chabad schools from nursery to high-school level were opened around the country (and beyond), and criteria for acceptance into them were virtually non-existent.[45] All of the Merkos activities were

[41] Ferziger, *Beyond Sectarianism*, 151–74; id., *Training American Orthodox Rabbis*.

[42] Several other notable exceptions to the broader ultra-Orthodox pattern during the second half of the twentieth century are Aish HaTorah and Ohr Somayach, two ultra-Orthodox institutions founded in the 1970s specifically for *ba'alei teshuvah*, and the Rabbinical Seminary of America/Yeshiva Chofetz Chaim of Queens, New York, a Lithuanian-type yeshiva that has a specific outreach component.

[43] Since this is a sociological analysis, the focus is on Chabad and its impact on Orthodox Judaism in the United States. Questions about Menachem Mendel Schneersohn before he became the seventh and last *rebbe* are not germane to the analysis here. Likewise, the issue of the *rebbe*'s messianism will not be discussed. That issue is pertinent here insofar as, since his death in 1994, the movement has experienced struggles internally as well as with some other Orthodox groups because of its increasingly assertive proclamations of him as the messiah, a notion which others view as antithetical to Judaism. See Belcove-Shalin, *New World Hasidim*; D. Berger, *The Rebbe, the Messiah, and the Scandal of Orthodox Indifference*; S. S. Deutsch, *Larger Than Life*; Fishkoff, *The Rebbe's Army*; L. Harris, *Holy Days*.

[44] Kraus, *The Seventh* (Heb.), 183–223.

[45] I was witness to a 'graduation' ceremony at a Chabad nursery school in a remote town in California where it was questionable whether, among the parents and teachers, there was a sufficient number of halakhically defined adult Jewish males for a *minyan*, a quorum for congregational prayer service. The president of the nursery school, who addressed the audience, was married to a Jew but was not himself Jewish.

geared to reaching out to Jews, however remote, and bringing them closer to Judaism. Among the controversial but creative techniques he devised was what became known as 'mitzvah tanks', pickup trucks and adapted mobile homes that drove through the streets or were stationed at heavily trafficked areas in city centres, and broadcast hasidic or other Jewish music through loudspeakers. The objective was to attract the curious and encourage them to perform religious acts, *mitsvot*, especially—for men—donning tefillin, and for women lighting sabbath and festival candles. This was in line with Schneersohn's aim of 'turning Judaism outward', of making it public rather than restricting it to the private sphere.[46]

Along with the educational activities geared primarily to children, Schneersohn developed a notion devised on a limited scale by his father-in-law, namely a sophisticated system of *shluchim*—emissaries charged with the task of bringing Judaism to all Jews, even in the farthest corners of the earth.[47] By 2013 there were well over 5,000 *shluchim* in Chabad houses worldwide engaged in giving Judaism a global presence.[48] Whatever this may have accomplished for Chabad and for Judaism in general, it had a great impact on Orthodoxy.[49] It gave it a public presence and reduced some of the wider population's xenophobia concerning Orthodox Jews. It also enabled the Orthodox to travel worldwide with the knowledge that they would find an Orthodox Jewish presence, albeit a small one, and be able to obtain kosher food at a Chabad house wherever they went. This contributed to the development of a significant travel industry geared to this market.

The ultra-Orthodox turned outward not only in terms of religious outreach but also more broadly by actively engaging with society on issues which it saw as having a Jewish dimension. Beth Medrash Govoha, the largest yeshiva in the United States, and possibly the world, holds an annual event in which several hundred individuals gather to pore over classical texts and hear talks and discussions on a broad range of halakhic and ethical issues involving relations between Jews and society, as well as those within the Jewish community.[50]

---

[46] Ch. Miller, *Turning Judaism Outwards*. The phrase was apparently first used by Rabbi Jonathan Sacks, who, in June 1994, eulogized the Lubavitcher Rebbe as 'The Man Who Turned Judaism Outward'.

[47] Kraus, *The Seventh* (Heb.), 92–131; Ch. Miller, *Turning Judaism Outwards*.

[48] Shwayder, 'More than 5,000 Chabad Emissaries Convene in Crown Heights'. The worldwide presence of Chabad is expressed in a popular joke that the two things one can find all over the world are Coca-Cola and Chabad.

[49] In 2005 Michael Steinhart, the philanthropist who co-founded Taglit-Birthright Israel, called Chabad 'the most effective movement in the Jewish world today'. See Becker, 'Chabad, a Success Story'. In 2011 it was labelled by the *Daily Beast* and *Newsweek* as 'the fastest-growing denomination in Judaism' (Pogrebin, 'America's 50 Most Influential Rabbis').

[50] Goldman, 'The Jewish "Newsroom"'.

Agudath Israel became very active in the public sphere during the second half of the twentieth century. It has a full-time office in Washington DC, as well as others across the United States, and actively lobbies all branches of federal, state, and local government on issues that it views as having a Jewish interest. Its public relations specialist frequently writes columns in Jewish newspapers across the country and internationally, expressing the Agudath Israel perspective. The indications are that most ultra-Orthodox are increasingly attached to the surrounding society and view living their Orthodox lifestyle within it rather than set apart from it as a right. This was demonstrated in their reaction to the destruction of the World Trade Center on 9/11. There was a widespread display of the American flag outside homes and businesses in heavily Orthodox neighbourhoods, while the national office of Agudath Israel sent out strongly worded letters imploring members to contribute to the fund for families of the firefighters and police who had been victims of the attack. Another striking manifestation of their identification with American society was the cover-page colour image of the American flag on the US edition of the ultra-Orthodox newspaper *Hamodia*, published on Independence Day 2012, with the heading in bold letters, taken from the US national anthem 'O'ER THE LAND OF THE FREE'.[51]

The coming of age of Orthodoxy in American society manifested itself in a host of developments during the second half of the twentieth century. One such development was the growth of the kosher food industry. Until recently, it was indeed *shver tzu zayn a yid*, difficult to be an observant Jew, especially keeping to a kosher diet. As a result of a combination of cultural and structural factors, this is no longer the case. Hasidim were among the first to focus on improving the standard and availability of kosher foods, and they helped develop new lines of kosher products. Cultural patterns in the larger society which made it increasingly likely that both spouses in the family worked outside the home precipitated an increasing need for ready-made foods and, for observant Jews, these had to be kosher. This sparked technological developments in the food-processing industry that dramatically increased the range and availability of kosher foods, and this in turn removed the stigma attached to them; most of those who buy kosher foods today are not Orthodox or even Jewish. An annual trade show, Kosherfest, is attended by thousands of international trade buyers, including top buyers for supermarket chains, restaurants, caterers, hotels, hospitals, and universities. By the end of the century, one frequently ate kosher food whether one knew it or not.[52] The sheer scale

---

[51] *Hamodia: The Daily Newspaper of Torah Jewry* (4 July 2012), 1.
[52] http://www.kosherfest.com/.

of this industry is evidence, among other things, of the socio-economic mobility of American Orthodox Jews. In addition to the now worldwide presence of Chabad, the improved socio-economic status of many Orthodox Jews, coupled with the expansion of the kosher food industry, has enabled the emergence of the kosher tour industry. One can now go on kosher tours and cruises worldwide, and celebrate the Jewish festivals at lavish hotels with the finest cuisine.[53]

Another industry which has developed dramatically since the Second World War is English-language Orthodox publishing, pioneered by ArtScroll and Mesorah Publications, who publish a wide array of translations, including the popular prayer book, the ArtScroll Siddur, as well as hagiographical biographies, commentaries, and a range of children's books.[54] Critics have argued that ArtScroll censors its books to present only strictly Orthodox accounts and perspectives,[55] but by the turn of the century most observers agreed that, whatever its faults, ArtScroll had revolutionized Jewish learning in America and raised it to unprecedented heights by bringing many previously obscure sacred texts to the attention of the public in attractive editions.[56] In addition, through its publication of an English translation of the Talmud, it has played a key role in the popularization in America of the Daf Yomi, an endeavour that encourages the study of Talmud at the rate of a page a day, which was initiated in eastern Europe in the 1920s by Rabbi Meir Shapiro and was adopted by the Agudath Israel movement there. The English translation of the Talmud is frequently consulted, even by many who study it primarily in its original Aramaic. At a page a day, the cycle of study takes seven and a half years, and the completion of each cycle is marked by a major celebration, the Siyum Hashas, sponsored by Agudath Israel. The first Siyum Hashas was held in 1968, attended by about 700 people. This figure has risen year by year: to 3,200 in 1975; more than 5,000 in 1982; about 26,000 in 1991; 70,000 (including those who participated via satellite) in 1997; and more than 100,000 (again including participants via satellite) in 2005, while in 2012 the

[53] There are numerous kosher travel companies whose websites provide detailed information on the high quality of the hotels and cuisine offered in their travel packages.

[54] Stolow, *Orthodox by Design*.

[55] Marc Shapiro, *Changing the Immutable*.

[56] A more recent player in the field of English-language Orthodox publishing is the Israeli-based firm Koren and its subsidiary, Maggid Books. Originally a publisher of religious texts in Hebrew, the company was purchased and reorganized to include major English-language divisions that have appeal to the Modern Orthodox. The English-language Steinsaltz Talmud, first published by Random House, was picked up and developed by Koren, and it also publishes a growing number of English-language books on classic Jewish texts as well as on Jewish thought.

celebration, at which most of the speeches, lectures, and salutations were in English, reportedly involved the world's largest ever gathering of Jews.[57]

It may be that this adaptation to American society by the ultra-Orthodox is an expression of a basic difference between it and fundamentalist Christianity. In contrast to evangelical Christianity, which engages with society and strives to change it, for fundamentalist Christians a key symbol is the 'mighty fortress' which, according to Luther, is God, who acts as a trusty shield and weapon, an image interpreted as an injunction to remove oneself from involvement in the larger society.[58] For Orthodox Jews, the objective is to build a 'fence' (seyag) around the Torah, to shield it from distortion, but not to refrain from societal involvement. Socio-historical circumstances in eastern Europe did encourage an isolationism that carried over to Jews' initial perceptions of American society. However, once they felt physically secure and legitimately autonomous religiously, the Orthodox began to feel themselves part of society and to praise the political system that made that participation possible. They also began to feel comfortable about taking part in some aspects of popular culture that had previously been alien to traditional Judaism, such as sport and music. As Jeffrey Gurock indicated, the notions of 'recreation' and 'leisure time' were alien to Jewish immigrants[59] and, it may be added, to traditional Judaism at large. With respect to sport, it is now commonplace to find American ultra-Orthodox yeshiva students intimately involved as ardent fans and even participating in betting pools as well as engaging in athletics, albeit not professionally.[60] Exercise and sport are now kosher.[61]

With respect to music, there is today what might be called a parallel structure to the American pop culture music industry, with a broad new genre of American ultra-Orthodox music being created, much of which closely resembles popular music more generally, but with a Jewish twist.[62] This is

[57] Bruni, 'Thousands Celebrate Completion of Talmud Study'; Otterman, 'Orthodox Jews Celebrate Cycle of Talmudic Study'.

[58] As George Marsden indicates, 'Though outsiders to the movement sometimes use the term broadly to designate any militant conservative, those who call themselves fundamentalists are predominantly separatist' (Understanding Fundamentalism and Evangelicalism, 4).

[59] Gurock, Judaism's Encounter with American Sports.

[60] Caplan, 'Haredim and Western Culture'. Caplan highlights the involvement in sport as one of the distinguishing characteristics shared by American and Israeli haredi and ultra-Orthodox yeshiva students. He does, however, indicate the growing presence and influence of American ultra-Orthodoxy in the haredi public sphere in Israel (p. 274). The influence on American Orthodoxy of travel to Israel is discussed below. On American ultra-Orthodox students' involvement in sport while studying in Israeli yeshivas, see Raub, 'For American Expats, a Home Away From Home'.

[61] Gross, 'Exercising to a Rabbinic Beat'; Wilson, 'Ultra-Orthodox Jews Find Gym to Call Their Own'.

[62] See, by Mark Kligman, 'Contemporary Jewish Music in America', 'On the Creators and Consumers of Orthodox Popular Music', and 'Recent Trends in New American Jewish Music'.

most pronounced in the hasidic branch of American ultra-Orthodoxy, from which a variety of new types of Orthodox music have developed, from Shlomo Carlebach's hasidic hippie to 'neo-hasidic',[63] 'hasidic pop',[64] and others. Ultra-Orthodox Jews have also developed a genre of literature which had been alien to conservative traditional Orthodoxy, namely, fiction.[65] All of this is possible in an American society which tolerates, and even encourages, both religion and religious diversity.

Ultra-Orthodox Jews have now adopted modern methods of inspirational self-help. Agudath Israel conventions and ultra-Orthodox publications are replete with 'cutting-edge' psychological, educational, and medical topics. The producers and the consumers of these materials are not isolated and do not retreat from the larger society and culture; they are very much engaged in them. They have learned to operate within the culture and to use it for their own ends.[66] When the ultra-Orthodox legal scholar Aaron Twerski became the dean of a law school in New York, it warranted an article in the 'Long Island' section of the *New York Times*, but only because of his atypical appearance, including his mode of dress. Twerski emphasized that 'We are insular in terms of our private lives and our institutions and all the rest, but we are not insular in terms of being a vital part of society.'[67]

By the close of the century, it not only seemed acceptable to be Orthodox: for many it appeared to be the 'in' way to be Jewish. As suggested, this dramatic turn was precipitated by a variety of internal Jewish as well as broader societal developments. Perhaps the most dramatic example of this occurred in the summer of 2000, when Senator Joseph I. Lieberman, an Orthodox Jew, was nominated as the vice-presidential running mate on the Democratic ticket. No 'inside, outside' Jew,[68] he so frequently made reference to God and traditional religion that he was asked by a number of national organizations—and even a Jewish one—to tone down these references lest he be seen to undermine the constitutional separation of religion and state. Four years later, Lieberman was a candidate in the Democratic presidential primaries. Although there was some question as to his support among American Orthodox Jews,[69] his nomination, support, and praise, even from many of those who did not vote for him,

[63] Blumberg, 'The Hasidic Hipsters of Zusha'.
[64] Werdiger, 'Lipa Schmeltzer'.   [65] Finkelman, *Strictly Kosher Reading*.
[66] See, for example, the highly popular books by the psychiatrist Abraham J. Twerski, especially *Getting Up When You're Down*, *The Shame Borne in Silence*, and *Successful Relationships*. See also such works as Tatz, *Anatomy of a Search* and Kelemen, *To Kindle a Soul*.
[67] Fischler, 'Hofstra's Law Dean Stands Out, But Still Fits In'.
[68] See Herman Wouk's novel *Inside, Outside*, in which the main character has a high position in the American government and keeps his private traditional Jewish life and public political life completely separate and compartmentalized.   [69] Bronner, 'The Lieberman Syndrome'.

suggested that Orthodox Judaism is broadly accepted in American society. Little more than a decade later, another Orthodox Jew, Jacob Lew, was named US Secretary of the Treasury, making him the first Orthodox Jew ever to achieve such high office in the American government.[70] It would thus appear that Orthodox Jews and American society have come to terms with each other.

[70] Guttman, 'Jack Lew's Life Shaped by Faith and Service'.

FOUR

AMERICAN ORTHODOXY ADOPTS STRINGENCY

D URING the second half of the twentieth century many observers of American Orthodoxy were struck by what was labelled as a move to the right. This was manifested in a variety of ways, including the increasing insistence on what was termed 'glatt kosher'[1] and stricter rules of *kashrut* in general; a growing number of married women covering their hair in public;[2] increasing insistence on separation of the sexes not only in the synagogue during services but in a wide array of venues; a narrowing of outlook in which works that referred to non-Jewish or even non-Orthodox scholarship, such as the Hertz Pentateuch (*ḥumash*),[3] were discarded in favour of those which offered only Orthodox views, such as ArtScroll; and a distinct inward turn and decreasing co-operation with the Conservative and Reform branches of American Judaism.[4] A small group of social scientists offered a number of basic sociological factors to explain why Orthodoxy in modern society is adopting a stance of greater isolation from the wider Jewish community and, especially, of ritualistic stringency. Perhaps the first to point to this trend was Charles Liebman in his pioneering 1965 analysis of American Orthodox Judaism in the *American Jewish Year Book*.[5]

---

[1] The term originally referred to a stringency adopted by some to use only meat from animals whose lungs were smooth and entirely unblemished. It has evolved into an all-encompassing term that refers to all food that is purported to meet the strictest standards of *kashrut*.

[2] On the changes in practice and the halakhic issues involved, see Broyde, 'Hair Covering and Jewish Law'; Shulman and Broyde, 'Hair Covering and Jewish Law: A Response'.

[3] J. H. Hertz, *The Pentateuch and Haftorahs*.

[4] Perhaps the most dramatic manifestation of this trend was on 1 February 1956, when eleven prominent Orthodox rabbis issued a prohibition on Orthodox participation in interdenominational organizations such as the New York Board of Rabbis, the Synagogue Council of America, which represents the interests of the American Jewish religious community, and 'similar groups in other communities, which are composed of Reform and Conservative "rabbis"'. For the text of the prohibition, see Rakeffet-Rothkoff, *The Silver Era*, 291–2.

[5] Liebman, *Aspects of the Religious Behavior of American Jews*, 150. See also Liebman's essay 'Orthodoxy in American Jewish Life'. In 1983 Liebman published a seminal essay, 'Extremism as a Religious Norm', which explained religious extremism in general and Jewish religious extremism in particular, but it did not specifically deal with American Orthodox Judaism and, if anything, focused more on Orthodox Judaism in Israel.

A paper that I published in 1998 focused specifically on American Orthodoxy. In it, I distinguished between ultra-Orthodox Judaism and Modern Orthodoxy in terms of three important variables: attitudes towards the surrounding society and the broader Jewish community; attitudes towards modernity; and attitudes towards Zionism.[6] I presented a number of examples of what I described as 'haredization', but perhaps its most conspicuous manifestation was a greater punctiliousness, perceived by many to be excessive, in ritual observance and the inward turn noted above. These tendencies reached the point where a journalist who is a keen observer of the American Jewish scene perceived the existence of a conflict within the Jewish community, with the Orthodox opposing non-Orthodox in a 'struggle for the soul of American Judaism'.[7]

It is clear that religious stringency is not new. It has been prevalent for centuries, and is probably endemic to the social psychology of the religious person. Following the sociology of religion of Émile Durkheim[8] and Peter Berger,[9] we know that religion strives towards self-denial and that asceticism is inherent to the religious sphere. As they saw it, no society can exist unless its members accept a degree of self-control and, as Durkheim suggests, such control requires training. Religion, in that it relates to the sacred, that which is by definition 'set apart and forbidden',[10] necessarily implies renunciation, and it is thus in the practice of religion that members of society acquire the self-control necessary for society to function. Despite arguments to the contrary by Max Weber,[11] asceticism has long been a theme within Judaism. In addition, there is a centuries-old tradition within Judaism that measures an individual's religious status—both intellectual and behavioural—as inversely related to the time separating them from the divine revelation at Sinai. We thus have the statement, 'If earlier generations were as sons of kings, then we are sons of [ordinary] men. And if earlier generations were as sons of men, then we are like asses.'[12] Rabbi Norman Lamm avers that there is no consensus on the meaning or existence of generational decline.[13] Be that as it may, it is nevertheless

---

[6] Waxman, 'The Haredization of American Orthodox Jewry'; for more details of these differences see pp. 77–8 above. At the suggestion of Tovah Lichtenstein, I would add that another very important distinction between the ultra-Orthodox and the Modern Orthodox is to be found in their respective attitudes towards Jewish education for women, with the latter being egalitarian and the former being discriminatory.   [7] Freedman, *Jew vs. Jew*.

[8] Durkheim, *The Elementary Forms of Religious Life*.   [9] P. L. Berger, *The Sacred Canopy*.

[10] As the son of a rabbi (see Lukes, *Emile Durkheim: His Life and Work*, 39), Durkheim may well have been familiar with the translation of the term *kadosh* as 'set apart' (see Rashi on Leviticus 19: 2).   [11] Weber, *Economy and Society*, ii. 611–34.

[12] *Im rishonim kivnei malakhim, anu benei anashim, ve'im rishonim benei anashim anu kahamorim*: BT *Shab.* 112b; JT *Shek.* 5: 1. Cf. Maimonides, *Mishneh torah*, introduction.

[13] Lamm, *Torah Umadda*, 86–100. For a lucid analysis of Maimonides' approach to the notion of generational decline, see Kellner, *Maimonides on the 'Decline of the Generations'*.

held to be true by many, for whom it follows that later generations must be more stringent if they aspire to be considered religiously worthy. Hence the popularity through the ages of the *ḥumrah*, or religious stringency.[14]

However, history provides many examples of opposition to the adoption of unprecedented stringencies, on the grounds that this might create an impression that the innovators consider themselves holier, more religious, than their predecessors. Israel Ta-Shma, for instance, cites numerous medieval Ashkenazi halakhic authorities who scoffed at those who adopted unduly stringent ritualistic behaviour.[15] Nor was that attitude limited to either Ashkenazim or the eleventh century. For example, Rabbi Joseph Karo wrote a caustic critique of a person who wanted to be what would today be called 'super-*frum*', that is, one who adopts and encourages others to adopt an unprecedented stringency.[16] Likewise, although there are manifestations and expressions of asceticism and zealous piety in the Talmud and in the geonic and post-geonic periods, these too were minority expressions which were frequently condemned by the authoritative scholars of the day.[17]

On the other hand, it is also true that there was a change among Ashkenazi Jews from the thirteenth century on. As both Ta-Shma and Haym Soloveitchik indicate, stringency was prevalent in Ashkenaz during the era of the Tosafists.[18] However, there is a basic difference between stringent behaviour in medieval Ashkenaz and the type of stringency which is prevalent today. Today there is a conscious, almost ideological, drive to be highly discriminating in certain areas of halakhah. To some extent, this is what the late Rabbi Simcha Elberg, editor of the now defunct Torah journal *Hapardes* and a prolific writer who espoused ultra-Orthodoxy, had in mind when he described what he labelled 'Benei Berakism', following the strict interpretation of halakhah prevalent in that preponderantly ultra-Orthodox city:

The character and stature of Benei Berak express themselves not only in religiosity and traditional piety . . . Benei Berakism . . . consists of its own unique and independent approach . . . A yeshiva student under the spiritual influence of the

---

[14] See e.g. Horowitz, *Shenei luḥot haberit*, i. 19*a*, wherein the author gives a somewhat mystical reason for what he describes as the increasing prevalence of sin. He says this is actually the constantly spreading venom of the snake, for which he prescribes *ḥumrot*, stringencies, as the 'anti-toxin', defined not as rabbinic stringencies but as ordained by the Torah: 'Therefore, in each generation when it is proper to add stringencies, then all of that is from the Torah [*mide'orayta*].'   [15] Ta-Shma, *Early Franco-German Ritual and Custom* (Heb.), 82–3.

[16] The critique was with respect to tithing of fruits grown in land owned by a gentile: see *Kesef mishneh* on Maimonides, *Mishneh torah*, 'Hilkhot ma'aser', 1: 11.

[17] See e.g. *Mishneh torah*, 'Hilkhot de'ot', 3: 1. For an elaborate discussion of this, see Sperber, *Jewish Customs* (Heb.), chs. 3 and 4.

[18] Ta-Shma, *Early Franco-German Ritual and Custom* (Heb.); Soloveitchik, 'Religious Law and Change', in *Collected Essays*, i. 239–57.

Hazon Ish of Benei Berak actually lives and breathes the *Shulḥan arukh* with all of its *ḥumrot*. When he takes the *Shulḥan arukh* to look up any question, his perspective leans towards the strict, and he will neither seek out nor favour the more lenient opinion. His intention is not to be lenient but to be more stringent. He constantly makes an effort to search and dig: perhaps one of the commentaries tends towards greater stringency. And when he finds a more stringent opinion, it is as if his very being is refreshed and rejuvenated, and this *ḥumrah* becomes the norm which he establishes in his home and which he realizes in his daily life.[19]

Elberg attributed the growth of 'Benei Berakism' to the continuing influence of the powerful, almost charismatic quality of the late Rabbi Avraham Yeshayahu Karelitz, the Hazon Ish. He was one of the most widely revered halakhic authorities of his time, and although many of his rulings were lenient, his disciples tended to emphasize and follow his more stringent rulings as the norm. The most glaring examples are those which relate to the measurements required in the fulfilment of certain *mitsvot*, especially the amounts of wine and matza to be consumed at the *seder*, the festive meal on the eve of Pesach.[20] The Hazon Ish specified much larger measurements for the required four cups of wine as well as much larger amounts of matza to be eaten than had been the accepted tradition. With the spread of his prestige and influence, increasing numbers of his followers adopted his stringent measurements as obligatory and attempt to impose those measurements on others as well.

Menachem Friedman astutely argues that the source of Benei Berakism goes far beyond any individual, even one as influential as the Hazon Ish. Rather, he suggests, it is to be found in the very structure and culture of the higher yeshiva, the *yeshivah gedolah*, of which the model is the yeshiva in Volozhin. Among its many features, the *yeshivah gedolah* 'is a total-like institution whose students are, for the most part, alienated from their surroundings and cut off from their families for most of the year, as a result of which they are united amongst themselves, especially around the figure of the *rosh yeshivah* (head of the yeshiva) and his family'.[21] In addition, as Friedman points out, the *yeshivah gedolah* of the Volozhin type 'is not an institution *of the community*, but rather an economically independent organization supported by the contributions of individuals from many regions', and 'the vast majority

---

[19]   Elberg, 'Benei Berakism' (Heb.). For a somewhat different rendition of Elberg's concept, based perhaps on the translation of another version of his editorial which also appeared in the Israeli Agudat Israel periodical *Diglenu* (Nov./Dec. 1964), see Menachem Friedman, 'Life Tradition and Book Tradition', 235.

[20]   Friedman, 'Life Tradition and Book Tradition', 236–8. See also Singer, 'Thumbs and Eggs'.

[21]   Friedman, 'Life Tradition and Book Tradition', 242.

of the yeshiva students are not from the community but come from near and far for the purpose of studying there'.[22]

Although not in quite the same way as Friedman, I argue that these characteristics of the 'world of the yeshiva', which has grown significantly in the United States and Israel since the Second World War, play a significant role in the emergence of 'Benei Berakism', as well as in the widely observed 'shift to the right' within Orthodoxy. Whereas in the past the traditions of the family and the local community played a central role in setting the standard of behaviour within the religious realm—that is, *minhag*, custom, often took on the authority of halakhah[23]—with the growth of the *yeshivah gedolah* a new pattern has emerged. The *rosh yeshivah* now determines behavioural norms, and the folkways and mores of the family and local community are often not taken very seriously. Likewise, whereas traditionally the local rabbi was the halakhic authority for his community, the emergence of the *yeshivah gedolah*, the high-level seminary, has resulted in a growing struggle between the rabbi and the *rosh yeshivah* for halakhic authority.

Until the beginning of the nineteenth century, there was no struggle between the local rabbi and the *rosh yeshivah* because the yeshiva was a local institution and the roles were usually filled by the same person. Not only did they not conflict, they frequently augmented each other and compensated for conflicts in other areas. As Jacob Katz analysed the pre-nineteenth-century yeshiva:

The identity of purpose of the rabbi and yeshiva head, which was customary in this period, was another typical feature . . . Since the nucleus of the yeshiva consisted of students whose only loyalty was to their rabbinic head, an atmosphere was created conducive to the creation of a close personal link between them. These circumstances facilitated the formation of an educational framework of an unusually intensive nature. The combining of the tasks of president of the local rabbinic court and yeshiva head decreased rather than increased the prospects that this would happen. The advancement of the yeshiva was, after all, only one of the rabbi's many tasks . . . The relationship of the *kehilla* to the rabbi, which was not lacking in conflict and tension, was likely, for its part, to have its equilibrium restored through the halo which surrounded the rabbi in the line of his yeshiva duties. The honor accorded the rabbi as head of the yeshiva and as disseminator of learning among the people, values that were universally esteemed, also strengthened his hand as he carried out his function as arbiter of the values of the entire community.[24]

By 1802, when Rabbi Hayim of Volozhin established the yeshiva there, the

---

[22] Ibid. (emphasis added).
[23] On the status of *minhag*, see Dinari, *The Rabbis of Germany and Austria* (Heb.), 190–228.
[24] Katz, *Tradition and Crisis*, 197–8.

basic roles had changed because the relationships had radically altered.[25] Although Rabbi Hayim was the rabbi of Volozhin, when he wanted to establish a yeshiva there he went outside his community to raise the requisite financial resources. Although that is the common pattern today and many strong arguments can be made in its defence, such as that it eases the financial burden on the local community, it radically restructured some traditional relationships: between the yeshiva and *rosh yeshivah* and the local community, and between the *rosh yeshivah* and the local rabbi. The broadening of the base of financial support for the yeshiva meant that it was no longer under the direct control of the community within which it was located, and that the *rosh yeshivah*, too, was now much more independent. Moreover, not only were the *rosh yeshivah* and rabbi no longer one and the same, they were now potentially in conflict with one another for the loyalties of the members of the community as well as of the yeshiva students. As Rabbi Dr Immanuel Jakobovits put it,

The denigration and usurpation of the role of practicing rabbis by *yeshivah* deans had virtually eliminated the traditional place and functions of the rabbinate in the spiritual government of the religious community, resulting in the disappearance of the public Torah image in the community at large . . . The transfer of rabbinic jurisdiction from communal rabbis to academic scholars confined to *yeshivot* had severely limited the scope of contemporary Halakhah and caused substantial deviations from the traditional pattern in the methods used to determine Jewish law.[26]

Not infrequently, each attempted to enhance his own stature at the expense of the other. Within this development, the tendency towards stringency played a special role in that the more stringent ruling was frequently posited as and viewed as the more 'authentic' one.

Haym Soloveitchik's analysis of the unique role of printed texts suggests another source for the growth of the pattern of stringency. He argues that the technology of modern publishing has transformed much of traditional religious practice, particularly in ultra-Orthodox enclaves.[27] Indeed, the condition of modernity transformed a traditional religious society and culture into a voluntary Orthodox sub-society and subculture in which what had previously been recipes for living which were transmitted in a mimetic manner, via

---

[25] Etkes, *Rabbi Israel Salanter and the Mussar Movement*; Stampfer, *Lithuanian Yeshivas of the Nineteenth Century*.

[26] Jakobovits, 'Deans and Rabbis', 74.

[27] Soloveitchik, 'Rupture and Reconstruction'. Soloveitchik suggests that part of the tendency towards stringency may also lie in the 'group's need for self-differentiation', a need that became acute with modernity, as will be discussed shortly, as well as in 'religious one-upsmanship' (p. 72).

custom, have now become ritualistic beliefs, objects, and practices which require accuracy. Although Soloveitchik differs somewhat from Menachem Friedman, who sees this increased stringency as rooted in structural factors, especially since the emergence of the east European type of yeshiva,[28] he also considers it to be a predominantly post-Second World War phenomenon which, by the mid-1970s, had become 'the dominant mode of religiosity'.[29]

Another element in the pattern involves certain structural conditions of modernity itself which inevitably lead to stringency. In large measure, this is a consequence of the process of religious pluralization,[30] which manifests itself in the emergence of denominations, each of which claims legitimacy and authenticity. Accordingly, there is a need for each to develop techniques of boundary maintenance to clearly distinguish itself from other denominations. Religious orthodoxies in particular, as James Davison Hunter points out, have a special interest in establishing and maintaining symbolic boundaries:

orthodoxies are unique because of the *special significance* bestowed upon the symbolic boundaries which constitute the tradition. Those boundaries are regarded as timeless . . . The claim of the orthodox, then, is that they alone are the keepers of the tradition; they alone are the protectors of the true faith. Their stake in keeping the tradition sound and unqualified is high because their very identity and purpose as religious people (both collectively and individually) are bound to that mission . . . For the orthodox, the symbolic boundaries mean everything.[31]

A number of points connected with *ḥumrah* and its application require elaboration. For starters, the vast majority of authoritative halakhic experts define it as applicable, at most, to rabbinic laws (*mitsvot derabanan*), but not laws from the Torah (*mitsvot de'oraita*). The authority to impose *ḥumrot* is viewed as rooted in a term in Leviticus 18: 30,[32] and over the centuries, when rabbis thought that strictures were necessary to prevent further lapses in religious life, they did not hesitate to impose them. Since most prominent traditional rabbis viewed modernity itself as threatening, they not infrequently imposed strictures against any and all innovations, seeing them as inherently

[28] Friedman, 'Life Tradition and Book Tradition', 235. Also see Waxman, 'Toward a Sociology of *Pesak*'.

[29] Soloveitchik, 'Rupture and Reconstruction', 74.   [30] P. L. Berger, *The Sacred Canopy*.

[31] Hunter, *Evangelicalism*, 159; Liebman, 'Extremism as a Religious Norm'. Brown, 'Stringency' (Heb.), argues in a similar vein in his analysis of stringency in recent generations. He points to five types of halakhic decisor who represent different motivations and sources for halakhic stringency in the contemporary era. A common denominator found by Brown is the attempt to establish boundaries, which is a reaction to manifestations of modernization, secularization, and pluralization.

[32] See BT *Yev.* 21a: 'And you shall guard my charge'. In a play on *mishmeret*, the Rabbis derived from this the authorization to provide extra safeguards for their charge, Jewish law.

destructive. Perhaps the most explicit expression of this is that of Rabbi Moses Sofer (known as the Hatam Sofer), who famously proclaimed, 'that which is new is proscribed by the Torah'.[33] He opposed all innovation, and at times adopted stringencies, particularly deriving from his staunch opposition to the incipient Reform movement in Judaism.[34] Subsequently, almost all religious conservatives who ideologically oppose modernity and innovation have legitimated their opposition under the banner of the Hatam Sofer's declaration. This may be one of the major reasons why, in the nineteenth century, militant ultra-Orthodoxy was much stronger and more widespread in Hungary than in Russia. Modernity and secularization were already present in Hungary at the end of the eighteenth century but their influence was not felt in Russia until the end of the nineteenth century.[35]

Although the number of secondary and higher institutions in eastern Europe increased greatly during the nineteenth and early twentieth centuries,[36] the most dramatic growth, both in the number of institutions and in the number of students, occurred during the last three decades of the twentieth century. In 1945, there were nine yeshiva high schools in the United States. Thirty years later, in 1975, that number had grown to 138.[37] At post-high-school level, the growth was even more pronounced. In 1976, David Singer indicated that 'the number of students studying Talmud on an advanced level in the United States compares quite favourably with the number who were enrolled in the great yeshivot of Eastern Europe during their heyday'.[38] Since then, the numbers and percentages have continued to increase significantly. Among Orthodox Jews in the United States, Modern as well as ultra-Orthodox, at least twelve years of yeshiva day-school education is the norm, and a significant number of the graduates of those institutions continue their studies for a year or more in yeshivas and seminaries in which Talmud study is a part of the curriculum, in the United States or in Israel. There has also been a dramatic increase in adult Torah learning in American Orthodox communities, evidenced in the popularity of the

[33] *Ḥadash asur min hatorah*. See e.g. Sofer, *Teshuvot haḥatam sofer*, 'Oraḥ ḥayim', 181, and 'Yoreh de'ah', 91. For biographical analyses of R. Sofer, see J. Katz, *Divine Law in Human Hands*, 403–43; Samet, *Chapters in the History of Orthodoxy* (Heb.), 310–18.

[34] Meyer, *Response to Modernity*; Ferziger, *Exclusion and Hierarchy*.

[35] Silber, 'The Emergence of Ultra-Orthodoxy'.

[36] Stampfer, *Lithuanian Yeshivas of the Nineteenth Century*; S. K. Mirsky, *Jewish Institutions of Higher Learning in Europe* (Heb.).

[37] Mayer and Waxman, 'Modern Jewish Orthodoxy in America', 99.

[38] Singer, 'The Yeshivah World', 70. See also Bomzer, *The Kollel in America*. It should be emphasized that this does not mean that the amount and level of Talmud learning in the United States is the same as it was in eastern Europe, where a much higher percentage of Jews devoted several hours daily to Talmud study. No less certain is the fact that religiously observant Jews comprise a much smaller segment of American Jewry than was the case in eastern Europe.

ArtScroll edition of the Talmud, as well as translations of many other classic Jewish texts, and the popularity of the Siyum Hashas, the celebration of the completion of a cycle of Talmud study which takes place every seven years.[39]

The significant increase in the numbers of American Orthodox Jews studying at yeshiva high schools and post-high-school yeshivas, together with the dramatic increase in adult Torah learning, have impacted on American Orthodox religious behaviour in a number of ways. One of the characteristics of Jewish Orthodoxy, indeed of all religious orthodoxies, is submission to the authority of the tradition as espoused by its 'experts'. Authority and tradition are prerequisites for religious orthodoxy. Within an orthodoxy, the individual is expected to so internalize tradition as to perceive that he or she has no choice but to conform to all of its dictates. As Peter Berger elucidates, the notion that the individual has the ability to choose is 'heretical': 'The English word "heresy" comes from the Greek verb *hairein*, which means "to choose." A *hairesis* originally meant, quite simply, the taking of a choice.'[40] From the perspective of religious orthodoxy, individuals should feel that they have no choice,[41] and from the perspective of traditional Jewish Orthodoxy, the absence of choice included the inevitable submission to the ultimate authority of the rabbinic scholarly elite even as Judaism encourages everyone to learn and analyse the texts for themselves.

Learning in a yeshiva socializes one to greater punctiliousness in the observance of *mitsvot*.[42] Concern with precision and punctiliousness often leads to greater rigidity and stringency in religious behaviour because this is seen as ensuring that a *mitsvah* will be performed properly. As a result, the 'world of the yeshiva' in the United States is overwhelmingly the world of stringency. With respect to halakhic questions, the greater numbers of people who have studied in a yeshiva are, presumably, turning to their yeshiva head for guidance and, for a variety of reasons,[43] the positions of those heads are typically more stringent than those of the local rabbi. When it comes to which halakhic positions will have the greatest weight in the broader Orthodox population, therefore, the more stringent ones will, because the ultra-Orthodox are the most scrupulously observant, and this is what is of greatest concern to

---

[39] On Siyum Hashas see pp. 85–6 above, and Newman, 'Orthodox Jews Celebrate End of a True Sabbatical'.   [40] Berger, *The Heretical Imperative*, 27.

[41] This is one interpretation of the verse, *Lo tukhal lehitalem* ('You will not be able to avoid it': Deut. 22: 3).

[42] I use the term 'learning', rather than 'studying' because of the unique character of the process in higher yeshivas. It is perhaps best captured in Samuel Heilman's *The People of the Book*, wherein he uses the term *lernen*.

[43] As indicated above, *rashei yeshivah* may be less sensitive than local rabbis to communal pressures; their halakhic proficiency may be greater than that of local rabbis; and they have much less familiarity with daily communal problems and issues.

most Orthodox Jews. As discussed in Chapter 1, they are more likely to attend synagogue services, to participate in Torah-learning groups, to contribute to charity on a regular basis, and to visit the sick; and they are much more likely to be the ones who will abide by halakhic decisions. It seems reasonable to assume that increased Jewish knowledge will lead to a greater awareness of halakhah, and that awareness may lead to changes in types of behaviour which may have been widespread in the community but which are not halakhically sanctioned. For example, during the first half of the twentieth century, many Orthodox synagogues held dinners and balls which included mixed-gender dancing, frequently with non-spouses. Likewise, it was quite typical for Orthodox Jews to eat dairy foods or fish at restaurants which had no *kashrut* supervision, and many even ate in restaurants where non-kosher food was served. With increased Jewish knowledge, such behaviour is now much less common, and is widely frowned upon in the American Orthodox community. To those who recall the earlier days, the shift may appear as reflecting an eagerness to adopt the excessive stringency of a *ḥumrah* when, in actuality, this is not a matter of 'excessive stringency' but, rather, of straightforward halakhah.

In addition, technological developments in the food industry have made food production much more complex. As Haym Soloveitchik put it,

Frequently, a new practice was being labeled a '*ḥumra*' not because it was the more stringent of two valid views, but simply because it made stricter demands than what had been habitually required. More often than not, '*ḥumra*' meant simply 'more than what one had been accustomed to.' . . . Modern technology had created a cornucopia of new products which required religious definition, and the growing complexity of food technology had transformed many hitherto harmless products into questionable ones, from the point of view of kashrut.[44]

Indeed, there is historical precedent for the development of greater awareness and, thus, stricter behaviour with increased levels of education, especially with the opening of yeshivas. As Judah Galinsky has shown, there was a growth of yeshivas, a number of which became quite prominent, in Spain during the late thirteenth and the fourteenth centuries. They, in turn, attracted increasing numbers of students, who went on to become learned scholars. A scholarly class grew and an increasing number of authors emerged from that scholarly class. They, in turn, contributed to greater interest in religious instruction and practice within the Jewish community:

---

[44] Soloveitchik, 'Clarifications and Reply', 137. Rabbi Gideon Sylvester informed me that the development of quality Israeli wines made it easier for English *kashrut* authorities to insist that kosher wines be served at functions where the food supplied is under their supervision.

The growth of academies, in places where they did not exist previously or had been unsuccessful, had the potential of changing not only individuals but entire families. In forming learned young men, one in essence created many new 'textual communities'. The young scholar served as the conduit of the written word to a religiously unschooled community, largely unable to understand the Hebrew language. Many more individuals, in various communities, could perform the task of being communal 'readers', explaining in a variety of forums the contents of the books. Even the student that did not become a rabbi or a judge, was nevertheless, somewhat of a local authority on all aspects of the written lore. In short, as the academies expanded so did the pool of potential readers, at the primary and secondary level.[45]

Finally, the social organization of the ultra-Orthodox community supports its strength in influencing the diffusion of stringency within American Orthodoxy. The importance of boundary maintenance was indicated above. The Orthodox Jewish community of Frankfurt in Germany in the nineteenth century under the leadership of Rabbi Samson Raphael Hirsch is an example of the relationship between boundary maintenance and stringency. Hirsch's approach led him to separate himself and his community from the larger Jewish community, the *Grossgemeinde*, which was dominated by Reform leaders.[46] Whatever else might be said about that action, it had the advantage of setting firm and clear boundaries between the *Gemeinde*, the Hirschian Orthodox community, and the rest of Jewry. Through this overt separation it achieved a very high level of self-consciousness as a distinct community and a highly honed sense of itself as the true bearer of a very special tradition.[47] Although very different from today's ultra-Orthodox community, it is this type of traditional sectarianism that ultra-Orthodoxy has been successful in maintaining and even strengthening. Its members' primary identification is with the community, and they have a clear religio-cultural sense of communal responsibility. For example, members of the community pitch in to help make celebratory meals for such occasions as a circumcision, a barmitzvah, or a wedding. They welcome newcomers with invitations to meals and offer them assistance in becoming established. They provide services for the hospitalized and their families; they volunteer for emergency medical services; and they provide financial assistance to a broad range of needy Jews.[48] Ḥesed (acts of kindness to others) is a religious value that is internalized and becomes a

---

[45] Galinsky, 'On Popular Halakhic Literature'.
[46] Breuer, *Modernity Within Tradition*, 294–303; Ellenson, *Rabbi Esriel Hildesheimer*, 61–2.
[47] Although Hirsch himself was definitely not ultra-Orthodox according to the criteria indicated in this book, his secession from the larger Jewish community paved the way for his sectarian community to become ultra-Orthodox and, at least in the United States, it has by and large done so. See also J. Katz, *With My Own Eyes*, ch. 3.   [48] Oppenheimer, 'Beggarville'.

personal value.[49] By contrast, although there may be many individuals who define themselves as Modern Orthodox, Modern Orthodoxy does not seem to have established itself as a real movement in the way that ultra-Orthodoxy has, nor is it likely to do so. There are a number of basic sociological reasons for this.

Many of those who consider themselves Modern Orthodox are so behaviourally rather than philosophically.[50] They do not define themselves as modern because of an ideological commitment to worldly knowledge or any other value. As the evidence indicates, it is through their very selectivity in observance that the Modern Orthodox manifest their modernity.[51] However, that selectivity is for them almost solely a matter of *personal* choice. They do not usually seek to legitimate their behaviour halakhically. Thus, although they feel free to choose, they do not challenge the halakhic authority of the ultra-Orthodox scholarly elite, and since they do not constitute a challenge to that authority, they are tolerated by that elite and can still feel themselves part of the broader American Orthodox community.[52] As a result, the ultra-Orthodox have a major hold on authority. Indeed, it may be argued that the deviance of Conservative Judaism, as defined by ultra-Orthodoxy, is not so much that they do not behaviourally conform to the norms as prescribed by Orthodoxy— although many do not—but that they reject the authority of the Orthodox. Orthodoxy can tolerate deviance when it is so recognized by the actor; what it cannot tolerate is the legitimation of what it considers to be deviance through the rejection of the authority of its rabbis.[53] For the philosophical Modern Orthodox, however, matters are much more complex. First of all, even if they

---

[49] Partly this is because it is much easier to be motivated to do good deeds when the recipients are one's own friends and neighbours. The Modern Orthodox community, whose members are generally wealthy, do not have the same motivation to get involved.

[50] Although there are also many ultra-Orthodox who are so behaviourally rather than philosophically, this is not an issue within ultra-Orthodox communities because they place much more emphasis on behaviour than on philosophy.

[51] S. C. Heilman and Cohen, *Cosmopolitans and Parochials*, 39.

[52] See Breuer, *Modernity Within Tradition*, for evidence of such a situation in nineteenth-century Germany.

[53] Cf. Ellenson, *Tradition in Transition*. Benjamin Brown relates that Rabbi Shlomo Cohen, who had been a student of and remained very close to the Hazon Ish, recalled that while they were learning together in Lithuania he once asked his teacher what was so bad about the Mizrahi, especially since the Hazon Ish was personally rather tolerant of mediocre Jews and recognized that they were an inevitable fact of life. The Hazon Ish responded, 'The existence of mediocre Jews does not in and of itself make for a unique ideology. The mediocre ones also know that it is better to be a tsadik and that one must strive for all Jews to become perfect tsadikim. However, he thinks that he himself is unable to achieve that, either because of uncontrollable desires or for other reasons. The Mizrahi, by contrast, presents an ideology of mediocrity whose aspira-tion is merely that Jews should be mediocre' (Brown, 'From Political Fortification to Cultural Fortification' (Heb.), 408).

do not challenge the halakhic authority of the ultra-Orthodox elite—and they do in fact do so at times—there are specific areas in which they overtly challenge them philosophically. These members of Modern Orthodoxy are, therefore, vilified and shunned by the ultra-Orthodox community.

Above and beyond the specific issues on which they challenge the ultra-Orthodox, the Modern Orthodox, being modern, are at least suspicious of the very notion that human beings can wield virtually complete authority in the field of religious belief. In addition, their understanding of halakhah reinforces the Orthodox Jewish rationalist priority of truth over authority.[54] Even if it is gaining in numbers, it is much more diffuse than ultra-Orthodoxy because, being philosophically modern, it emphasizes a measure of personal autonomy as well as rationalist truth. The Modern Orthodox reject monarchy and oligarchy just as they are sceptical of all human authority, which may be one reason why, unlike the ultra-Orthodox, they possess no 'Council of Torah Sages'.[55]

On the other hand, some Modern Orthodox rabbis experience a need for acceptance by the ultra-Orthodox yeshiva world, which is the core of the traditional ultra-Orthodox community. Since stringency, punctiliousness, and zeal in ritual observance are the prescribed norms in that world, those Modern Orthodox rabbis who seek its approval may likewise adopt stringent stances. However, in the process, they may lose the support of precisely the Modern Orthodox group that they seek to lead. In addition, the ability of Modern Orthodoxy to attract a large following and become a movement is inherently inhibited by the fact that it is highly rational and intellectual and thus has built-in tensions and frequently requires its adherents to live with inconsistency. As Sol Roth wrote with respect to synthesis, 'The task of realizing synthesis in personality is a very difficult affair, primarily because it requires the development of an attitude that enables an individual to adopt different perspectives.'[56] To the philosophically Modern Orthodox the tension of synthesis may not be a weakness but rather an ideal—a religious mission to live with challenge in a world that is replete with challenges—but for many, the challenges are too difficult. They prefer what they view as consistency and clarity.

[54] Cf. Lamm, *Torah Umadda*, 100–2.

[55] Cf. Jonathan Sacks's observations as to why Modern Orthodoxy rejects the manner in which the slogan *da'at torah* ('Torah opinion') is used by the sectarian community: '*daas Torah* in its modern sense tends to be opposed by many within Orthodoxy who see halakhah as a rational discipline operating in the empirical world, open to argument and counter-argument and the development of consensus. They also see the new charisma with which the yeshivah head has been invested as subverting the traditional authority of the *mara d'atra*, the local rabbi' (Sacks, *Traditional Alternatives*, 136). For analyses and critiques of the concept, see Bacon, *The Politics of Tradition*; Brown, 'The Polemic of Da'at Torah' (Heb.); L. Kaplan, '*Daas Torah*'.

[56] Roth, *The Jewish Idea of Community*, 145.

Also, the very fact that Modern Orthodoxy is much more open than ultra-Orthodoxy[57] severely limits it attractiveness for most people. For better or worse, most people prefer, if they do not demand, very specific, black or white concepts which can easily be differentiated from others. If an analogy may be permitted, they prefer either meat or dairy to what they view as *parve*, neutral or grey areas. As the British anthropologist Mary Douglas suggests, 'the yearning for rigidity is in us all. It is part of our human condition to long for hard lines and clear concepts.'[58] Accordingly, the American legal scholar and a leader of the National Council of Churches Dean M. Kelly argues that membership of the liberal Protestant denominations has declined because they are weak religiously. They allow for a diversity of theological viewpoints and are undemanding of their members. Conservative religions grow because they provide clearly defined doctrines as well as clear and straightforward answers to the most basic questions about the meaning of life. They demand that their members behave in accordance with distinct codes and they provide strong common bonds by means of which they are able to rally their followers to further their common objectives.[59] Modern Orthodoxy, in both its content and its structure does not have the 'hard lines and clear concepts' possessed by ultra-Orthodoxy, and it is therefore viewed by those unfamiliar with its philosophy as an inauthentic compromise.

Moreover, being largely rationalist rather than romanticist, Modern Orthodoxy has limited potential for attracting the masses. Social movements in general, and religious movements in particular, are built on emotional, passionate commitment, and an ability to radiate a strong sense of family-like, communal warmth. The somewhat distant intellectual coolness of the philosophically Modern Orthodox is much less amenable to translation into a movement that generates warmth and devotion. For the same reasons, it is difficult to establish primary and secondary schools capable of socializing children to this type of Modern Orthodoxy.

None of this should be taken as criticism of Modern Orthodoxy. All that is being argued is that its characteristics render it weak in terms of being able to develop a highly organized following. That may well be the fate of any approach that does not view complexity and even uncertainty as negative features. Those who take Modern Orthodoxy seriously would probably agree with the approach of Rabbi Joseph B. Soloveitchik, the most prominent ha-

[57] The openness referred to here is openness to new ideas. As for openness to 'others', Adam Ferziger shows that the ultra-Orthodox are currently much more open to others, i.e. non-observant Jews, than they were previously, and Modern Orthodoxy is much less engaged in outreach to the non-observant Jewish population than in the past. See Ferziger, *Beyond Sectarianism*.   [58] Douglas, *Purity and Danger*, 162.

[59] See Kelley, *Why Conservative Churches Are Growing*.

lakhic authority and intellectual leader of American Modern Orthodoxy in the twentieth century. He argued that 'religious consciousness in man's experience which is most profound and most elevated . . . is exceptionally complex, rigorous and tortuous. Where you find its complexity, there you find its greatness.'[60] That may well be one of the reasons that Rabbi Soloveitchik perceived the life of the man of faith as lonely. Be that as it may, the characteristics of Modern Orthodoxy inhibit its becoming a strong and cohesive social organization.[61] It appears that we are therefore left with what might be called an 'iron law of *ḥumrah*'. Where the sociologist Robert Michels averred that one 'who says organization, says oligarchy',[62] we may add, 'He who says organization, says *ḥumrah*', because organization requires boundaries, commitment, and submission to human authority.

Finally, two related developments in the larger American culture probably contributed to the growth of Orthodox stringency. First, there has been an increasing relaxation of moral norms. Standards of acceptable portrayal and speech became looser and looser in American cinema, radio, and television during the second half of the twentieth century. This led increasing numbers of Orthodox Jews to avoid those cultural media. Some undertook to use the technology of the media for cultural productions which reflected what they perceived as 'authentic' Jewish values. For example, rather than banning fiction they created 'kosher' fiction and 'kosher' videos. These reinforced the distinctiveness of Orthodoxy—i.e. ultra-Orthodoxy. The greater the ritualistic stringency, the greater the distinctiveness. Second, it was not only Orthodox Jews who began reacting against what they saw as the moral laxity of American society and culture; many American Christians did so as well. To the surprise of many, it was revealed that conservative Christianity was rather widespread in the country, and many Christians began manifesting their conservative beliefs and values. By the third quarter of the twentieth century, it had become acceptable to manifest one's religiosity in public. America was no longer a country where religion was relegated and limited to the private domain. Under these conditions, increasing numbers of Orthodox Jews felt comfortable developing and living in accordance with ultra-Orthodox beliefs and values. Thus the expansion of ultra-Orthodoxy was assisted not only by their higher birth rate but by changes in the cultural patterns of the surrounding society, which encouraged many to search for a more secure Jewish identity.

[60] J. B. Soloveitchik, *Halakhic Man*, 141.
[61] This may be one of the reasons for the failure of Edah, an organization whose motto was 'The Courage to be Modern and Orthodox', which is discussed in the following chapter.
[62] Michels, *Political Parties*, 365.

TENSIONS WITHIN
MODERN ORTHODOXY

THE PREVIOUS CHAPTER analysed the growing stringency within American Orthodoxy and discussed how the inherent characteristics of Modern Orthodoxy place it at a structural disadvantage in becoming an organized movement. This does not mean, however, that Modern Orthodoxy is a spent force. The last half-century has seen developments indicating significant ritualistic departure not only from ultra-Orthodox norms and values but from what had been traditional Jewish religious behaviour as well. As will be indicated from an examination of both formal organizational and institutional developments and informal sources, the Modern Orthodox sector is still a significant component of American Orthodoxy and is itself quite heterogeneous. The chapter concludes with a tentative prognosis.

The Role of Women

One of the most discussed and pressing concerns for many Modern Orthodox Jews is the role of women. With the broad societal awareness and growing acceptance of gender equality, increasing numbers of modern Jewish women feel that they have a very limited or no place in the Orthodox synagogue or the organized community.[1] Historically, few opportunities existed for women to pursue higher levels of Judaic studies within Orthodox institutions. In an Orthodox synagogue, women are not counted for the quorum (*minyan*) required to

Parts of this chapter are based on Turetsky and Waxman, 'Sliding to the Left? Contemporary American Modern Orthodoxy'. I am grateful for the partnership with Yehuda Turetsky in the original article and for his permission to use material from it in this chapter.

[1] A 2010 *Forward* survey of seventy-five major American Jewish communal organizations found that less than one in six were run by women, and that those women were paid 61 cents for every dollar earned by male leaders. The numbers are especially striking when compared with the overall composition of the Jewish communal workforce. Women comprise about 75 per cent of those employed by federations, advocacy and social service organizations, and religious and educational institutions, but occupy only 14.3 per cent of the top positions. Of the eleven female leaders identified in this survey, three were in interim roles. Ferst and Eisner, 'Jewish Women Lag Behind Men in Promotion and Pay'.

allow prayer and, until recently, they were not able to lead mixed prayer services or even pray together in the same way as their male counterparts. Since the
1960s, when gender equality became a national issue in the United States, a
variety of attempts have been made to expand the educational opportunities
available to Orthodox women and give them a greater role in synagogue life.

Perhaps the first major innovation along these lines was the organization of a women's *tefilah* (prayer) group on 1 October 1972, in the Orthodox
Lincoln Square Synagogue in New York City. That date was the Jewish festival
of Simhat Torah, and the organizers gained permission and support from the
synagogue's rabbi, Shlomo Riskin, to hold their own service there and dance
with the Torah. One prominent local rabbi had already announced that if the
synagogue allowed this, it could no longer be considered an Orthodox synagogue. Riskin immediately consulted with Rabbis Joseph Soloveitchik and
Moshe Feinstein, both of whom told him that allowing the women's service
was halakhically legitimate. The Lubavitcher Rebbe went even further and
told him that he must repeat the women's Simhat Torah service the following
year.[2]

Within a decade there were more than half a dozen women's *tefilah* groups
in the United States, most gathering in private homes but two meeting in
prominent Modern Orthodox synagogues in New York: the Hebrew Institute
of Riverdale, headed by Rabbi Avi Weiss, and Congregation Kehilath Jeshurun,
headed by Rabbi Haskel Lookstein. While the numbers were small at first, by
2015 there were several dozen Orthodox/observant women's *tefilah* groups
across the United States, as well as many more in Israel, Canada, the UK, and
Australia.[3]

The staunchest opposition to women's increased participation within the
Modern Orthodox community came from Rabbi Herschel Schachter, a *rosh
yeshivah* at Yeshiva University's Theological Seminary since 1967 and a widely
recognized Talmud scholar. In 1985, Rabbi Schachter and four other faculty
members of the Theological Seminary sent a brief responsum to the president
of the Rabbinical Council in which they declared unequivocally that women
dancing with the Torah on Simhat Torah and organizing *tefilah* groups were
halakhically prohibited.[4] Rabbi Bronspiegel followed the responsum with a brief

---

[2] Riskin, *Listening to God*, 194–6.

[3] On women's *tefilah* groups, see Frimer and Frimer, 'Women's Prayer Services'; M. Meiselman,
Jewish Woman in Jewish Law; Nusbacher, 'Efforts at Change in a Traditional Denomination';
A. Weiss, *Women at Prayer*.

[4] The responsum appeared in *Hadarom*, 54 (1985), 49–50. It was signed by Rabbis Nissan
Alpert, Abba Bronspiegel, Mordechai Willig, Yehuda Parness, and Hershel Schachter. Of the
five signatories, two, Rabbis Schachter and Willig, are still at the seminary, where they continue
to be leaders of the more conservative sector of Modern Orthodoxy, especially with respect to
women's place in Orthodox Judaism. Rabbi Alpert passed away in 1986. In 2000, Rabbis

article in which he provided documentation for the reasons for the prohibition given in the responsum.[5] At the same time, Rabbi Schachter wrote a
lengthy article in the seminary's Torah journal in which he questioned the
religious credentials of those who participated in women's prayer groups and
asserted that they were motivated by self-aggrandizement. He stated that 'in
some places the intention in starting a women's "minyan" is to publicly demonstrate that women are as important as men'.[6] A heated debate ensued between
those Modern Orthodox rabbis who either frowned upon such prayer groups
or prohibited them outright on halakhic and sociological grounds and those
who strongly defended them on both counts. To a great extent, the debate was
and continues to be over meta-halakhic, public policy issues rather than purely
halakhic ones. The opponents fear the 'slippery slope' effect, that legitimating
women's prayer groups may lead to innovations which are clearly unacceptable
halakhically. The supporters, by contrast, argue that the non-Orthodox branches
of Judaism are no longer a threat to Orthodoxy and that there are no longer any
grounds for questioning the religious motivation of Orthodox women or for
barring them from prayer groups.[7]

A driving force behind many of these efforts is the Jewish Orthodox
Feminist Alliance (JOFA), an organization of women and men that seeks 'to
expand the spiritual, ritual, intellectual and political opportunities for women
within the framework of halakha'.[8] Beginning as a small group, JOFA has
grown to more than 5,500 members. It held its first international conference
in 1997 and has held one every two years since. These are major conferences
with more than a thousand attendees, from which have emerged numerous
scholarly articles and books.

A further innovation and, some emphasize, more serious deviation
from tradition was the establishment of 'partnership *minyanim*', modelled on
Kehillat Shira Hadasha, a congregation established in 2002 in the German
Colony neighbourhood of Jerusalem.[9] That congregation's synagogue has a
divider, a somewhat opaque hanging curtain that runs from above head level
down to the floor, which separates men and women, but women as well as

Bronspiegel and Parness left the Theological Seminary for the Talmud studies branch of Lander
College for Men in Brooklyn, which appeals to ultra-Orthodox young men who want to get a
college degree.

[5] Bronspiegel, 'Separate Prayer Quorums for Women' (Heb.).

[6] Schachter, 'Go Out and Walk in the Footsteps of the Flock' (Heb.). For a penetrating analysis
of Rabbi Schachter's perspective and style, see Ferziger, *Beyond Sectarianism*, 114–29.

[7] See e.g. A. Weiss, *Women at Prayer*, 99–122.

[8] http://www.jofa.org/Who_We_Are/Mission.

[9] See http://www.shirahadasha.org.il/english/index.php?page=25. On partnership *minyanim*,
see Mendel Shapiro, '*Qeri'at ha-Torah* by Women'; Sperber, 'Congregational Dignity and Human

men lead parts of the services on Friday night and sabbath morning, and take the Torah out of the ark and read from it to the congregation on sabbath morning. They are also honoured with the role of taking out the Torah and returning it at the end of the service. Some Modern Orthodox rabbis have written opinions legitimating these innovations, but most, including those who permit women's prayer groups, prohibit them.[10] As of the end of 2015 there were no partnership *minyanim* housed in an Orthodox synagogue.

Whatever the impact of larger social and cultural forces, the growing feminist awareness of Orthodox Jewish women is probably also related to their increased levels of Jewish education over the past half-century.[11] Renewed ideological validation of higher Jewish learning for women was provided by Rabbi Joseph B. Soloveitchik when, in 1977, he gave the inaugural lecture at the opening of the Beit Midrash programme at Yeshiva University's Stern College for Women, thereby indicating his support for educational equality at the highest levels. Indeed, almost forty years earlier, he had espoused the goal of equal Jewish education for women in the Maimonides School which he founded in Boston.[12]

In 1979 Drisha, an institution which achieved not only legitimacy but a reputation for providing first-class higher education for Jewish women, was founded in New York City,[13] and in 2000 Yeshiva University established its Graduate Program for Women in Advanced Talmudic Studies with the explicit goal of developing 'an elite cadre of female scholars of Talmud and *Halakha* who will serve as leaders and role models for the Orthodox Jewish community'.[14]

In Jerusalem, Orthodox programmes that teach Talmud at a high level have had a significant impact on the Jewish education of Orthodox women. They include Michlelet Bruria (now Midreshet Lindenbaum), founded by Rabbi Chaim Brovender, who immigrated from New York in 1965, and Matan and Nishmat, which were established by American-born women living in Israel,

Dignity'; id., *The Path of Halakhah* (Heb.); id., *The Ways of Pesikah* (Heb.); Tamar Ross, *Expanding the Palace of Torah*; Rothstein, 'Women's Aliyyot in Contemporary Synagogues'.

[10] Shlomo Riskin, although he permits women's prayer groups and advocates on behalf of women as halakhic decisors, opposes partnership *minyanim*, in which women are called up for the Torah reading: see Riskin, 'Women's *Aliyah* to the Torah' (Heb.). For an Orthodox feminist analysis of the issue, see Irshai, 'Dignity, Honor, and Equality in Contemporary Halachic Thinking'.

[11] Women's prayer as a significant religious phenomenon has recently become a major subject of discussion and analysis. A widely recognized contributor to its development is the book by Aliza Lavie, an Israeli political scientist and social activist, *Tefilat nashim* (Women's Prayer). It quickly became a best-seller, and has been translated into English as *A Jewish Woman's Prayer Book*. In 2008 it won the National Jewish Book Award in Women's Studies.

[12] S. Farber, *An American Orthodox Dreamer*, 68–87. On the school, see above, p. 16.

[13] http://drisha.org/aboutus/.   [14] http://yu.edu/stern/graduate-talmud/.

and are attended by significant numbers of American Orthodox women, both immigrants to Israel and those studying there for a year or two.[15] For many young American women and men the experience of the post-high-school 'year in Israel' yeshiva and seminary study has led to higher levels of religious observance.[16] This may help explain a pattern of growing observance among Modern Orthodox women in the United States. For example, it has become more popular for married women to cover their hair in public to the extent that there is now a sense that those who don't do so need to justify their decision.[17] In view of this it seems likely that a growing number of such women have developed a clearer consciousness of themselves as Jewish and thus have aspired to greater involvement and presence in the public spheres of the Orthodox community.[18] Indeed, this is one of the underlying reasons for the call, in August 2015, by a prominent rabbi and *rosh yeshivah* at Yeshiva University's Theological Seminary to re-evaluate, and probably reject, 'the inclusion of Talmud in curricula for all women in Modern Orthodox schools'.[19]

One of the major issues separating the Orthodox from the non-Orthodox had been the ordination of women. Recently, that line of separation has been blurred. In March 2009, Daniel Sperber and Avraham Weiss bestowed the title 'rabba' (female rabbi) on an Orthodox woman who had served as a religious guide and spiritual and pastoral counsellor in Weiss's congregation.[20] The act was greeted with scorn in the Orthodox community, but that largely came from men who are active in the public sphere. What is not yet known is how the Modern Orthodox, men and women, who have not made public statements perceive this development. It appears that opposition may not be as widespread as was initially believed: three more women were ordained at Yeshivat Maharat, New York, in 2013, although they were titled 'maharat', a Hebrew acronym meaning halakhic and spiritual leader, as a concession to the Rabbinical Council, which is opposed to giving the title 'rabbi' to women. Significantly, that opposition is not necessarily halakhic but, rather, sociological. According to Mark Dratch, executive vice president of the Council, 'In addition to the *halakha*, there are broader implications for the community.

---

[15] See the websites of these organizations: http://www.midreshet-lindenbaum.org.il/; http://www.matan.org.il/eng/about.asp; https://ots.org.il/program/midreshet-lindenbaum/; https://www.nishmat.net/about-us/.

[16] S. Z. Berger, Jacobson, and Waxman, *Flipping Out?*, 35–46.

[17] Broyde, 'Hair Covering and Jewish Law'; Shulman and Broyde, 'Hair Covering and Jewish Law: A Response'; Pachter, 'Head-Covering for Women' (Heb.).

[18] See e.g. Tamar Ross, *Expanding the Palace of Torah*, p. xii.   [19] Willig, 'Trampled Laws'.

[20] Weiner, 'Todah "Rabba"?' Several women had actually already been ordained in Israel by Orthodox rabbis. Miriam Sara Feigelson was ordained in 1994 by Rabbi Shlomo Carlebach, and Haviva Ner-David was ordained in 2006 by Rabbi Aryeh Strikovsky. Neither of them, however, serves in a synagogue or in any other Orthodox institution.

Traditional rabbinic roles have not been in the domain of women . . . Even if it were permissible, it might not be good policy.'[21] As he apparently sees it, to have women assume traditional rabbinic roles is too divisive, and therefore not politically acceptable. What he did not say is what the Rabbinical Council policy would be if increasing numbers of Orthodox Jews said they would be happy to have a woman serve as a rabbi. Michael Broyde and Shlomo Brody similarly suggested that they

believe that the technical halakhic questions regarding women rabbis remain debatable, but that ultimately a reasonable case can be made that it is not forbidden to issue qualified women *semikhah* [ordination] and let them perform many rabbinic functions. Yet this does not necessarily make it appropriate or advisable in the current context. As with all cases of changes in normative halakhic practice, one needs to weigh and address other meta-halakhic or non-halakhic issues. This calculation plays a central role in determining whether we should deviate from traditional practice and begin to ordain women.[22]

They present a detailed analysis of the halakhic and meta-halakhic issues, and are receptive to the possibility of Orthodox women rabbis in the not too distant future.

However, in 2015 the Rabbinical Council voted to extend its previously stated opposition to the ordination of women by prohibiting its members from ordaining women into the rabbinate 'regardless of the title used'. It was forbidden 'to hire . . . a woman into a rabbinic position at an Orthodox institution' or to 'allow a title implying rabbinic ordination to be used by a teacher of Limudei Kodesh in an Orthodox institution'.[23]

In the face of strong statements by the Rabbinical Council and most senior Talmud faculty at Yeshiva University's Theological Seminary asserting that the ordination of women is against tradition and halakhah, one *rosh yeshivah* there, Jeremy Wieder, suggested in 2015 that 'it is important to follow the stream [of Jewish tradition] in order to follow Jewish law, but in terms of women rabbis, the stream only started ninety years ago, so there is no mesorah (tradition) to talk about'. Although there are halakhic limitations on certain aspects of women's rabbinic functioning, 'such as being a witness in Jewish court or for a marriage, leading prayer services in shul, reading the Torah in shul, and serving as judge on a court' which all involved would have to be aware of, he nevertheless thinks that 'in light of the success of the

[21] Unger-Sargon, 'Orthodox Yeshiva Set to Ordain Three Women'. Two women were ordained in June 2015 in Jerusalem by Rabbi Herzl Hefter, founder and head of Har-El Beit Midrash. See Hefter, 'Why I Ordained Women'.

[22] Broyde and Brody, 'Orthodox Women Rabbis?', 42.

[23] Rabbinical Council of America, '2015 Resolution: RCA Policy Concerning Women Rabbis'.

yoetzet halacha program in increasing overall observance in the communities that he has observed, it may be very beneficial to have women rabbis'.[24] How much authority Wieder has in the seminary and among Modern Orthodox Jews remains to be seen.

Religio-political policy aside, in the realm of sociology, change is taking place. A year after the ordination of the three maharats, Alissa Thomas-Newborn received a one-year appointment as 'kehilla intern' from the Orthodox Congregation B'nai David-Judea, and after receiving her ordination at Yeshivat Maharat in 2015 she became the first Orthodox female member of the clergy in Los Angeles, with the title *moratenu* (our teacher).[25] Even in the more traditional, 'Centrist' Modern Orthodox community women are taking on other religious leadership roles. For example, *yo'atsot* are increasingly normative in American Modern Orthodox communities. In Israel, at the Susi Bradfield Women's Institute for Halakhic Leadership, fellows are being given a historic opportunity 'to master an expansive curriculum in Talmud and *Halakha* identical to that studied by men who are training for rabbinical ordination'.[26]

Torah Umada

Since the turn of the century there have been several significant and interrelated developments in American Modern Orthodoxy, both internally and in response to changes in the surrounding society and culture. The origins of some of these recent developments can be traced to subtle changes in the ideals espoused by leaders of Yeshiva University over the course of its history.

The university's first president, Bernard Revel, saw the introduction of secular studies at the university as an inescapable concession to the realities of American society. As Aaron Rothkoff puts it, 'Revel was only concerned with his attempts to guide the Yeshiva successfully through the labyrinths of American life' if it 'was to retain it brightest high school graduates'.[27] The institution's second president, Samuel Belkin, took this further, seeing *torah umada*—the combination of Torah learning and secular education—as a guiding principle of the institution. In his inaugural address he declared:

---

[24] May, 'YU Roshei Yeshiva Address the Topic of Women Rabbis'. Yo'atsot ('yoetzet') are women who are recognized as authorities capable of providing information on halakhic aspects of family purity, sexuality, and reproduction.

[25] Kustanowitz, 'Morateinu Alissa Thomas-Newborn Joins the Clergy'.

[26] https://ots.org.il/program/susi-bradfield-wihl/.

[27] Rakeffet-Rothkoff, *Bernard Revel*, 72; though Jacob Schacter disagrees with this interpretation, arguing that the evidence indicates that Revel saw the combination of Torah and secular learning not merely as a compromise but, rather, an acknowledgement that the two are intrinsically related within the Jewish perspective (Schacter, 'Torah U-Madda Revisited', 18 n. 14).

it is not our intention to make science the handmaiden of religion nor religion the handmaiden of science. We do not believe in a scientific religion nor in a pseudo-science. We prefer to look upon science and religion as separate domains which need not be in serious conflict and, therefore, need no reconciliation. If we seek the blending of science and religion and the integration of secular knowledge with sacred wisdom, then it is not in the subject matter of these fields but rather within the personality of the individual that we hope to achieve the synthesis.[28]

Norman Lamm, Belkin's successor, developed the concept of *torah umada* analytically at greater length and with much more intellectual sophistication. From his perspective,

advocates of Torah Umadda do not accept that Torah is fundamentally at odds with the world, that Jewishness and Jewish faith, on the one side, and the universal concerns and preoccupations of humanity, on the other, are fundamentally in-apposite, and that Torah and Madda therefore require substantive 'reconciliation.' Rather, whereas it may be true that effectively Torah and culture have become estranged from each other . . . in essence they are part of one continuum. Hence, the motivating mission of Torah Umadda must be to reunite and restore an original harmony.[29]

Some of the most prominent Theological Seminary faculty members went so far as to emphasize the biblical obligation to 'Be fruitful and multiply and replenish the earth and subdue it' (Gen. 1: 28)—and that, they argued, could only be done by studying it. Those supporting this view included Rabbi Ahron Soloveichik, in a speech at Yeshiva College's senior dinner in 1963. Shortly thereafter, his elder brother Joseph developed the meaning of that mandate within the context of his analysis of the two aspects of Adam.[30] Joseph Soloveitchik's son-in-law, Rabbi Dr Aharon Lichtenstein, who had been a faculty member at three branches of Yeshiva University—its Theological Seminary, Yeshiva College, and Stern College for Women—before he immigrated to Israel, proclaimed the value of modern culture, not out of pragmatics but for religious reasons. According to him,

General culture can be a genuinely ennobling and enriching force . . . For what is it that such culture offers us? In relation to art—profound expressions of the creative spirit, an awareness of structure and its interaction with substance and, consequently, the ability to organize and present ideas; in relation to life—the ability to understand, appreciate and confront our personal, communal and cosmic context, sensitivity to the human condition and some assistance in coping with it; in relation to both—a literary consciousness which enables us to transcend our own milieu and place

---

[28] Belkin, *Essays in Traditional Jewish Thought*, 16–17.   [29] Lamm, *Torah Umadda*, 142–3.
[30] J. B. Soloveitchik, *The Lonely Man of Faith*, 10–20. The essay originally appeared in 1965.

it in a broader perspective. Above all, culture instills in us a sense of the moral, psychological and metaphysical complexity of human life.[31]

It should be emphasized that neither Yeshiva University nor Modern Orthodoxy has ever been limited to any particular perspective on the relationship between Torah learning and worldly knowledge. The faculty at the Theological Seminary has always contained a range of attitudes towards both *torah umada* specifically and Modern Orthodoxy in general. For example, a senior member of the faculty, Rabbi David (Dovid) Lifshitz, who arrived at the seminary two years after Joseph B. Soloveitchik, taught a Talmud class which, like Soloveitchik's, was at the highest level in the institution's structure. They were good friends but they had very different perspectives. Following the approach innovated by his grandfather, Rabbi Soloveitchik's classes were wholly within the Brisker tradition and widely adopted within the world of Lithuanian higher yeshivas, which entailed sophisticated analysis and a focus on Maimonides' halakhic codex, *Mishneh torah*.[32] Rabbi Lifshitz followed the approach of his teacher and mentor Rabbi Shimon Shkop, who for almost two decades was a leading Talmud teacher at the higher yeshiva in Telz (Telšiai), Lithuania. This approach became known as 'the Telzer *derekh*'. It was also analytical but much more detailed in its focus than the Brisker approach,[33] and frequently had some grounding in or relevance for moral behaviour, in contrast to the much more cerebral Brisker approach. These differences were reflected in how the two men were seen. Rabbi Soloveitchik was perceived as a *gaon*, a great intellectual who was somewhat removed from most of his students, many of whom feared his temper; Rabbi Lifshitz too was known for the breadth and depth of his talmudic knowledge, but also for his warmth and deep personal caring for all of his students and, indeed, many who were not his students.[34] Rabbi Soloveitchik had a much more modern appearance: he spoke English, he had a doctorate in philosophy, his beard was trimmed, and he wore regular suits. Rabbi Lifshitz projected the rabbi of eastern Europe: he spoke in Yiddish and Hebrew, had no formal secular education, had a full beard, and wore a black frock and hat. He was comfortable with his students obtaining secular education along with their Torah learning, but he was not an advocate of the Modern Orthodox notion of *torah umada*. He saw general education as necessary for making a living but not as a value in and of itself.

[31] Lichtenstein, *By His Light*, 210. Although the book was published after Lichtenstein had left for Israel, the ideas it contains are not essentially different from those that he professed throughout his tenure at Yeshiva University.

[32] See Blau, *The Conceptual Approach to Jewish Learning*; Marc Shapiro, 'The Brisker Method Reconsidered'; Solomon, *The Analytic Movement*; Taragin, '*Limud torah she-ba'al peh*'.

[33] Bechhofer, 'Telshe: 120 Years since the Founding of the Yeshiva'; id., 'An Analysis of *Darchei HaLimud*'.   [34] M. Berger, 'Brisk and Telz'.

Though he maintained close ties with many ultra-Orthodox 'rejectionists', he was not one. He was also a passionate Zionist. His erudition and his great personal caring for his students made him a very influential figure in the Theological Seminary, and his influence became increasingly clear around the turn of the century.[35]

A perusal of the Yeshiva College yearbooks from 1960 to 1965 suggests that its students had a range of interests and reasons for enrolling. Those who went solely out of what the early American sociologist Thorstein Veblen called 'idle curiosity'[36] were a very small minority. Some went simply as a means to getting a job, and most probably aspired to careers and professional advancement. Hardly anyone engaged in higher education *lishemah* (with no ulterior motive). This impression was bolstered by a survey of Yeshiva College and Stern College students that I conducted in the late 1980s. Not surprisingly, the students overwhelmingly viewed receiving a secular education as a Jewish value. More than 80 per cent disagreed with the statement, 'Ideally, a Jew should study Torah only, without any secular study.' More than 75 per cent disagreed with the statement, 'Secular study is permissible only insofar as it is important for one's livelihood.' More than 80 per cent agreed with the statement, 'It is a Jewish value to learn as much as one can, including secular study'; 85 per cent disagreed with the statement, 'Some types of secular study, such as the natural sciences, are important for the observant Jew, but not such fields as literature, history, philosophy, and fine arts.' And 80 per cent agreed with the statement, 'All spheres of knowledge are intrinsically important for the observant Jew.'[37]

When asked why they had gone to Yeshiva University, quite a few students reported that they wanted to be able to continue their talmudic and halakhic studies in a Jewish environment while gaining a secular college education. As one Yeshiva College student expressed it, 'I wanted to combine the college education and to be able to continue learning in a yeshiva setting. I had experienced a special kind of learning in an Israeli yeshiva, and I wanted to continue that kind of learning while getting a broad-based liberal arts education.' When asked if that kind of combination was not basically the same as that of those who learned in other yeshivas, such as Chaim Berlin, Mir, or Ner Israel, since they too managed to learn in the yeshiva and get a college degree, one

[35] Full disclosure: he was my father-in-law. See Waxman, 'Reb David'.

[36] '"Idle" in the sense that a knowledge of things is sought [for its own sake] apart from any ulterior use of the knowledge so gained', which he viewed as the true mission of the university: Veblen, *The Higher Learning in America*, 5.

[37] The survey was not published. The sample size, 435, represented about a third of the student body.

student responded,

'I'm familiar with that. I was at the XYZ Yeshiva for two years, where people do that. Precisely because I saw the kind of college education they were getting, I chose not to do that. I found that they were getting a very narrow summary of what college was. They only took courses that were specifically for their career goals, and they never really went to college; they attended classes.'

Responses such as these indicate an undergraduate body of students who are Modern Orthodox but for whom there are various meanings to *torah* and *mada*.

The fact that, for most Yeshiva University undergraduates, higher education is job-oriented should be no surprise. It is a reflection of patterns in the broader American society, where the vast majority of those who go to college or university do so for pragmatic purposes. As indicated by the president of the American Association of Higher Education, 'When asked why they go to college, most students put "getting a good job" high on their list.'[38]

Although securing the qualifications necessary for a good job has apparently always been the dominant reason for going to Yeshiva University, there were some in the faculty and administration who developed philosophies of Modern Orthodoxy to accompany secular studies; presidents Belkin and Lamm and yeshiva heads Soloveitchik and Lichtenstein developed sophisticated approaches to basic human issues. Since their departure, the approach Yeshiva University largely projects is one of retreat from synthesis to a curriculum that includes both *torah* and *mada* but as separate entities. As Tovah Lichtenstein, a social work supervisor, wife of Rabbi Aharon Lichtenstein, and daughter of Rabbi Joseph Soloveitchik, puts it,

there are former students, notable among them a number of faculty members or former faculty members at RIETS, who have not only turned their backs on the complex worldview the Rov [R. Joseph B. Soloveitchik] espoused but are anxious to claim that the Rov himself turned his back on this view. It has even been claimed that 'Whatever he [the Rov] did aside from learning Torah came to him coincidentally.' It is, indeed, preposterous to think that his major philosophical essays, which interweave general philosophy and science, are 'coincidental'.[39]

Likewise, there has been a distinct theoretical void which has enabled the predominance of a much more limited, cautious, and self-conscious focus within Yeshiva University and within Modern Orthodoxy.[40]

---

[38] M. A. Miller, 'The Meaning of the Baccalaureate', 6, in *About Campus*, the quarterly publication of the National Center for Public Policy and Higher Education.

[39] T. Lichtenstein, 'Reflections on the Influence of the Rov', 21.

[40] The one Modern Orthodox project which prevailed was the Orthodox Forum, a think-tank

Modern Orthodoxy is perceived as experiencing a 'declining hierarchalism' since the early 1990s. By then, its two outstanding halakhic authorities had passed away: Rabbi Feinstein in 1986 and Rabbi Soloveitchik in 1993.[41] As a result, there is now a pluralization of perspectives on three levels: elite, institutional, and among ordinary community members. Among the elite, there are some halakhic scholars who view themselves as the exclusive heirs of the leadership of Rabbi Joseph B. Soloveitchik and who wish to maintain his halakhic authority, while others, who accepted the authority of Rabbi Feinstein and Rabbi Soloveitchik while they were alive, view them as having been unique and without equal in their generation but now want to move on and develop their approach in new ways.

Similarly, although Yeshiva University was the heart and hub of American Modern Orthodoxy—its Theological Seminary was the pre-eminent Modern Orthodox rabbinical seminary, and the Rabbinical Council of America was *the* Modern Orthodox rabbinic organization—none of them now has a monopoly on Modern Orthodox life and education. Talmud study, and Jewish studies courses—as well as a host of basic necessities such as kosher food—which enable students to maintain and even grow in Modern Orthodoxy, are now available in a variety of colleges and universities in the United States, and between 1970 and the end of the century there was a dramatic increase in the number of classes offering Jewish studies on campuses across the country.[42] In the ten years between 1993 and 2003, the Association for Jewish Studies doubled its membership of professors who teach Judaic studies from approximately 800 to 1,500. In conjunction with this, Jewish centres and campus organizations such as Hillel became much more active, and provided an inviting institutional setting for religiously observant students. Harvard, Yale, Columbia, Princeton, Rutgers, and the University of Pennsylvania, as well as

established by Norman Lamm and administered by his senior adviser, Robert Hirt, who is also vice president emeritus of Yeshiva University's Theological Seminary. Participants, who include academicians, *rashei yeshivah*, Jewish educators, and Jewish communal professionals, meet in an annual conference during which scholarly papers invited from among forum participants and beyond and dealing with a designated theme are discussed. The stated goal of the forum is 'to create and disseminate a new and vibrant Torah literature addressing the critical issues facing Jewry today'. The literature is mainly disseminated through the volumes in the Orthodox Forum series, some two dozen of which have so far been published. Impressive as these conferences may be, their critics argue that they are severely limited because attendance is by invitation only and they are closed to the public. Moreover, restrictions are placed on who is invited to submit a paper, and even presented papers may be subject to censorship, which can result in their not being published in the series. See Tamar Ross, *Expanding the Palace of Torah*, pp. xii–xiii. Full disclosure in the interests of transparency: I was part of the Orthodox Forum and was a member of its steering committee from its inception.

[41] Turetsky and Waxman, 'Sliding to the Left?'
[42] Cattan, 'Judaic Studies Classes See Enrollment Boom'.

Brandeis, to name just a few in the north-east, have energetic observant sub-communities of students and faculty, and the restrictions and limitations on those young college-age adults who wish to be both modern and religiously observant are much fewer than they were in past decades. Indeed, the Orthodox Union established a joint programme with Hillel called the Jewish Learning Initiative on Campus, which has brought Jewish educators to more than twenty campuses to further invigorate and be a source of inspiration and assistance to observant students and faculty already there.[43] Some higher yeshivas which previously prohibited or severely restricted their students from college and university studies are now somewhat more amenable to their studying at these institutions.

Organizational Developments

In response to what some viewed as a growing tendency towards halakhic rigidity in Yeshiva University and the Rabbinical Council, there have been moves towards organizational decentralization. As discussed above, women's prayer groups emerged in the 1970s and their numbers have grown since, indicating that the issue of women's greater public involvement in Jewish religious life was very real. The reactions to this within Modern Orthodoxy, both negative and positive, led to a split, and there are now effectively two movements: I will refer here to the more traditional sector as 'Centrist Modern Orthodoxy',[44] and to the less traditional as Modern Orthodoxy. In 1997, two organizations committed to supporting women's role in Judaism were founded: JOFA, mentioned above, and Edah. Both held conferences which attracted wide interest. Two years later, in 1999, Rabbi Avi Weiss established a new rabbinical school, Chovevei Torah (YCT), in New York with the statement that 'the future of Orthodoxy depends on our becoming a movement that expands outward non-dogmatically and cooperatively to encompass the needs of the larger Jewish community and the world'. Despite predictions of its imminent demise it has continued to grow.[45]

Initial reaction at Yeshiva University, especially within the Theological Seminary, was scorn and rejection. YCT was rejected as being unworthy of serious consideration and those associated with it were condemned as traitors not only to the university, to which it presented serious competition, but to Orthodoxy as

[43] http://jliconline.org/jlic-overview/. The programme was founded by Rabbi Menachem Schrader, an American immigrant to Israel who was ordained at Yeshiva University's Theological Seminary.

[44] The label here has a somewhat different meaning than that intended by Norman Lamm in his 'Some Comments on Centrist Orthodoxy'.

[45] http://www.yctorah.org/content/blogcategory/13/49/.

a whole. After the 2003 installation of Richard Joel as president of Yeshiva University there was a marked change. Joel, the first non-rabbi to serve as Yeshiva's president, had been the president and international director of the Hillel Foundation for the previous fifteen years and was credited with revivifying that organization. He brought to bear his wide and deep ties within the entire American Jewish community, as well as his highly regarded administrative skills, in his mission to familiarize that larger community with Yeshiva and its activities, as well as to make it more responsive to both Orthodox and non-Orthodox Jews. Soon after his inauguration, Joel named Kenneth Brander, an energetic and highly successful rabbi,[46] as dean of the soon-to-be-established Center for the Jewish Future (CJF).[47] The CJF, which went into operation in 2005, aimed at harnessing and exploiting the intellectual resources of the university in order to stimulate and strengthen Jewish communities across the country and abroad. Significantly, throughout all of these efforts to reach out to the larger Orthodox and non-Orthodox communities, Joel maintained positive relations with the rabbis at the Theological Seminary and he belied the predictions of some of his detractors as well as supporters that he and the rabbis, and especially the dominant figures among them, would clash over irreconcilable differences. In 2008, however, the financial condition of Yeshiva University deteriorated significantly and Joel was apparently preoccupied with that to the exclusion of other concerns.[48] Since then, a number of episodes have suggested not only a hardening of halakhic positions but also distinct expressions of disrespect and disdain from members of the Theological Seminary for those who disagree with them.

Although Modern Orthodoxy's major synagogue organization, the Orthodox Union, has shown various signs of 'haredization', it still is a lay organization which needs to present a Modern Orthodox position and reflect the entire Modern Orthodox community. Accordingly, it has undertaken efforts to resist the haredi influence and to bolster Modern Orthodoxy's self-confidence. One major step was an alliance with a prominent Israeli publishing company which caters to the Modern Orthodox market. It began with the publication of

[46] Brander played a major role in the rapid development of the Modern Orthodox community in Boca Raton, Florida, during his fourteen-year tenure there.

[47] The selection of this name was, perhaps, not coincidental. The former CJF, the Council of Jewish Federations, had renamed itself the United Jewish Communities (UJC), so the well-known initials, CJF, were available. In 2009 the UJC changed its name again, this time to the Jewish Federations of North America (JFNA).

[48] The Madoff scandal and the world financial crisis in 2008 were major reasons for the university's financial crisis. According to an article in *University Business*, 'Yeshiva's investment was valued at about $110 million, which represents 8 percent of its endowment . . . [its] endowment is currently estimated to be approximately $1.2 billion, down from $1.7 billion on January 1, 2008'. See Herrmann, 'Behind the News: Yeshiva Hit Hard by Madoff Scam'.

a new translation of the prayer book, the *Koren Sacks Siddur*, that challenged the dominance of the ArtScroll prayer book which, despite its clear haredi perspective, was by far the most widely used prayer book even in Modern Orthodox congregations. The new prayer book and new translations of other sacred texts, as well as a growing series of books on a variety of topics reflecting Modern Orthodox interests and perspectives, appear to have been met with enthusiasm and suggest that Modern Orthodoxy is producing and promoting its own scholars and does not have to turn to the ultra-Orthodox for insight and guidance.[49]

That these efforts have reportedly been successful suggests that there are receptive individuals and communities across the United States with a variety of perspectives, and that they have not all 'haredized'. This was suggested by the large number of attendees at the JOFA and Edah conferences mentioned above, and is further supported by the data amassed, in 2002, by political scientist Milton Heumann and David Rabinowitz in a Young Israel synagogue in the New York/New Jersey area,[50] which found that a minority held 'conservative' or 'very conservative' views on the eight issues presented, while an approximately two-thirds majority held 'modern' to 'very modern' views.[51]

[49] Stolow, *Orthodox by Design*; Lockshin, 'Get Ready for Duelling Prayerbooks'; Finkelman, 'A Prayer Book of One's Own'. Significantly, the *Koren Sacks Siddur* was promoted by the Orthodox Union some time after the Rabbinical Council announced the impending publication of the 'revised RCA siddur'. To some observers, the belated arrival of the revised RCA siddur was taken as a manifestation of basic organizational weakness and the decision to publish the new siddur with ArtScroll as a sign of the Rabbinical Council's rightward leanings. In the end, that new siddur was not published.

[50] The Young Israel Synagogue Organization was started as a youth group in 1913 by a small group of 'upwardly mobile' college age young adults whose goal was to combat indifference to Judaism and Jewish issues, especially among young people. It began as an independent movement covering a broad range of issues of concern to Judaism and was initially supported by some faculty and students at the Conservative Jewish Theological Seminary. It subsequently cut all ties with both Conservative Judaism and the JTS. In 1915 a group of Orthodox Jews, including some of those affiliated with Young Israel, initiated the 'Model Synagogue', an effort to retain Orthodoxy while making the synagogue service attractive to young Americans. It merged with Young Israel in 1918 as the Young Israel Synagogue. In the following years, a number of other Young Israel synagogues developed, and in 1922 they united to form the Young Israel Synagogue Organization, with a Council of Young Israel, which was to co-ordinate the organization's activities. It soon gained widespread support within the Orthodox community and, at least until the second half of the twentieth century, was widely viewed as the national Modern Orthodox movement. According to Shulamith Z. Berger, curator of special collections at Yeshiva University, 'Young Israel's special mission was to prove that becoming American did not mean abandoning Judaism' (Berger, 'The Early History of the Young Israel Movement'). I thank Shulamith Berger for sharing this important unpublished paper with me. A full-scale study of the Young Israel movement throughout the twentieth century is yet to be written.

[51] Waxman, 'American Modern Orthodoxy', 2. The survey focused on issues including pluralism/tolerance; the religious meaning of Israel; attitudes towards and behaviour between

It is difficult to determine how pervasive the phenomenon of inconsistent identification within Orthodoxy is. However, a recent study by Yael Steinmetz has supplied some information on the situation within Modern Orthodoxy.[52] She found that, on social media and especially in the Jewish blogosphere which deals with religious identity, thought, and behaviour, there are many who identify emotionally with Orthodoxy but are independent when it comes to belief and/or behaviour, and that many American Orthodox Jews select a diversity of identifications with a variety of versions of Orthodoxy. For example, at times they may pray in a hasidic *shtiebl* while at other times they may pray in a Modern Orthodox synagogue; they may regularly engage in traditional Lithuanian yeshiva-type Talmud study as well as academic Talmud study; they may read ultra-Orthodox Jewish thought as well as modern biblical scholarship; and they may participate in a hasidic *rebbe*'s *tish* combining Torah study with a meal and singing hasidic songs while having subscriptions to the theatre or the local pool club. Jewish identification increasingly encompasses a 'collective of individuals' who have deep memories and emotions that help define them as human beings and are thus strongly attached to their Orthodoxy, even if communal.[53]

The Role of Israel

Israel has played a significant role in the increasing heterogeneity of American Orthodoxy. On the one hand, Israeli Judaism is much more traditional than American Judaism,[54] and both Orthodox identification and traditional religious observance are increasing in Israel.[55] On the other hand, Israeli Orthodoxy, especially the non-ultra-Orthodox parts, appears to be more open and tolerant of diversity, both ideological and institutional, than American Orthodoxy, including Modern Orthodoxy.[56] The strong connections between American Orthodox Jewry—ultra-Orthodox as well as Modern Orthodox —and Israel have influenced American Orthodox Judaism in a variety of

---

Jews and non-Jews; rabbinic authority, including *da'at torah*; Torah and secular study (*torah umada*); religious stringency (*ḥumrah*); women and halakhah; and religious outreach.

    [52] Steinmetz, 'Let's Talk About It' (Heb.).
    [53] Ibid. 177.   [54] Levy, Levinsohn, and Katz, *A Portrait of Israeli Jewry*.
    [55] Arian and Keissar-Sugarmen, *A Portrait of Israeli Jewry*, 32–5.
    [56] As indicated above, partnership *minyan* and more egalitarian synagogues first emerged in Jerusalem without much oppositional fanfare, and institutions of higher learning for Orthodox Jewish women are much more developed and prevalent in Israel. Indeed, the greater flexibility of Israeli Orthodoxy is not limited to women's issues but extends to gay groups, such as Havruta (see p. 70 above). Likewise, the Israeli television series *Serugim*, which focused on young religious people in Jerusalem, portrayed a wide range of behaviour, including homosexuality.

spheres,[57] and it seems difficult to imagine that behaviour which is accepted in religious Zionist communities in Israel will be judged deviant in the American Modern Orthodox community in general, even though it may be so judged by some Centrist Orthodox rabbis. This is especially so because Israel has become the centre of creative thinking in Modern Orthodoxy.[58]

Israel serves as a source of rigidity for American ultra-Orthodoxy and as a source of moderation for American Modern Orthodoxy. Israeli ultra-Orthodox yeshivas are considered to be superior to their American counterparts, and many ultra-Orthodox yeshiva students go to study in Israeli yeshivas for a year or more before entering a *kolel* in America. The heads of the Israeli ultra-Orthodox communities, the most revered rabbis in ultra-Orthodoxy (the *gedolim*),[59] such as Rabbi Aharon Leib Shteinman and Rabbi Shmuel Auerbach, are also viewed as the authorities by American ultra-Orthodox Jewry. They are much more rigid in their approach than the American ultra-Orthodox, who live socially as equals in a more heterogeneous and open society, because they do not perceive themselves as equals in Israel and they are opposed to the openness of the Jewish society in Israel. Although their opinions are not necessarily definitive for American Orthodoxy, they do tend to influence it in the direction of greater rigidity because the American ultra-Orthodox also view themselves as essentially being part of the same collective religious group and perspective.[60]

By contrast, Israeli Modern Orthodoxy is broader and more diverse as a result of a number of significant sociological factors. One is the near-absence of denominations in Israeli Judaism, especially among Mizrahim, as Jews from Middle Eastern and North African communities are known, and Sephardim. They comprise about half of Israel's Jewish population, and the notion of

---

[57]   Waxman, 'If I Forget Thee, O Jerusalem'.

[58]   There are in Israel numerous institutions, organizations, books, journals, and weekly publications in which a wide array of issues in Modern Orthodoxy are analysed and discussed on various intellectual levels that cater to various audiences. There is nothing approximating this, either quantitatively or qualitatively, in American Orthodoxy. This is probably related to the fact that a significant percentage of young American Modern Orthodox Jews with high levels of Jewish education and communal commitment choose to live in Israel, leaving American Orthodoxy with a brain drain. Since 1967, between 1,500 and 3,000 American Jews annually have made *aliyah*. The vast majority of them are Orthodox, and they arrive in Israel with a high level of Jewish education (figures taken from data at Israel's Central Bureau of Statistics). There are no firm data on the percentage who return to the United States, but evidence over the past twenty years indicates that less than 20 per cent return.

[59]   See Leon and Brown (eds.), *The Gdoilim* (Heb.).

[60]   P. L. Berger, *A Rumor of Angels*, 7. In a conversation I had with Menachem Friedman several decades ago, we agreed that the connections between the ultra-Orthodox in the United States and in Israel are so strong that they can be analysed within the context of the 'haredi global village'.

denominations is alien to both groups. They exhibit a wide variety of religious behaviour, but those differences do not make for significant social barriers between them. As sociologist Nissim Leon indicates in *Gentle Ultra-Orthodoxy*, even their haredism is 'gentle'. Since the majority of Israeli Orthodox have an open, welcoming approach, and there are no other major religious ideologies which reject the core religious beliefs of all Orthodox Jews, neither the Modern nor the ultra-Orthodox in Israel therefore feel a need to establish firm boundaries to distinguish themselves from other religious branches, as they do in the United States. In addition, religious practice in Israel differs from that of Orthodoxy in the diaspora in a number of ways. What is considered correct synagogue attire, for example, is very different in Israel than in the diaspora, and the informality of most Israeli synagogues strikes some visitors as strange. Similarly, the period for which religious festivals need to be observed is shorter in Israel than in the diaspora and there is some dispute as to how visitors to Israel should behave on the extra 'free' day of Pesach or Sukkot, for example. A fundamental source of difference between Israeli and American Jews is that in Israel Sephardim are in the majority, whereas the American Orthodox are overwhelmingly of Ashkenazi background. This means, for example, that visitors to Israel find that Sephardi Jews will eat certain grains and legumes, called *kitniyot*, at Pesach, whereas these are forbidden to Ashkenazi Jews. American Orthodox Jews, especially young people, who are exposed to these Israeli norms may question whether they need to observe so strictly when they return home, and may be critical of other patterns of behaviour they previously accepted as definitive. There are also reports of a growing number of Israeli Modern Orthodox Jews, particularly American *olim*, who no longer conform to the centuries-old Ashkenazi ban on *kitniyot* at Pesach.[61] One reason for this, and for why some diaspora visitors to Israel readily cease observing the extra day of the major holidays, is rooted in some approaches to religious Zionism, especially those deriving from the thought of Rabbi Abraham Isaac Kook. According to this, the State of Israel is not only an 'old-new land' but one with radical religious and mystical significance.[62] The uniqueness of Israel requires it to be returned to its pristine character, and this involves unshackling it from some of the religious norms which have developed in the diaspora.[63] Even within overt mystical interpretations, some religious Zionists view the special status of Israel as grounds for unique halakhic norms. Thus, for example, Rabbi Shlomo

[61]   Ahren, 'Efrat Rabbi Tilts against Passover Food Restrictions for Ashkenazi Jews'.
[62]   See Herzl, *Old-New Land*; for an analysis of Rabbi Kook and his thought, see Y. Mirsky, *Rav Kook*.
[63]   It is within this framework that some religious Zionists strive to elevate the authoritative status of the Jerusalem Talmud at the expense of the Babylonian Talmud.

Goren introduced a number of major innovations to the process of religious conversion while he was Israel's chief rabbi.[64]

Given the increasing influence of Israel on American Modern Orthodoxy, the boundaries of acceptable norms and values within Modern Orthodoxy are expanding, and there seems less reason for the leaders of 'Open Orthodoxy'[65] to leave Modern Orthodoxy today. Rejection of Modern Orthodoxy is made even more unlikely by the pluralization of authority in the Modern Orthodox community and, indeed, in Orthodox Judaism as a whole.[66] As indicated above, Modern Orthodoxy is increasingly fragmented and lacks a single source of authoritative leadership, especially but not exclusively in the area of halakhic decision-making. Ironically, this partly results from the approach of Rabbi Joseph B. Soloveitchik, who encouraged his students to become learned scholars in their own right and to make their own decisions. In addition, modernity and postmodernity have contributed to many feeling a growing sense of autonomy. Enormous collections of rabbinic literature, much of it in translation, can now be accessed online, enabling many more people to acquire knowledge previously available only to a small minority. But Internet search engines can only indicate the sources that are available; it is the individual who then chooses which ones to adopt as authoritative.[67] Indeed, Avraham Bronstein argues that we are now in 'the bold new era of big Torah', and

novel interpretations, challenges, or ritual innovations that arise anywhere are now instantly available to the entire world, open for criticism, adoption, or adaptation. With so many more diverse voices chiming in, the conversations move faster, and make a greater impact . . . Therefore, we should not be lamenting the lack of a singular, top-down authority that tells us what to do. We should, rather, all be spending more time using the unprecedented resources and capabilities at our disposal to carefully evaluate the options that so many preeminent thinkers and scholars are making

[64] Waxman, '*Giyur* in the Context of National Identity'; id., 'Multiculturalism, Conversion, and the Future of Israel'.

[65] An approach which, with Modern Orthodoxy, has a welcoming stance towards all Jews, greater religious equality between women and men, an emphasis on spirituality, and, in general, greater halakhic openness and flexibility. See Weiss, 'Open Orthodoxy' and 'Defining "Open Orthodoxy"'.

[66] It is more than just interesting to note that, although the ultra-Orthodox community has in the past been characterized by strict obedience to central rabbinic authority, *da'at torah*, today that is much less the case. There are now a significant number of individuals who are ultra-Orthodox in observance but do not accept such authority unquestioningly. This development is, in large measure, a reaction to bans pronounced by prominent ultra-Orthodox rabbis on books such as those of Rabbi Natan Slifkin (*Mysterious Creatures, The Science of Torah*) and Rabbi Nathan Kamenetsky (*Making of a Godol*).

[67] Rosensweig, 'The Study of the Talmud in Contemporary Yeshivot'.

available to us, and taking a real sense of responsibility for the choices we make, both as individuals and communities.[68]

Over the course of the last thirty years, enrolments at Yeshiva University's Theological Seminary and the size of the graduating classes have been growing. Whatever else they may reflect, these enrolments do not necessarily indicate the increased prestige and/or authority of rabbis within the Jewish world. An analysis of those ordained by the seminary between 1998 and 2002 indicated that only 16 per cent expected to enter the pulpit rabbinate. Most (52%) planned to enter the field of Jewish education at the primary, secondary, or post-high-school level. Another 21 per cent planned to enter secular professions; 7 per cent planned careers in the Jewish organizational field; and 3 per cent planned to enter the chaplaincy in either a hospital or university setting.[69] It might be suggested that being ordained is becoming a rite of passage in the Orthodox community and, for some, a prerequisite of entry into an Orthodox scholarly subculture. Rabbis may no longer be an elite group. Within American Orthodoxy, rabbinic ordination may now be akin to a bachelor's degree in secular society; it once conferred prestige, but as it became common it lost its lustre, although the requirement to get the degree became greater.

There are some scholars who have suggested that 'the sliding to the left' in Modern Orthodoxy may result in the emergence of a new denomination, especially after the founding, in November 2009, of a new Orthodox rabbinical organization, the International Rabbinic Fellowship (IRF), created by Rabbis Avi Weiss of Yeshivat Chovevei Torah and Marc Angel, rabbi emeritus of New York's Congregation Shearith Israel, the oldest congregation in the United States. The IRF, which claims a membership of more than 200 rabbis across the country, sees its mission as 'to bring together Orthodox Rabbis for serious study of Torah and Halacha, for open and respectful discussion, and to advocate policies and implement actions on behalf of world Jewry and humankind'.[70] At its first conference, it focused on two of the most controversial issues in contemporary Orthodoxy: it appointed a committee to examine conversion procedures with an eye towards a more lenient and welcoming approach than that of the Rabbinical Council of America and the Israeli rabbinate, and it urged the Fellowship to consider admitting women members.

Responding to the establishment of the IRF, Jonathan Sarna is quoted as saying, 'In American religion, when you have a new seminary and a new board of rabbis, including many who are not acceptable to the Rabbinical

---

[68]   Bronstein, 'On Leaders and Followers in the Age of Big Torah'.
[69]   Waxman, 'The Role and Authority of the Rabbi', 103–4.
[70]   http://internationalrabbinicfellowship.org/.

Council, one begins to wonder if in fact we are seeing the development of two movements that use the term Orthodox.'[71] There are a number of reasons to be sceptical of the emergence of a new denomination. For one, most of those affiliated with the IRF and Yeshivat Chovevei Torah identify as Orthodox and wish to remain so. As Jeffrey Gurock said, 'A wing of Orthodoxy is just a wing . . . Members can be loyal members of the RCA and part of their own organization.'[72] Although YCT's founder, Avi Weiss, did actually resign from the Rabbinical Council in protest at its refusal to admit rabbis ordained by his institution,[73] and although its current president, Asher Lopatin, also resigned over this and also in protest at the Council's increasingly exclusionary practices and policies,[74] both he and Weiss continue to identify as Modern Orthodox. In fact, Lopatin appears to be engaged in efforts to strengthen Modern Orthodoxy rather than leave it.[75] The establishment, in 1935, of the Rabbinical Council of America, whose stance contrasted with that of the ultra-Orthodox Agudat Harabanim, did not result in a new denomination,[76] and it is not anticipated that the establishment of the International Rabbinic Fellowship will either.[77] Just as, in 1935, the fact that many Rabbinical Council members were also members of Agudat Harabanim helped to prevent an irreparable split, so today many of the members of the IRF are also members of the Rabbinical Council, and many on the faculty of YCT have strong ties with Yeshiva University. In addition, the fact that a group or institution is viewed as beyond the pale by one segment of Orthodoxy does not mean that Orthodox Jews as a whole will view it as such. Modern Orthodoxy itself is an example. It has been vociferously critiqued by some prominent ultra-Orthodox rabbis but its adherents are still perceived as Orthodox. Moreover, although the notion of obedience to higher authority is more pronounced in Orthodox Judaism than in other denominations, it is structurally more diverse than the non-Orthodox. Ironic as it may appear, the Orthodox have many more seminaries and rabbinic organizations than the non-Orthodox. Even among the Modern Orthodox, although Yeshiva University has the 'flagship' seminary it has no

---

[71] Quoted in Breger, 'Do 1 Rabba, 2 Rabbis and 1 Yeshiva = a New Denomination?', 38.

[72] Quoted ibid.

[73] Jewish Telegraphic Agency, 'In Protest, Rabbi Avi Weiss Quits Rabbinical Council of America'.   [74] http://www.yctorah.org/content/view/961/17/.

[75] Lopatin, 'How to Rejuvenate Modern Orthodoxy'.

[76] Liebman, 'Orthodoxy in American Jewish Life', 33, 51–4; Rakeffet-Rothkoff, The Silver Era, 105, 294.

[77] It is interesting to note that, in his pioneering study of American Orthodoxy, which originally appeared as a lead article in the American Jewish Year Book in 1965, Liebman had observed that the 'RCA has moved to the right in recent years'. See Liebman, 'Orthodoxy in American Jewish Life', 53.

monopoly. Many who identify as Modern Orthodox, including some of its prominent rabbis, have never studied there. Moreover, many affiliates of the International Rabbinic Fellowship and Yeshivat Chovevei Torah have close bonds with Modern Orthodox groups and organizations in Israel. They may feel that they get their legitimacy from there and that they are therefore part of Modern Orthodoxy, even if Yeshiva University and the Rabbinical Council do not accept them. Also, just as there are many Centrist Orthodox American Jews who eschew labels and identify simply as 'Orthodox', so there are probably many who do not wear the label 'Modern Orthodox' but are so nevertheless. Any attempt to develop a new movement would be to risk leaving behind these covert Modern Orthodox, weakening the new movement. Precisely because of its perspective on modernity, which is viewed as essentially positive even as it poses challenges, Modern Orthodoxy is viewed by many adherents as able to encompass diversity. Increasingly, it appears that Modern Orthodox American Jews are not concerned with in-depth philosophy; rather, they are comfortable with a sense of commonality with all those who promote Torah learning in its broadest sense: public basic halakhic observance; ethical behaviour as defined by Jewish tradition and modern values; compassion for 'others'; and devotion to Zionism and the State of Israel—though not necessarily support for all the actions of its government. In short, working to improve the state of Jews and Judaism and making the world a better place. Many of those are thought to be specific goals and values even if they do not form part of a sophisticated philosophy.

Finally, this does not appear to be a propitious moment for establishing new denominations. This seems to be indicated by the experience of the Union of Traditional Judaism (UTJ), which began within Conservative Judaism but broke away and formed its own rabbinic organization and seminary. It has not developed into a distinct denomination even though the cleavages between the founders of UTJ and mainstream Conservative Judaism seem to be significantly wider than those between the founders of the International Rabbinic Fellowship and mainstream Orthodox Judaism.[78] The present, if anything, is an era of trans-denominationalism, post-denominationalism, and/ or non-denominationalism, in which increasing numbers of younger Jews are eschewing denominational labels.[79] Additionally, as indicated, Steinmetz's research suggests that among young American Jews who do identify as Orthodox there are significant manifestations of individuality and wide

[78] It should also be noted that, in addition to being a former president of the Rabbinical Council of America, IRF co-founder Marc Angel is of Sephardi heritage, and the Sephardi tradition has always been much more tolerant of religious variation than the Ashkenazi tradition (Angel, *Foundations of Sephardic Spirituality*).

[79] S. M. Cohen, 'Non-Denominational and Post-Denominational'.

variations in the behaviour and belief that accompany that identification.[80] Identity is much less defined by membership of formal groups and is much more self-defined, subjective. There are those in the community who think that Modern Orthodoxy need not condone 'Social Orthodoxy',[81] 'Half Shabbos',[82] or any other deviation from strict halakhic Orthodoxy, but it also need not condemn and exorcize. Such measures may work in very traditional societies and groups where the individual needs the group. Ostracism is a powerful sanction in such groups because it undermines the very basis of the individual's identity. In modern societies and groups such as Modern Orthodoxy, however, where identity is not conferred but is subjectively created, individuals do not fear being ostracized because they are free to seek out other groups as they wish. Adam Ferziger has written on the 'Chabadization' of 'Haredi Orthodoxy', arguing that the Lakewood yeshiva and others like it have adopted the approach and methods of Chabad in outreach to the non-observant.[83] Modern Orthodoxy has incorporated some aspects of Chabad and other variations of hasidism. Whether this will lead it to return to its orientation of outreach through openness remains to be seen.[84]

---

[80] Steinmetz, 'Let's Talk About It' (Heb.).   [81] Lefkowitz, 'The Rise of Social Orthodoxy'.

[82] The term refers to a phenomenon reportedly found among a growing number of Modern Orthodox Jews, especially teenagers, who otherwise observe Jewish law but do text on the sabbath (see Lipman, 'For Many Orthodox Teens'). The phenomenon has led to efforts to develop a 'shabbat app' which, its designer and promoters claim, will enable halakhically legitimate texting on the sabbath (see 'Sacred Texts'). Although critics argue that the app does not resolve serious halakhic issues, it does have its halakhic defenders. If the experience with the 'Kosher Switch'—a device designed to enable lights and other electrical appliances to be turned on and off in a halakhically legitimate way on the sabbath—is any indicator, use of the shabbat app may well spread within the Modern Orthodox community (see U. Heilman, 'Is Kosher Switch Really Kosher for Shabbat?'). Despite initial opposition, the Kosher Switch is sold widely, and advertises that it is 'Endorsed by leading Poskim & Orthodox Rabbis'; perhaps the same will occur with the shabbat app. The diffusion of both would significantly change the character of the sabbath in Orthodox communities. One's view of such change is rooted not only in halakhah but also in how one regards change more widely. For some, all change in the religious realm, even if it is halakhically sanctioned, is seen as negative. Others may feel it has positive consequences, so long as it is halakhically sanctioned.   [83] Ferziger, *Beyond Sectarianism*, 175–94.

[84] Ch. Miller, *Turning Judaism Outwards*, 291–2.

SIX

HALAKHIC CHANGE AND META-HALAKHAH

I N   A   V O L U M E on Judaism written for the general public, a prominent English theologian, Rabbi Dr Louis Jacobs, asserted that 'the Torah did not simply drop down from heaven but is the result of the divine–human encounter through the ages'.[1] This is a statement that strongly lends itself to rejection by traditionalists, especially the Orthodox. In a later work, in which he provided an in-depth analysis of the development of halakhah, Jacobs appeared to modify his earlier assertion in such a way as to be more acceptable to some Orthodox thinkers. He indicated that, when he used the term Torah, he included the Written Law, Oral Law, and halakhah, which 'has grown through the tender care and skill of responsible gardeners instead of, as in the view of many fundamentalists, growing of its own accord solely by divine command'.[2] His clarification did not, however, mollify those, typically ultra-Orthodox, Jews who insisted that both the Written and the Oral Law as we know them were given at Sinai, and that any mention of halakhic development is heresy. Jacobs went even further and asserted that the very notion that the halakhah has a history and developed over time is anathema to the traditional halakhist, who operates on the massive assumption that the Torah, both in its written form, the Pentateuch, and its oral form, as found in the talmudic literature, was directly conveyed by God to Moses either at Sinai or during the forty years of wandering through the wilderness. Furthermore, the traditional halakhists accept implicitly that the talmudic literature contains the whole of the Oral Torah, that even those laws and ordinances called rabbinic are eternally binding, and that the Talmud is the final authority and can never be countermanded.[3] This chapter clarifies current attitudes to Jacobs's assertion, based on a review of changes in American Orthodox Judaism from the end of the nineteenth century to the beginning of the twenty-first in the sphere of halakhah, that is, what is deemed to be religiously acceptable within the observant community. It does this primarily through an examination of the responsa of Rabbi Moshe Feinstein, who was widely perceived as the

---

[1] Jacobs, *The Jewish Religion*, 3.   [2] Jacobs, *A Tree of Life*, p. xv.   [3] Ibid. 222.

foremost halakhic authority in the American Orthodox community during the second half of the twentieth century. It concludes with a consideration of the meta-halakhic and theological differences between American and British Orthodoxy through a discussion of Louis Jacobs and his notorious departure from the British Orthodox rabbinate.

Developments in Observance in the United States

Decorum in Shul

The first major attempt to reform Jewish religious services in the United States took place in Charleston, South Carolina, in 1824. Forty-seven members of Congregation Beth Elohim who were unhappy with the synagogue service attempted to reform it by abbreviating it, having parts of the service read in both Hebrew and English, eliminating the practice of auctioning synagogue honours, and having a weekly discourse, or sermon, in English. These reforms were radical at the time, and the leadership of Beth Elohim rejected them, which led to the group splitting from the parent congregation and forming a separate community which then introduced more radical reforms.[4] Ironically, the group's initial demands are quite compatible with contemporary Centrist Orthodox synagogue services in America.

Attitudes to Women

Before the twentieth century it was axiomatic that women should neither be taught nor engage in Torah study. This was based on the opinion of Rabbi Eliezer, in the Babylonian Talmud and reiterated by Maimonides.[5] But in the first half of the twentieth century, Rabbi Israel Meir Hacohen, author of the *Mishnah berurah*, and the Lubavitcher Rebbe, Menachem Mendel Schneersohn, asserted that since young women no longer remained in their parents' home until they were married and religious tradition was no longer as strong as it had been, women were now obligated to study the Written Law and those laws which specifically pertained to them. By the 1970s, as outlined in Chapter 5, women's role was increasingly supported by major figures such as Rabbi Joseph B. Soloveitchik.

Another development is the adoption of the bat mitzvah as a coming-of-age ritual for girls. In his first responsum dealing with the issue, written in 1956, Rabbi Moshe Feinstein asserted that there was no halakhic source justifying the celebration, that the idea was simply nonsense (*hevel be'alma*), and that it was a violation of the sanctity of the synagogue to hold the ceremony

---

[4] Waxman, *America's Jews in Transition*, 12–13.
[5] BT *Sot.* 21b; Maimonides, *Mishneh torah*, 'Hilkhot talmud torah', 1: 17.

there. A quarter of a century later he reiterated his opposition to holding the ceremony in the sanctuary of the synagogue but relented somewhat and permitted, albeit warily, a kiddush to mark the event in the synagogue's social hall.[6]

A careful reading of his responsa on the subject suggests that his underlying objection was to holding the ceremony in the synagogue, a reflection of his steadfast opposition to the changes in synagogue ritual introduced by Conservative and Reform Judaism. If the bat mitzvah celebration was held within the home he did not object. Indeed, a number of his elders and colleagues are reported to have held such celebrations, even in Lithuania.[7] Be that as it may, increasing numbers of ultra-Orthodox and Modern Orthodox now celebrate bat mitzvah in a communal setting, most typically in a social hall and frequently as a women-only ceremony. Some are also finding ways to hold the ceremony in the sanctuary in ways that are now deemed to be halakhically approved.[8]

Non-Observant Jews

Rabbi Feinstein's opposition to non-Orthodox Judaism was steadfast. He considered both Conservative and Reform Judaism heretical. Reform Judaism does not merit much discussion in his work, and he merely dismisses its rabbis as heretics. For example, in a responsum on whether it is proper to honour Reform and Conservative rabbis with blessings at Jewish organizational banquets, he asserts that even if they pronounce the blessing properly, since they are (obviously) heretics their blessings are invalid. Their heretical nature is deemed to need no elaboration.[9] He addressed Conservative Judaism in more detail, perhaps because he felt that it was a greater danger to Orthodoxy. In a number of responsa he consistently emphasized its heretical nature. For example, in a responsum on the question of whether one can organize a *minyan*, a quorum, to pray in a room within a synagogue whose sanctuary does not conform to Orthodox standards, he distinguished between Orthodox and Conservative synagogues. In a Conservative synagogue, he asserted, one should not make a *minyan* in any room, 'because they have announced that they are a group of heretics who reject a number of Torah laws'.[10] One should keep apart from them, 'because those who deny even one item from the Torah are considered deniers of the Torah', and one must distance oneself from heretics. However, in an Orthodox synagogue which is ritually unfit—for example, it has no *meḥitsah*

---

[6] *Igerot mosheh, Oraḥ ḥayim*, pt. 1, no. 104; pt. 4, no. 36.
[7] Joseph, 'Ritual, Law, and Praxis'; Pensak, 'Keeping the Bar Out of Bas Mitzvahs'.
[8] Eleff and Butler, 'How Bat Mitzvah Became Orthodox'.
[9] *Igerot mosheh, Oraḥ ḥayim*, pt. 2, no. 50.   [10] Ibid., pt. 4, no. 91: 6.

(partition to separate men and women), or it uses a microphone—the members 'are not heretics, Heaven forbid; they treat the laws lightly but they do not deny them', and thus there is no obligation to distance oneself from them.[11]

With respect to non-observant Jews, Feinstein adopted a more conciliatory position, and ruled in direct opposition to Rabbi Israel Meir Hacohen, whose multi-volume halakhic work *Mishnah berurah* is widely viewed as authoritative. Whereas the latter cites precedents and suggests that a sabbath violator cannot be counted as one of the minimum ten adult males necessary for a *minyan*,[12] Feinstein allows them to be counted.[13] In addition, he allows them to be called up to the Torah, unless they are professed atheists.[14] He also allows suspected sabbath desecrators to be appointed president of a synagogue; only those who publicly and brazenly desecrate the sabbath are barred.[15] Likewise, he ruled that a *kohen* (a male descendant of the priestly class) who does not observe the sabbath may be permitted to go up and bless the congregation.[16] In each case, Feinstein was apparently influenced by the social and cultural, including religious, patterns of American Orthodox Jewry. He was willing to accommodate non-observant Jews who did not challenge the authority of Orthodoxy. Only those who challenged the boundaries of Orthodoxy and its authority were deemed to be beyond the pale.

Medical Issues

Rabbi Feinstein wrote responsa on a wide range of questions related to health and medicine, all of which manifest compassion and deep concern for human life and well-being. Several of the responsa are presented here to indicate the impact of both material change, such as advances in technology, and cultural change, which includes norms and values.

Treating Non-Jews on the Sabbath

Rabbi Israel Meir Hacohen, living in eastern Europe in the early twentieth century, ruled that a doctor may not violate the sabbath to treat a non-Jew, and he strongly condemned those who did. He wrote,

[11] Feinstein was unwavering in his absolute rejection of deviance from what he viewed as authentic and basic Jewish belief. That was the reason he declared the Torah commentary of Rabbi Judah Hehasid, which contains a number of radical notions, to be heretical and an obvious forgery. See Marc Shapiro, *Changing the Immutable*, 56–7.

[12] Hacohen, *Mishnah berurah*, vol. i: *Hilkhot berakhot*, 55: 11. Benjamin Brown proposes that, although in his halakhic works Rabbi Hacohen took a very strong stance against sabbath violators and went so far as to equate them with apostates and gentiles, in other works he seemed to take a more benevolent attitude. Perhaps, Brown suggests, there is here a distinction between 'pure halakhah' and 'practical halakhah'. See Brown, 'The Hafets Hayim on the Halakhic Status of the Non-Observant' (Heb.).   [13] *Igerot mosheh, Oraḥ ḥayim*, pt. i, no. 23.

[14] Ibid., pt. 3, no. 12.   [15] Ibid., no. 11.   [16] Ibid., pt. i, no. 33.

And know that the most kosher contemporary doctors are not at all careful . . .
It happens every sabbath that they go several *parsa'ot* [many kilometres] to heal
gentiles, and they write [e.g. notes, medical reports, and prescriptions] and grind
drugs by themselves without any basis on which to rely, because even if we say that
it is permissible to violate the sabbath in a rabbinic prohibition in order not to pro-
voke the animosity of the gentiles, everyone agrees that a Torah prohibition must
definitely be obeyed, and the doctors are utter and wilful sabbath violators, may
Heaven protect us.[17]

In a detailed responsum written in 1979 dealing with how doctors should
behave on the sabbath, Feinstein rejected this position as astounding. In
small towns where the only doctor was Jewish, he argued, if the doctor didn't
treat Gentiles the townspeople would surely kill him and the legal system
there would not punish them. He concludes by citing sources indicating that
there is a basis everywhere, even in advanced countries, to allow Jewish doctors to treat non-Jews on the sabbath, even if a Torah prohibition is thereby
infringed.[18]

Artificial Insemination

One of Rabbi Feinstein's most heatedly debated decisions was also among the
earliest in his published works. Medical science had advanced and created
situations which it would have previously been unthinkable to consider halakhically permitted. In a 1959 decision, not published until a few years later,
Feinstein ruled that a childless woman whose husband's sperm count was
too low for him to be able to impregnate her was permitted to be artificially
inseminated with semen from a non-Jew.[19] Several years after the ruling's
publication, a responsum by Rabbi Joel Teitelbaum rejected Feinstein's responsum in its entirety.[20] Following the publication of Teitelbaum's responsum, a series of other responsa rejecting Feinstein's ruling was published,
primarily in the journal *Hamaor*, whose editor was known for his scathing

[17] Hacohen, *Mishnah berurah*, vol. iii: *Hilkhot shabat*, 330: 8.

[18] *Igerot mosheh*, *Oraḥ ḥayim*, pt. 4, no. 79.

[19] *Igerot mosheh*, *Even ha'ezer*, pt. 1, no. 71; see also ibid., pt. 2, no. 11; pt. 4, no. 32: 5. Many
halakhic issues were involved in this case. For example, if the sperm donor was Jewish: Since the
mother was a married woman who had become pregnant from another man, was that child
halakhically illegitimate (*mamzer*)? Should one fear the possibility that the child may someday
unknowingly marry his or her sibling and violate the prohibition of incest? If the donor was not
Jewish: Was the child a Jew in all halakhic aspects, i.e. may he or she later marry a *kohen*?
Another question was whether a woman may be impregnated during her menstrual cycle. Feinstein states in the responsum that he consulted with his son-in-law, Rabbi Dr Moshe D. Tendler,
a biologist.

[20] Teitelbaum, 'A Responsum on the Prohibition of Artificial Insemination from the Sperm
of a Different Man'.

attacks on those whose actions and/or opinions he rejected, and who was closely allied with Teitelbaum. There are some who suggest that, as a result of the critiques, Feinstein subsequently retracted his initial ruling and con- cluded that artificial insemination was not permitted. Examining his specific phraseology, however, Baruch Finkelstein argues that Feinstein did not in principle revise his opinion but only recommended against artificial insemi- nation as a general practice for the sake of peace in the home lest the husband become jealous.[21] What effect Rabbi Feinstein's basic decision has had on the use of artificial insemination in the American Orthodox community is a sub- ject worthy of study.

Heart Transplants

In 1968 Rabbi Feinstein wrote a responsum in which he categorically prohib- ited heart transplants. He unequivocally considered them a double murder: first, of the donor, because 'they murder with their own hands the person from whom they take the heart, because he is still alive not only according to the Torah laws which provide us with the calculation of death but even some of the doctors themselves who tell the truth that he is still alive', and second, of the recipient, because some people live a long time with their own weak heart and the doctors remove that and replace it, though all such recipients live only a short while after the transplant.[22] Two years later, he wrote a respon- sum reiterating his decision and emphasized that the doctors involved cannot be trusted, either with respect to the alleged death of the donor or with respect to the recipient, 'because we have seen that they are not experts in this and erred in their actions and some premeditatedly misled, because all those who received transplants died within a short time while with their originals hearts they clearly may have lived a lot longer than with the transplanted hearts. Therefore all the doctors involved are unequivocally murderers.'[23]

Setting aside Feinstein's mistrust of some doctors, with medical advances which greatly increased the survival rate of heart recipients the crucial halakhic issue became that of establishing the death of the donor. In a 1976 responsum to his son-in-law Rabbi Tendler, whom he usually consulted about medical matters, concerning establishing time of death—the responsum does not directly address transplants—Feinstein stated that death occurs with the ces- sation of respiration. Since there are situations in which a person who has stopped breathing and has been placed on a respirator is later able to start breathing again on their own, if there is someone on a respirator who in all other visible ways does not appear to be alive, one must wait until the oxygen in the

---

[21] Finkelstein, 'Characteristics and Patterns in Rabbi Moshe Feinstein's Rulings' (Heb.).
[22] *Igerot mosheh*, *Yoreh de'ah*, pt. 2, no. 174.   [23] Ibid., no. 146.

respirator is depleted before determining if the patient is breathing. Only then can the patient be deemed dead. He then relates that his son-in-law has informed him of a new method of determining death: a radioactive liquid is injected into the patient's vein, and this can show whether the connection between the brain and the body is severed and that the patient is therefore brain dead. Feinstein suggested, therefore, that in cases of sudden death, for example by car accident or by falling from a window, where the victim's breathing has stopped but perhaps only temporarily, one should be particularly stringent and use the new method as well.[24] This latter decision became the subject of a debate on whether brain death can be considered halakhically definitive.

In his own discussion of medical issues, Rabbi Ahron Soloveichik makes reference only to Feinstein's responsa that deal specifically with heart transplants. He asserts that 'all *rishonim* and *aharonim* [the early and later Talmud scholars and decisors] say that as long as a person has cardiac activity he is not considered dead'. However, he continues, 'it would be repugnant to the halakhah to impose one's halakhah-true opinion upon someone who follows a contrary view'.[25] Some, including Rabbi Tendler himself, argue that, once Rabbi Feinstein learned that it was possible to determine the absence of circulation and the complete separation of the brain from the body, he ruled the condition to be similar to decapitation. Accordingly, they aver, in the end Feinstein held that brain death is halakhic death and, under those circumstances, heart transplants are permissible.[26] On the other hand, J. David Bleich and others argue that Feinstein did not change his mind but merely introduced an additional requirement in the event of sudden death. Bleich forcefully argues that Feinstein's last responsum on the matter 'clearly adheres to the position enunciated in his earliest responsa regarding this subject'.[27] There is now a growing body of literature on the halakhic questions surrounding time of death and brain death,[28] which is not surprising since those issues are also subject to a variety of opinions in the fields of bioethics.[29]

[24] Ibid., pt. 3, no. 132.
[25] Soloveichik, 'Death According to the Halacha', 44. For a suggested new approach to transplants which would satisfy Soloveichik's objections, see Lopatin, 'Non-Heart-Beating Donation from Brain Dead Patients'.
[26] See e.g. Rosner and Tendler, 'Definition of Death in Judaism'; Tendler and Rosner, 'Communications: Brain Death'.
[27] Bleich, 'Of Cerebral, Respiratory and Cardiac Death'; id., *Time of Death in Jewish Law*.
[28] See e.g. the paper by the Halakha Committee of the Rabbinical Council of America, 'Halachic Issues in the Determination of Death', and Z. Farber (ed.), *Halakhic Realities*.
[29] Düwell, *Bioethics*, 213–17; A. L. Kaplan and Arp (eds.), *Contemporary Debates in Bioethics*, 369–400. On medical practice, see Sanghavi, 'The Last Decision'; S. Kaplan, 'When Are You Dead? It May Depend on Which Hospital Makes the Call'.

Whether a *Kohen* Can Go to Medical School

In 1974 Rabbi Feinstein was asked whether it was permissible for a *kohen* to attend medical school.[30] On the one hand, a *kohen* is forbidden to come into contact with a dead body (Lev. 21: 1), and a medical student is required to perform autopsies. On the other hand, the saving of human life is considered the most important religious obligation and takes precedence over almost every prohibition. Feinstein vehemently rejected the suggestion that this obligation plays any role in the issue because, although one who is a doctor has a duty to save lives, there is no duty for every individual to study medicine and become a doctor. There are many doctors in the world, he said, and there is no obligation for a *kohen* to drive himself to become a doctor. Therefore, he concluded, it is definitely forbidden for a *kohen* to go to medical school.

Until the late twentieth century it was indeed rare for an Orthodox *kohen* to go to medical school but, although there are no hard data, informal observation suggests that it has recently become much more common. One keen observer who is a member of Young Israel in New York said: 'Fifty years ago married women didn't cover their hair and *kohanim* knew they couldn't become doctors. Now the women are all covered and in my *shul* it seems that most of those called up for the *kohen aliyah* are doctors!'[31]

In this case, the change may be related to the close ties between the American Modern Orthodox community and Israel. In contrast to Feinstein, Rabbi Shlomo Goren, who was Israel's Ashkenazi chief rabbi from 1972 to 1983, offered a much more lenient decision. An official at Yeshiva University, Larry Wachsman, wrote to Goren in 1981 to ask whether students who are *kohanim* can study in medical school since they are required to study anatomy and perform autopsies. Apparently there were young *kohanim* at Yeshiva University who wanted to go to medical school and were unhappy with Feinstein's unequivocal decision less than a decade earlier. Goren wrote an extensive decision in which he found a method, under extenuating circumstances, to permit a *kohen* to study medicine.[32] However, it would seem that the limitations that Goren outlined were either overlooked or forgotten, and the drive to study medicine was so strong that it has become almost commonplace in the American Orthodox community for there to be a fair representation of *kohanim* among those who are medical doctors.

---

[30] *Igerot mosheh, Yoreh de'ah*, pt. 3, no. 155.

[31] Lawrence Grossman, personal communication, 3 Feb. 2015. *Kohen aliyah* refers to the practice of honouring a *kohen* in the synagogue by calling him up to read the first section of the weekly Torah reading.   [32] Goren, *Medical Torah* (Heb.).

'Change in Nature'

Rabbi Feinstein's condemnation of doctors who engage in heart transplants was not reflective of his general attitude towards physicians and the medical sciences. On the contrary, his responsa indicate his high regard for both, and he frequently consulted medical professionals on related halakhic matters. On a number of occasions he also invoked the concept of 'change in nature' as a way to deal more leniently with certain issues which had previously been ruled on more stringently.[33] For example, according to the Talmud and the *Shulḥan arukh*, a woman must refrain from sexual relations in the first three months of pregnancy at the times of what would have been her regular menstrual cycle, on the slight chance that she might menstruate. However, he asserted that 'nature had changed' and that women now cease menstruating as soon as they become pregnant; therefore, if a woman knows, instinctively or by having a medical examination, that she is pregnant, she does not have to refrain from marital relations.[34] He also invoked 'change in nature' in another case which entailed some of the same issues. Although the Talmud states that all women who convert to Judaism must wait three months before their conversion is approved so that the rabbinic court can certify that they were not pregnant when they actually converted, he ruled leniently for menstruating women when waiting the three months would have been burdensome. Part of his rationale was that we now know that menstruating women are definitely not pregnant.[35]

In 1962 he issued another decision in which he applied the notion of 'change in nature'. Jewish tradition abhors castration, vasectomy, and any other maiming of the male organs which renders a man unable to impregnate. The origin of the taboo is biblical: 'He that is crushed or maimed in his privy parts shall not enter into the assembly of the Lord' (Deut. 23: 2). Feinstein was asked whether a childless husband is permitted to undergo a biopsy on his testicles in the hope of finding a cure for his infertility, because there is a risk that the procedure may damage a testicle. After pointing out that this biopsy is to help overcome the patient's infertility, he proceeded to a lengthy analysis of all of the relevant talmudic and later sources, and indicated that, although the Talmud states that a man with a damaged testicle cannot have children, we know today that he can and this must be because of a 'change in nature'. He therefore allowed the biopsy.[36]

[33] The concept has a long history, going back to the Tosafists and others. For an in-depth analysis of the concept and the conditions under which it may be applied, see Gutel, *Natural Changes in Halakhah* (Heb.). See also Malakh, 'Changes in Nature' (Heb.).

[34] *Igerot mosheh*, Yoreh de'ah, pt. 3, no. 52.

[35] *Igerot mosheh*, Even ha'ezer, pt. 2, no. 4. See also *Igerot mosheh*, Yoreh de'ah, pt. 4, no. 4.

[36] *Igerot mosheh*, Even ha'ezer, pt. 2, no. 3.

In 1970, Feinstein was asked about several cases which entailed an obstetrician delivering a baby prematurely and the possible halakhic consequences. In a lengthy responsum, he made reference to a statement in the Talmud (BT *Yev.* 42a) that a woman who bears a child at nine months does not give birth until the all nine months are completed, and again referred to the 'change in nature', because we know that infants born at eight months do survive.[37] He also indicated a possible change in nature from the time of Maimonides, who expresses his strong scepticism about the possibility of a woman surviving a caesarean delivery.[38] He said that nature must have changed because this was now a very common phenomenon.

In the light of Feinstein's adoption of 'change in nature' on several occasions as a basis for ruling leniently, it is interesting that he cautioned against publicizing it. In 1981 he wrote a responsum to Rabbi Shimon Eider, who was writing a book in English on the laws pertaining to menstruation. In the responsum Feinstein amended his previous lenient ruling and told Eider to provide a stringent ruling in his book, namely, that during the first three months of pregnancy a woman must separate from her husband during what would have been her usual time of menstruation. The editor of the relevant volume of Feinstein's responsa reports that Feinstein had orally conveyed that the reason for his stringency in this instance was that Eider's book was being written for the newly Orthodox (*ba'alei teshuvah*), who were unfamiliar with the Talmud and the methods of halakhic decision-making, and the adoption of 'change in nature' as a basis for leniency would not be comprehensible to them; therefore they should be provided with a more stringent decision.[39] That rationale was provided before the digital revolution. However, the world, including the world of halakhah, has been revolutionized by the 'web of knowledge', and this rationale now seems completely untenable in a society in which everything is public and anyone who wishes has access to it.

Other Halakhic Issues

The *Eruv*

The phenomenon of the *eruv*, the symbolic enclosure of a neighbourhood or community to allow Jews to carry on the sabbath within its perimeters, is

---

[37] *Igerot mosheh, Yoreh de'ah*, pt. 2.

[38] Maimonides, *Commentary on the Mishnah, Bekh.* 8: 2.

[39] *Igerot mosheh, Yoreh de'ah*, pt. 4, no. 17. Feinstein applied the notion of 'change in nature' to physical changes in other areas as well. For example, in response to a question concerning one who slaughtered an animal while sitting, which some medieval and later rabbis prohibit lest the slaughterer crush the animal, Feinstein pointed to the Talmud, where sitting while slaughtering is not prohibited, and he suggested that there had been a change in the physical senses since talmudic times (ibid., pt. 1, no. 2).

another example of the impact of social change on traditional Jewish religious practice and halakhah. Many who are familiar with Orthodox Jewish life in America today might be surprised to learn that, until 1970, there were only two cities in the whole country that had an *eruv*, and both were highly controversial. The first, established in 1894, was in St Louis; the second (1905) was in New York, on Manhattan's East Side, but it was dismissed as unacceptable by many, who did not make use of it. In the 1940s the idea of erecting an *eruv* around the entire island of Manhattan stirred up years of controversy, from 1949 to 1962.[40] However, by 2011 there were more than 150 *eruvin* in communities across the USA. A variety of sociological factors, perhaps most significant among them being the social and geographical mobility of the Orthodox, many of whom moved to the suburbs in the 1970s and 1980s, contributed to the increased halakhic acceptability of *eruvin*.

Electric Timers

When electric timers were first introduced, there was resistance in the Orthodox community based on concerns about the permissibility of using them to control household appliances remotely on the sabbath. In the 1970s Rabbi Feinstein wrote two responsa in which he emphatically prohibited the use of timers, saying that they desecrated the sanctity of the sabbath by contravening the ban on igniting fire on that day. He did, however, reluctantly permit their use for setting lights to go on and off on the sabbath because there was precedent for this in synagogues and it contributed to the enjoyment, and thus the sanctity, of the sabbath. For all other appliances, however, he categorically prohibited them.[41] Today, however, it appears that such timers ('shabbos clocks') are widely used within the Orthodox community for a variety of purposes, such as home heating, air conditioning, and warming food, as well as other uses which it strains the intellect to consider as falling in the category of actions that contribute to the sanctity of the sabbath.[42]

Ḥalav Yisra'el

According to halakhah, milk must be produced under the supervision of an observant Jewish adult to ensure that it is indeed cow's milk, and not the milk of a non-kosher animal. Such supervised milk is known as *ḥalav yisra'el*. In a number of responsa written in 1954, Rabbi Feinstein ruled that, in the United States, milk that is under government supervision is surely cow's milk, because any accredited dairy would be severely penalized for violating

---

[40] For a social history and analysis of *eruvin* in the United States, see A. Mintz, 'Halakhah in America'. On the halakhic controversy concerning an *eruv* in Brooklyn, see id., 'A Chapter in American Orthodoxy'.   [41] *Igerot mosheh, Oraḥ ḥayim*, pt. 4, no. 60.
[42] See Chapter 5 n. 82 above on the 'shabbat app' and 'Kosher Switch'.

the law. Therefore, all milk sold under the label of a reputable company could be considered kosher.[43] In 1970 he reiterated this lenient ruling. However, he also added that it is proper for one who is punctiliously observant to be strict and use only *ḥalav yisra'el*. Principals in yeshiva day schools, he asserted, should certainly provide only *ḥalav yisra'el* to their students, even if it cost more, because the students would learn that observant Jews should be stringent even if an action entails only a slight chance of involving something prohibited.[44] This is an example of Feinstein bowing to social pressure for greater stringency despite having a more lenient position himself: in this case, there were already a number of dairies selling *ḥalav yisra'el* and a growing number of consumers requesting it.

It is commonly assumed that the influence of American society and culture is towards greater leniency in religious practice. Indeed, this is often the case; however, the impact of the American experience cuts both ways, as can be seen from the example of *ḥalav yisra'el*. Another interesting example is found in one of the posthumously published volumes of Feinstein's responsa. When asked if prayer in a place not designated as a synagogue requires a *meḥitsah* between men and women, he responded that 'in all the generations it was typical that occasionally a poor woman entered the study hall to receive charity, or a woman mourner to say Kaddish, and the actual halakhah in this matter needs consideration and depends on many factors'.[45] In most American Orthodox study halls, let alone synagogues, not only would a woman not be permitted to enter into the men's section, in many she would also be discouraged, if not prohibited, from saying Kaddish.[46]

*

The phenomenon of the 'haredization' of American Orthodox Judaism was discussed in Chapter 4 above. What is now called for is an analysis identifying and explaining the criteria under which stringency emerges and those under which there are moves to leniency. Tentatively, it might be suggested that, as the result of a real or perceived breakdown in social norms, many Orthodox Jews sense a need for increased stringency in those areas in which boundary maintenance is viewed as critical. This includes boundaries between males and females, Jews and non-Jews, 'Torah-committed' Jews and those who are not.

[43] *Igerot mosheh, Yoreh de'ah*, pt. 1, nos. 47–9.
[44] Ibid., pt. 2, no. 35.   [45] *Igerot mosheh, Oraḥ ḥayim*, pt. 5, no. 12: 2.
[46] In Modern Orthodox synagogues it is now increasingly acceptable for women to recite the Mourner's Kaddish, but this is still frowned on in most American ultra-Orthodox synagogues.

Halakhah and Meta-Halakhah

In the introduction to the second edition of his book *A Tree of Life*, Louis Jacobs reiterated his argument regarding human involvement in halakhah. He contrasted two 'exemplars of opposite approaches to the halakhic process—respectively, the dynamic and subjective versus the static and objective'.[47] The latter he portrayed as the Orthodox approach and the former as that of Conservative Judaism. In point of fact, there is variety in Orthodox approaches with respect to the relationship between the decisor and his halakhic decision.

Jacobs cites David Bleich as the exemplar of 'the static and objective' approach, and indeed, Bleich has portrayed halakhah as a science, in which 'there is no room for subjectivity'.[48] More recently, he has elaborated and clarified his position:

halakhic decision-making is indeed an art as well as a science. Its kunst lies precisely in the ability to make judgment calls in evaluating citations, precedents, arguments etc. It is not sufficient for a halakhic decisor to have a full command of relevant sources. If so, in theory at least, the decisor par excellence would be a computer rather than a person. The decisor must have a keen understanding of the underlying principles and postulates of Halakhah as well as of their applicable ramifications and must be capable of applying them with fidelity to matters placed before him. No amount of book learning can compensate for inadequacy in what may be termed the 'artistic' component. The epithet 'a donkey carrying books' is the derisive reference employed in rabbinic literature to describe such a person.[49]

Rabbi Joseph B. Soloveitchik presented his conception somewhat differently:

the mutual connection between law and event does not take place within the realm of pure halakhic thought, but rather within the depths of the halakhic man's soul. The event is a psychological impetus, prodding pure thought into its track. However, once pure thought begins to move in its specific track, it performs its movement not in surrender to the event, but rather in obedience to the normative-ideal lawfulness particular to it . . . To what is this comparable? To a satellite that was launched into a particular orbit. Although the launching of the satellite into orbit is dependent on the force of the thrust, once the object arrive[s] at its particular orbit, it begins to move with amazing precision according to the speed unique to that orbit, and the force of the thrust cannot increase or decrease it at all.[50]

---

[47] Jacobs, *A Tree of Life*, p. xvii.
[48] Bleich, *Contemporary Halakhic Problems*, p. xiii.   [49] Bleich, '"Lomdut" and "Pesak"', 88.
[50] Soloveitchik, *Matters of Contemplation and Appreciation* (Heb.), 77–8. For a very different approach which rejects the notion of a method or path in halakhic decisions, see the method of Rabbi Moses Sofer as presented by Maoz Kahana in his article 'The Hatam Sofer' (Heb.). Kahana claims that, according to Sofer, the decisor does not arrive at truth through any method or formula; rather, truth announces itself, as a light or a bolt of lightning.

Soloveitchik's approach is reminiscent of Max Weber's thinking with respect to the place of values and emotions in sociological research; that is, that the sociologist's values clearly influence the areas and topics he or she selects to study. However, once the work actually begins, the rules of scientific research dominate, and all evaluations are made solely on the basis of empirical evidence. The researchers must be value-free and ignore their personal thoughts and prejudices.[51] Of course, as anyone who has engaged in social research knows, neutrality of values and emotions is very difficult, if not impossible, to achieve. Humans are influenced in many ways of which they are frequently unaware. Along these lines, Aharon Lichtenstein points to the distinction his father-in-law, Rabbi Joseph B. Soloveitchik, drew between psychosocial elements and pure thought in the halakhic process, and declares, 'It is a nice distinction, and I confess that I am not certain it can be readily sustained in practice.'[52]

Haym Soloveitchik suggests other influences on halakhah in his analysis of the issue of suicide and the killing of one's children in the face of forced apostasy in the Ashkenazi community during the period of the Crusades. He suggests that, although until that time, 'one knows of no allowance for committing suicide to avoid forced conversion', the scholars of the Ashkenazi communities

evolved, in the course of time, a doctrine of the permissibility of voluntary martyrdom, and even one allowing suicide. They did this by scouring all the canonized and semi-canonized literature for supportive tales and hortatory aggadah, all of dubious legal worth. But by massing them together, Ashkenazic scholars produced, with

[51] Weber, *The Methodology of the Social Sciences*, 49–112. Joshua Berman has suggested that perhaps the parallel between the halakhic decisor and the social scientist 'is not accidental; that something about the climate of German thought at the beginning of the century is what lies behind each one's [i.e. Soloveitchik's and Weber's] statement; the endeavor of converting the humanities into science; the ideal of the mechanical and the efficient' (personal communication, 15 Dec. 2013).

[52] Lichtenstein, *Leaves of Faith*, i. 173. Interestingly, Soloveitchik himself was apparently aware of this. In a letter to the president of Yeshiva University in 1951 he wrote, 'The halakhic inquiry, like any other cognitive theoretical performance, does not start out from the point of absolute zero as to sentimental attitudes and value judgments. There always exists in the mind of the researcher an ethico-axiological background against which the contours of the subject matter in question stand out more clearly. In all fields of human intellectual endeavor there is always an intuitive approach which determines the course and method of the analysis. Not even in exact sciences (particularly in their interpretive phase) is it possible to divorce the human element from the formal aspect. Hence this investigation was also undertaken in a similar subjective mood. From the very outset I was prejudiced in favor of the project of the Rabbinical Council of America and I could not imagine any halakhic authority rendering a decision against it. My inquiry consisted only in translating a vague intuitive feeling into fixed terms of halakhic discursive thinking' (Helfgot, *Community, Covenant, and Commitment*, 24–5).

a few deft twists, a tenable, if not quite persuasive, case for the permissibility of suicide in times of religious persecution. For murder of one's children few could find a defense, and almost all passed that over in audible silence.[53]

The innovations of the Ashkenazi scholars were not undertaken to conform with the demands of an increasingly secularized community. On the contrary, 'the Franco-German community was permeated by a profound sense of its own religiosity, of the rightness of its traditions, and could not imagine any sharp difference between its practices and the law that its members studied and observed with such devotion'.[54] Soloveitchik avers that, until the era of the Crusades, there was no known halakhic permission (*heter*) to commit suicide in the face of forced conversion to Christianity; indeed, he says, 'The magnitude of this halakhic breach is enormous.' However, the notion that such suicide is actually murder became untenable and events made it essential for the sages of Ashkenaz to search the entire body of traditional Jewish writing, including varieties of aggadah, to find some way of justifying suicide during eras of religious persecution.[55] Soloveitchik does not claim that the sages of Ashkenaz completely redefined the halakhah; he argues, rather, that the experiences, trials, and tribulations of the Jewish people guided them and influenced their rulings in ways that legitimated existing practices.[56] He does not indicate whether this aligns with what his father, Rabbi Joseph B. Soloveitchik, meant by 'the launching of the satellite into orbit', or, rather, with the situation 'once the object arrives at its particular orbit', but it does appear that Haym Soloveitchik attributes greater halakhic legitimacy to the roles of experience and perspective than did his father. He was a student of Jacob Katz, who emphasized the impact of the economy on halakhah,[57] and Soloveitchik's works on usury and wine are examples of that approach.[58]

There are few today in the fields of philosophy and the social sciences who think that it is possible to make decisions that are value-free. Israel Lipkin of Salant, known as Israel Salanter, who initially headed a yeshiva and subsequently became the father of the Musar movement,[59] agreed. As he explained,

---

[53] H. Soloveitchik, *Collected Essays*, i. 244.   [54] Ibid. 246.

[55] Ibid. 243–4. Soloveitchik subsequently states that such instances are the exception and limited to very specific circumstances (ibid. 258–77).

[56] Avraham Grossman, on the other hand, argues that the sages of Ashkenaz relied on midrashic *agadot* in their halakhic considerations, and that they found *agadot* which not only justified but required suicide in similar situations. See Grossman, 'The Origins of Martyrdom in Early Ashkenaz' (Heb.).   [57] See e.g. Katz, *The 'Shabbes Goy'*.

[58] See his *Halakhah, Economy, and Self-Perception* (Heb.); *Principles and Pressures* (Heb.); and *Wine in Ashkenaz in the Middle Ages* (Heb.).

[59] The Musar movement was a nineteenth-century movement among Lithuanian yeshivas that strove for ethical and spiritual self-discipline. See Brown, *The Lithuanian Musar Movement* (Heb.); Etkes, *Rabbi Israel Salanter and the Mussar Movement*; Y. Mirsky, 'Musar Movement'.

Man, inasmuch as he is man, even though it is within his capacity and power to strip (*lehafshit*) his intellect from the arousal of his soul-forces until these soul-forces are quiescent and resting (unaroused, so that they do not breach the intellectual faculty and pervert it), nonetheless man is human, his soul-forces are in him, it is not within his power to separate them (*lehafrisham*) from his intellect. Thus it is not within man's capacity to arrive at True Intellect (*sekhel amiti*) wholly separated (*hamufrash*) and disembodied (*hamuvdal*) from soul-forces, and the Torah is given to man to be adjudicated according to human intellect (it being purified as much as possible; see [BT] *Bekhorot* 17b: 'Divine Law said: Do it, and in whatever way you are able to do it, it will be satisfactory').[60]

Indeed, it appears that the sages of the Talmud recognized the human inability to separate subjective forces from adjudication and, therefore, the sages of the mishnaic era declared that certain people should not be appointed as judges to the Sanhedrin, the supreme court: 'We do not appoint to the Sanhedrin an old man, a eunuch, or one who is childless.'[61] Maimonides suggested the reasoning involved: 'We should not appoint to any Sanhedrin a very old man or a eunuch, for they possess the trait of cruelty, nor one who is childless, so that the judge should be merciful.'[62]

Differences between American and British Orthodoxy

In 1961 Chief Rabbi Israel Brodie caused a storm in British Jewry when he vetoed the appointment of Louis Jacobs as principal of Jews' College in London and then, in 1963, refused to authorize his reappointment as minister (rabbi) of London's New West End Synagogue.[63] Brodie claimed that, although Jacobs had earlier expressed unorthodox ideas, he had allowed his appointment as tutor at Jews' College as 'an act of faith'.[64] Brodie's 'faith' in Jacobs was probably based, in part, on the fact that, as a young man Jacobs had studied at the Gateshead yeshiva, where he developed a warm relationship with its head, Rabbi Eliyahu Dessler.[65] Although Jacobs did not agree with all of Dessler's ultra-Orthodoxy, he spoke fondly of him throughout his life.[66] Nevertheless,

[60] Hillel Goldberg, *Israel Salanter*, 119.
[61] BT *San.* 36b.   [62] *Mishneh torah*, 'Hilkhot Sanhedrin', 2: 3.
[63] There are various and varied accounts of what came to be known as 'the Jacobs affair', and reference will be made to some of them in the analysis that follows.
[64] Brodie, *The Strength of My Heart*, 348.
[65] Dessler wrote of him, 'I would not be exaggerating in the slightest if I were to say that I have never seen a genius with such depth and all the other aptitudes that he possesses; he is a truly great scholar and it is almost impossible to fathom the depth of his knowledge' (Dessler, 'Letters' (Heb.), 311). I thank my son-in-law, Noam Green, who completed a doctorate on Dessler's thought, for bringing this reference to my attention. For a hagiographic biography of Dessler, see Rosenblum, *Rav Dessler*.   [66] Jacobs, *Helping with Inquiries*, 40–59.

Brodie asserted, his own subsequent rejection of Jacobs was caused by the latter's increasingly public expression of ideas that were 'incompatible . . . with the most fundamental principles of Judaism'.[67]

It would be surprising, to say the least, if Jacobs's writings were the sole reason for this rejection. More than a decade later, the philosopher Menachem Kellner analysed several of Jacobs's works for the journal of the Orthodox Rabbinical Council of America and found them to be stimulating and valuable, even if problematic.[68] It seems difficult to imagine that American Orthodoxy, even Modern Orthodoxy, was that much more tolerant of unconventional ideas than Britain's United Synagogue. Very possibly, inter-Orthodox politics and a 'haredization' of British Orthodoxy played a major role. According to Miri Freud-Kandel, the immigration of east European Jews resulted in dramatic changes in British Judaism. As in the case of the immigration to the United States discussed above, the Judaism of the newcomers was very different to what was the British norm at the time. The east European rabbis were different, and so were their synagogues. The rabbis entered the British rabbinic establishment via the Beth Din, which until then had been subservient to the chief rabbi, but as the rabbis' power increased, they challenged even him. Brodie, according to Freud-Kandel, was weaker than his predecessors and was not able to stand up to this shift to the right and maintain Anglo-Jewry's moderate Orthodoxy. He thus rejected Jacobs.[69]

Jacobs eventually left the United Synagogue framework as well as Jews' College, and founded the New London Synagogue and later Britain's Masorti (Conservative) movement, with the New London as its flagship. He remained an observant Jew throughout his life, and frequently stressed that his radical ideas concerning revelation and halakhic development should have no impact on halakhic observance. As he put it, 'the Jewish rituals are still mitzvot and serve the same purpose as prayer. They link our individual strivings to the strivings of the Jewish people towards the fullest realization of the Jewish spirit.'[70] However, he admitted that once the *mitsvot* are defined as human products, the probability of their being observed is substantially decreased. As he himself wrote, 'Psychologically, it is undeniable that a clear recognition of the human development of Jewish practice and observance is bound to produce a somewhat weaker sense of allegiance to the minutiae of Jewish law.'[71] Empirical studies of Jewish ritual observance in the USA indicate that it is not only allegiance to 'the minutiae of Jewish law' that is severely weakened when

[67]   Brodie, *The Strength of My Heart*, 349–50.
[68]   Kellner, 'Louis Jacobs' Doctrine of Revelation'.
[69]   Freud-Kandel, *Orthodox Judaism in Britain since 1913*.
[70]   Jacobs, *God, Torah, Israel*, 6.   [71]   Jacobs, *Beyond Reasonable Doubt*, 53.

they do not have religious legitimation of being divinely ordained. Sociological theory likewise recognizes the power of religious legitimation.[72] It should therefore have been no surprise that the chief rabbi would not allow someone who might undermine religious allegiance to serve as rabbi in an institution under the auspices of the Orthodox rabbinate.

That said, and in the light of my discussion of American Orthodoxy, one factor that may have sparked a strong reaction to Jacobs's work was the terminology he used. Although he repeatedly indicated that he used the term objectively, his constant reference to the more traditional Orthodox approach as 'fundamentalism', and to those who disagreed with his conception of the halakhic process as 'fundamentalists', was taken as offensive. Indeed, Brodie expressed his indignation at the use of the term when he wrote, 'we who hold to the validity of the Torah are called backward, stagnant, mediaeval and fundamentalist'.[73] Jacobs's intentions aside, the term 'fundamentalist' is now widely viewed as derogatory. Mark Juergensmeyer indicates several reasons for its contemporary inappropriateness, among them that 'the term is pejorative. It refers, as one Muslim scholar observed, to those who hold "an intolerant, self-righteous, and narrowly dogmatic religious literalism." . . . The term is less descriptive than it is accusatory: it reflects our attitude toward other people more than it describes them.'[74] In addition to the specific terminology he used, Jacobs presented perspectives in a black/white, true/false manner. In some of his work he appears to argue that there is only scientific truth or 'fundamentalist' falseness, and that the possibility of multiple truths does not exist. This exclusivist conception of truth, coupled with his loaded terminology, may well have triggered the strong reaction.[75]

Jacobs rejected the notion that it is 'only the application of the halakhah which changes under changing conditions', and that 'halakhah itself is never determined or even influenced by environmental or sociological factors'.[76] It is a notion presented by some Orthodox when confronted with the reality of change.[77] What that notion ignores or hides is the vast diversity within

---

[72] P. L. Berger, *The Sacred Canopy*, 33. [73] Brodie, *The Strength of My Heart*, 344.

[74] Juergensmeyer, *The New Cold War?*; id., *Global Rebellion*, 4. Michael Harris similarly found Jacobs's use of the term 'fundamentalism' demeaning, despite Jacobs's claim that this was not his intention. See Harris, *Faith Without Fear*, 91–3.

[75] Terminology and demeanour may also play a significant role within halakhic development. Aviad Hollander argues, in 'The Relationship Between Halakhic Decisors and Their Peers', that demeanour can be an important variable in the probability of a halakhic decision being accepted within the Orthodox rabbinic community. [76] Jacobs, *A Tree of Life*, p. xi.

[77] Jacobs specifically referred to my claim, in 'Toward a Sociology of *Pesak*', 223–4, that many earlier halakhic authorities would have asserted that notion. A more recent version of the notion is presented by Broyde and Wagner in 'Halachic Responses to Sociological and Technological Change', where they argue that, while results provided by halakhah can vary in response to

halakhah. There are varieties of circumstances, varieties of halakhic principles, varieties of halakhic precedents, and varieties of earlier authoritative decisors with which the contemporary decisor can and must reckon. The decision of what ruling to adopt in the contemporary situation is influenced not only by the decisor's knowledge but by his own values. Had Jacobs framed his argument in a manner which remained true to the notion of halakhic development without explicitly rejecting the heavenly authority of halakhah, as did those in the United States who advocated change but remained securely within the Orthodox orbit, perhaps his own career and the subsequent history of the British rabbinate would have been very different. On the other hand, given the growing tide of 'haredization', he might still have been rejected. The haredi sector of Orthodoxy is growing faster than any other sector of British Jewry;[78] its leaders are as self-confident as ever and see no reason to budge from their traditional approach.

With respect to growth patterns, there is a confluence between American and British Jewries. In the United States as well, the Orthodox are increasing faster than the non-Orthodox, and the ultra-Orthodox are increasing faster than the Modern Orthodox. A major difference between the two Jewries, of course, is their absolute size. American Jewry is estimated to number about 5.5 million, whereas British Jewry numbers under 300,000.[79] With regard to Jacobs, perhaps a more significant difference is in the fact that American Jewry has no official structure, and no organizational body has the power to exclude others. American Orthodoxy is perhaps the most pluralistic of American Jewish denominations, in that it comprises numerous seminaries, rabbinic organizations, and synagogue organizations, as well as synagogues that are independent and belong to no national organization. The Rabbinical Council of America is the best-known Orthodox rabbinic organization, but its authority has undergone significant change. In the past, it was more heterogeneous ideologically and no bloc had the power to exclude those with whom it disagreed. Today it is much more homogeneous, but its national stature and authority appear to have declined. Alternatives exist, and not being accepted into the Rabbinical Council of America no longer has the serious consequences it previously had. In the UK, by contrast, the chief rabbi and the United Synagogue are formal bodies with politically recognized authority. Whereas in the United States Jacobs would have been able to remain an Orthodox rabbi of a synagogue which did not take orders from any formal organization, that option was and continues

changed social and/or technological conditions, there can never be any variation in the fundamental principles on which the halakhah is based.

[78] See Graham, 'Enumerating Britain's Jewish Population'; and Boyd, *Strictly Orthodox Rising*.
[79] DellaPergola, 'World Jewish Population 2015'.

to be largely unavailable in the UK.[80] The advantages and disadvantages of politically recognized Jewish religious structures are widely debated in Israel, and some of the issues raised there might be applicable to some extent in the United Kingdom as well. American Jewry, including American Orthodoxy, has no politically mandated authority, and perhaps that helped American Orthodoxy develop as it has.

[80]   The ultra-Orthodox in the UK have their own synagogue structure.

SEVEN

REVIVAL OF THE BIBLE

UNTIL NOW we have been dealing with evolution in halakhah, and the focus has been on changing religious behaviour. This chapter focuses on changes within American Orthodoxy concerning interpretations of Orthodox Jewish beliefs. About fifty years ago, American Orthodoxy was united in its allegiance to the credo of *torah min hashamayim*, that both the Written Law and the Oral Law were given by God to Moses at Sinai. Although, with respect to the Oral Law, there may have been different interpretations of precisely what this meant, no one in Orthodoxy publicly demurred from a literal understanding of it with respect to the Written Law. Some, such as Joseph B. Soloveitchik and Moshe Tendler, went so far as to axiomatically assert a literal version of both parts of the credo, while others simply expressed a general allegiance to the credo itself without discussing the detailed implications. American Orthodoxy did not engage in academic biblical analysis, and certainly not biblical criticism. As Charles Liebman indicated, the belief that the Torah was 'given by God to Moses at Sinai requires no elaboration. It has always been an article of faith for the Orthodox Jew, and the meaning of the words and their historical referent seem simple enough. Biblical criticism has not challenged this belief; in fact, biblical criticism only becomes meaningful if this article of faith is denied.'[1]

The absence of any publicly voiced alternative to the literal interpretation of the credo is almost certainly rooted in explicit talmudic assertions which were reiterated by Maimonides. For example, the Mishnah lists among those who have no share in the World to Come those 'who say the Law is not from Heaven'.[2] Further elaboration in the Talmud asserts that,

even if he says that the whole Torah is from Heaven except for a particular verse which was not given by God but by Moses himself, he is included in [those not having a portion in the World to Come] because he scorned the word of God. And even if he says that the whole Torah is from Heaven except for a single extrapolation or

---

[1] Liebman, 'Orthodoxy in American Jewish Life', 46 n. 40. See also L. Grossman, 'In What Sense Did Orthodoxy Believe the Torah To Be Divine?' [2] Mishnah *San.* 10: 1.

deduction, he is included among those not having a portion in the World to Come because he scorned the word of God.[3]

Maimonides laid down the fundamental credo that the Torah is from God: 'we must believe that the entire Torah found in our hands is the same Torah given Moses in its entirety by God . . . Anyone who says that Moses wrote some passages on his own is deemed by our sages to be an atheist and the worst kind of heretic.'[4] Likewise, in the eighth of his famous Thirteen Principles Maimon-ides reiterated the obligation to believe that the Torah that is in our hands was given by Moses and that it was received by him in its entirety, word for word and letter for letter, from God.

There are, however, several problems with these and, indeed, most of the Principles of Faith. As Menachem Kellner and Marc Shapiro[5] have shown, they were not unanimously agreed upon and have only relatively recently come to be viewed as both 'necessary' and 'correct' beliefs.[6] Moreover, as Shapiro points out, they cannot be taken literally because we know there are differences between Ashkenazi and Sephardi Torah texts, which in turn differ from Yemenite Torah texts. 'This means that if contemporary Ashkenazim and Sephardim accept Maimonides' Eighth Principle with regard to *their* versions of the Pentateuch, they stand condemned as heretics by Maimonides himself for refusing to accept *his* version as the proper one.'[7] Nevertheless, Maimonides' Thirteen Principles have become the fundamentals of faith in the Orthodox world. Until the second half of the twentieth century, unanimity on the credo of *torah min hashamayim* and an avoidance of biblical criticism were the sine qua non of American Orthodoxy.[8]

Today the situation is dramatically different. This is illustrated by the emergence and development of the website TheTorah.com, an American-designed and operated forum for analysis of the Torah within the context of modern academic scholarship. Most of the contributors are religiously observant, including a high percentage who identify as Orthodox. The heterogeneity and openness manifested on the forum's site are a novelty, especially in the West, which is characterized by denominationalism, with boundaries erected to express and maintain the identity of each denomination. There are

---

[3] BT *San.* 99a.   [4] Maimonides, *Hakdamot leperush hamishnah, San.* 10 (pp. 144–5).

[5] Kellner, *Must A Jew Believe Anything?*; Shapiro, *The Limits of Orthodox Theology.*

[6] Maimonides, *Guide of the Perplexed*, iii. 28 (trans. Pines, pp. 513–14).

[7] Shapiro, *The Limits of Orthodox Theology*, 97.

[8] Louis Jacobs initiated a major controversy in the UK with the publication of his book *We Have Reason to Believe*, in which he argued that, although divinely inspired, the Bible was not given at one time nor written by one person. For a more contemporary interpretation of *torah min hashamayim* by a British scholar who defines himself as 'sceptically Orthodox', see Solomon, *Torah from Heaven.*

several discussion forums similar to TheTorah.com in Israel, as the non-denominational character of Judaism there allows for a variety of perspectives on theological and religious questions. Perhaps the most popular of these is the literary supplement to the newspaper *Makor rishon*'s weekend edition.[9]

The question I wish to explore is, Why now? Given the denominational divides in America, what led to the birth of TheTorah.com and similar forums at this particular time? The question cannot be answered exhaustively here, but some of the major factors will be indicated and discussed.

The Factors Influencing Change

The emergence of more open theological discussion exemplified by websites such as The Torah.com is an outgrowth of a series of developments in American Jewry in general and Orthodox Jewry in particular, as well as within religious communities in Israel.

The second half of the twentieth century witnessed the emergence of a generation of college-educated Orthodox Jews who studied in yeshivas. In my study of Jewish baby boomers based on the 1990 National Jewish Population Survey (NJPS), I found that more than 75 per cent of those who had received nine to twelve years of day-school education had gone on to obtain at least a bachelor's degree. Among those who had received thirteen to sixteen years of day-school education, more than 83 per cent had at least a bachelor's degree.[10] Although not all of the Jews surveyed here may be Orthodox, it is fair to assume that, at least for those with twelve or more years of day-school education, the overwhelming majority are. Data from the 2001 NJPS indicate that 66 per cent of Orthodox Jews aged between 18 and 50 had at least a bachelor's degree.[11]

The Development of Jewish Studies on College and University Campuses

The Association for Jewish Studies (AJS) was founded in 1969: by 2000 it had about 1,400 members,[12] and by 2011 nearly 1,900 members. Its annual conferences have likewise grown significantly over the years: between 1996 and 2010 the number of sessions more than doubled.[13] In 2000 it was estimated that there were between 800 and 1,000 positions in Jewish studies,

---

[9] *Makor rishon* is an Israeli newspaper with an overt Israeli nationalist bent. It is not formally religious Zionist but the overwhelming majority of its staff and readership probably are. Its expanded Friday edition contains a variety of magazines and supplements: 'Shabbat' includes essays, interviews, and book reviews on Jewish philosophy, history, society, and culture.

[10] Waxman, *Jewish Baby Boomers*, 28.   [11] I thank Uzi Rebhun for this information.

[12] Rona Sheramy, personal communication, 28 July 2011.

[13] Sheramy, 'From the Executive Director' (Fall 2010).

approximately 150 endowed chairs, and around 600 Jewish studies courses in American colleges and universities.[14] By 2011 there were more than 230 endowed chairs. Indications are that, despite a broad decline in job opportunities in the liberal arts, Jewish studies remained relatively stable until 2011.[15] Since then it has experienced some reduction in the number of positions as well as a small decline in enrolments.[16]

Orthodox scholars play a prominent role in the field. In an informal survey of around half a dozen colleagues who are active in the AJS, I asked them for their guesstimate as to the percentage of Orthodox in the organization. The range was between 10 and 25 per cent, with most perceiving it to be 15 per cent or higher. More official data are available from surveys: a 2008 membership survey of the AJS found that 21.3 per cent identified as Orthodox,[17] while a 2014 survey found that, among members from the United States and Canada, 14.8 per cent identified as Orthodox, and among members from countries other than North America, 34.2 per cent identified as Orthodox.[18] In Israel, the percentage of religious students enrolled in Jewish studies is apparently even higher. As David Berger suggests, 'a disproportionately large percentage of students in departments of Jewish Studies in Israel come from the religious sector'.[19] This is probably because students from the religious sector are more likely to be interested in subjects of a specifically Jewish nature.

The Year-in-Israel Programme

A significant percentage of graduates of American Modern Orthodox yeshiva high schools spend a year or more in Israeli yeshivas, and this has had a significant impact on American Judaism in general and American Orthodoxy in particular.[20] One important result, in terms of the question at hand, of the year-in-Israel experience is that it introduces American students to modes of Jewish thought that are new to them. I have in mind especially the study of hasidic thought, kabbalah, and entirely new approaches to the study of the Bible. Faculty members in the yeshivas which these students attended in the United States were, until recently, themselves products of American yeshivas in which the approach to learning emphasized clear definitions of what constituted correct behaviour and thought, leaving little room for variation or

[14] Eisen, 'Jewish Studies and the Academic Teaching of Religion'.
[15] Sheramy, 'From the Executive Director' (Spring 2011). S. M. Cohen, 'Profiling the Jewish Studies Profession in North America'.
[16] Cohen, 'Profiling the Jewish Studies Profession in North America'.
[17] S. M. Cohen and Veinstein, 'The 2008 Association for Jewish Studies Membership Survey', 4.
[18] S. M. Cohen, 'Profiling the Jewish Studies Profession in North America', 101.
[19] Berger, *Cultures in Collision and Conversation*, 210.
[20] This is discussed in Waxman, 'If I Forget Thee, O Jerusalem'.

individuality. This increasing tendency towards a rigid approach has been incisively analysed by Haym Soloveitchik.[21] Nor does such an approach limit itself to behaviour. There have also been efforts to ban works, such as books by Rabbi Nathan Kamenetsky[22] and Rabbi Natan Slifkin,[23] which contain ideas that do not conform to what some in the ultra-Orthodox yeshiva world consider proper. Although this type of censorship is not typical of Modern Orthodox yeshivas, there have been efforts at mind control even there.

Some of the graduates of these American institutions who go to Israel are exposed to 'radical' notions, such as the value of *hitbodedut* (praying in isolation rather than in a *minyan*); not being overly concerned with the correct times for reciting prayers such as the Shema and the Amidah;[24] the notion of *averah lishemah* (a sin committed with good intentions);[25] expressions of what to some appears to be determinism as opposed to the notion of free will which is primary for halakhah;[26] or a series of hasidic writings which view the Ninth of Av, the date marking the destruction of both temples, as an occasion for rejoicing rather than mourning.[27]

Many are also exposed to the writings of Rabbi Abraham Isaac Kook. In addition to his religious, mystical Zionist ideas, there are many aspects to Kook's approach that are antithetical to standard yeshiva thinking. For example, in contrast to the tradition of denigrating the arts, he wrote that 'Literature, painting and sculpture aim to actualize all the spiritual concepts impressed deep in the human soul.'[28] Rabbi Kook looked very favourably on the renewal of the Hebrew language by Eliezer Ben-Yehuda and, to the consternation of the

---

[21] Soloveitchik, 'Rupture and Reconstruction'.

[22] J. Berger, 'Rabbis Who Were Sages, Not Saints'.

[23] S. I. Weiss, 'Orthodox Rabbis Launch Book Ban'.

[24] Following the practice of Rabbi Jacob Isaac Horovitz of Lublin.

[25] Following the thought of Rabbi Tsadok of Lublin and Rabbi Mordecai Joseph Leiner of Izbetz, author of and known as *Mei hashilo'aḥ*.

[26] See, among others, Magid, *Hasidism on the Margin*, 120. For a different interpretation, see Hefter, '"In God's Hands"'.

[27] Yehuda Gellman also points to the hasidic penchant for removing the text from its historical context and applying it ahistorically. As he puts it: 'In the first Hasidic book ever published, R. Yaakov Yosef of Polnoye laid down a principle, attributed to Rabbi Israel Baal Shem Tov his teacher and founder of Hasidism, which was followed in the coming generations of Hasidism. The principle, let's call it "The Principle of the Mutable Eternity of the Torah", states that the Torah is eternal, and *therefore* must speak directly to each era, as needed . . . So, every person in every generation must have a way to perform every commandment, even if he cannot perform it as literally prescribed . . . For R. Yaakov Yosef and the Hasidim, this principle means that the very linguistic meaning itself can vary from one period of time to another. The eternity of the Torah involves the fact that the Torah can be read differently by every generation for all time to come. The Torah is eternal because [it is] eternally semantically flexible. Even though the Torah has textual *immutability*, it has *mutability* of linguistic meaning' (Gellman, *This Was From God*, 141–2).   [28] Y. Mirsky, *Rav Kook*, 19.

ultra-Orthodox, who considered Ben-Yehuda an evil sinner and instigator who defiled the holy language of Hebrew, maintained fairly good relations with him. Kook also wanted to translate works of kabbalah into modern Hebrew.[29] Most significantly in the context of this chapter, he had a relatively lenient attitude towards those sceptical of the principle of *torah min hashamayim*.[30]

New Approaches to Studying the Bible

In the Lithuanian yeshivas, Bible study was not really on the curriculum, and in so far as it was, it was almost entirely limited to the study of the Torah; the later books—those known collectively as the *nevi'im* (Prophets) and the *ketuvim* (Writings), referred to in Jewish studies circles by the Hebrew acronym Nakh—were largely ignored except through the writing of selected exegetes, most notably Rashi.[31] The roots of this neglect are considered by some authorities to be talmudic in origin, though others disagree;[32] but either way there seems to be an attitude, especially in the Ashkenazi world, that the study of the Bible is not of any great importance.[33]

Subsequently, the study of the Bible, and especially its later books, even came to be seen as having dangerous implications for religious perspectives. A contemporary work by Rabbi Moshe Shternbuch, a highly regarded authority in the ultra-Orthodox world, and one of the heads of the *beit din* (rabbinic court) of the Edah Haharedit, a prominent ultra-Orthodox organization in Jerusalem, expresses this very concern. In his multi-volume collection of responsa, the question is posed as to whether one should teach the Bible in primary school (*ḥeder*) before teaching Talmud. Shternbuch's view is that it has not been the custom to teach the Bible in junior school because the way it

[29] Rosenak, *Rabbi A. I. Kook* (Heb.), 52–3.

[30] Tamar Ross, 'Rabbi A. I. Kook and Postmodernism' (Heb.), 204. An earlier English-language version of Ross's article appeared as 'The Cognitive Value of Religious Truth Statements'.

[31] For a historical analysis see Brettler and Breuer, 'Jewish Readings of the Bible'. A rare recent exception was Rabbi Yaakov Kamenetsky, referred to as the 'protagonist' by his son Nathan in the aforementioned banned work, *Making of a Godol* (see Chapter 5 n. 66 above); Yaakov Kamenetsky not only studied Tanakh but also wrote unique commentaries, for example *Emet leya'akov*.

[32] Rabbi Joel Sirkis, in his commentary on the *Shulḥan arukh*, claims that Rashi was actually the exception and that most authorities maintained that the father's obligation included the teaching of *nevi'im* and *ketuvim*.

[33] Rabbenu Tam, one of the major Tosafists, went even further than his grandfather Rashi, and was of the opinion that one can fulfil one's obligation to learn Torah as well as *nevi'im* and *ketuvim* by learning Talmud, because they are all included there (BT *Kid.* 30a). Although his opinion was the exception rather than the rule, it may have influenced the trend. It may also be one of the reasons that, though men did not generally study Tanakh, women, who did not study Talmud, did study Tanakh and typically knew it better than men.

is likely to be understood at that age may cause children to anthropomorphize God and lead to other heresies. He further warns of contemporary heretics (*apikorsim*) who undertake Bible study with the sole objective of demonstrating that people sinned even in biblical times, thereby minimizing the extent of contemporary sinfulness. Since we cannot understand the true meaning in the Bible, he claims it is best to refrain from teaching it to young children.[34]

Until relatively recently, when the Bible was taught in Orthodox schools it was in the context of a highly literal interpretation of the doctrine of *torah min hashamayim*, according to which the Torah as we have it is exactly the same Torah as that conveyed by God to Moses at Sinai, who then wrote it down completely and precisely. Moreover, it was emphasized that the text cannot be taken literally. Rather, the exegesis relied heavily on the homiletic approach known as *derash*. Orthodox Jewish education also emphasized the great gap between contemporary humans and biblical figures, especially those portrayed heroically, who were assumed to be on such a high spiritual level that they were actually free of human weaknesses and, especially, sin. For example, the statement by Rabbi Shmuel bar Nahmani in the name of Rabbi Yohanan, 'Whoever says that [King] David sinned is mistaken', was taken as authoritative, the final word.[35]

The second half of the twentieth century witnessed significant changes in the approach to biblical exegesis. In her broad analysis of trends in that period with respect to the study of medieval exegetical works from northern France based on the plain meaning of the text, Sara Japhet suggests that it had declined as a result of the waning of interest in the scientific study of Judaism (Wissenschaft des Judentums).[36] Zionism and the founding of the State of Israel changed that. Secular Zionism looked to the Bible as the basis for the 'old-new' Hebrew culture and rootedness in Erets Yisra'el, thus justifying the return to Israel and the establishment of Jewish sovereignty there.[37] David Ben-Gurion frequently quoted the Bible to foreign dignitaries, as when, in his

[34] Shternbuch, *Teshuvot vehanhagot hashalem*, ii, no. 457 (p. 386). Shaul Stampfer suggests that there are sound educational reasons for not teaching Tanakh in *ḥeder*, namely, 'the realities of teaching children—especially children who do not understand Hebrew. Even Hebrew-speaking adults today have great difficulty with books of the Bible such as Job and the prophetic books, with their sweeping and brilliant rhetoric' (Stampfer, *Families, Rabbis, and Education*, 155). For an overview of the neglect of Tanakh study in yeshivas, see Bin-Nun, 'On the Study of Tanakh in Yeshivas' (Heb.).

[35] BT *Shab.* 56a. For an analysis of the talmudic approach to David, see Medan, 'Anyone Who Says David Sinned Is Mistaken' (Heb.).

[36] Japhet, 'Major Trends in the Study of Medieval Jewish Exegesis in Northern France'.

[37] For somewhat different perspectives on the role of the Bible in secular Israeli society, see Simon, *Seek Peace and Pursue It* (Heb.), 23–46; Zakovitch, 'Scripture and Israeli Secular Culture'; and Zerubavel, 'A Secular Return to the Bible?'

testimony to the Peel Commission, the British Royal Commission sent to Palestine in 1936 to examine the causes of the violence and offer policy recommendations, he asserted, 'Our Mandate is the Bible.' As Anita Shapira indicates, the Bible became increasingly central both to Ben-Gurion's perspectives and to his actions.[38]

As a result of Ben-Gurion's public commitment, the Bible came to play a significant role in Israeli culture. Moreover, the approach to it was unquestionably one of *peshat*, interpreting in terms of the plain meaning, rather than *derash*. Over time, however, the Bible's lofty status in Israeli culture has apparently declined. At the Hebrew University, internal political and ideological disagreements over the correct approach to Bible studies stalled the establishment of the Bible Study Department for fifteen years, from 1925 to 1940,[39] and several years after Israel's independence the department was characterized by detached research and biblical criticism. At the same time, secular Zionism's dilution of the religious content and character of the Bible led to its content being viewed by an increasing number of non-religious Israelis as irrelevant and archaic.[40] By the end of the twentieth century, the Israeli public's interest in the Bible seemed to have waned.[41]

When Ben-Gurion was prime minister he established a Bible study circle which met regularly in his office. The Tanakh Circle of the Prime Minister's Residence continued until the resignation of Menachem Begin. When Ezer Weizman became president, it was reinstituted as the Tanakh Circle of the President's Residence, but subsequently met only very sporadically. There have been several not very successful efforts to revive it.[42] Most recently, it was reorganized by President Reuven Rivlin and headed by Hebrew University professors Avigdor Shinan and Yair Zakovitch, two scholars who have been

[38]   Shapira, 'Ben-Gurion and the Bible'.

[39]   Japhet, 'The Establishment and Early History of the Bible Department' (Heb.).

[40]   See Japhet, 'Major Trends in the Study of Medieval Jewish Exegesis in Northern France', and Simon, *Seek Peace and Pursue It* (Heb.).

[41]   There is some disagreement as to whether, when, and why this decline took place. In addition to the reasons cited by Japhet and Simon, Anita Shapira, in 'The Bible and Israeli Identity', argues that it was largely the result of 'appropriation of the Bible' by religious nationalism. Shapira's article is also the opening chapter in her edited volume of the same title, published in Hebrew. Curiously, in her article 'Ben-Gurion and the Bible', Shapira implies that the decline began before the Six Day War and the religious-nationalist 'appropriation of the Bible'. Izhak Laor, in a review of Shapira's book, 'Samson Was Lame in Both Legs' (Heb.), argues that the decline is connected to a linguistic matter, namely that the language of Tanakh is alien to modern non-religious Israelis and thus has little appeal. Yair Zakovitch, 'Scripture and Israeli Secular Culture', 301–4, suggests a series of reasons for the change. However, Yairah Amit, in another review of Shapira's volume, 'Has the Status of Scripture Declined?' (Heb.), asserts that in fact there has been no decline in the status of Tanakh in Israeli society.

[42]   Perhaps because he was a member, Yair Zakovitch is still somewhat optimistic that the

heavily involved in attempts to attract the broader Israeli public to the Bible.

Ben-Gurion also established the annual National Bible Contest, which was part of the national rituals on Israel's Independence Day. Subsequently, and particularly following the Six Day War of June 1967, the secular population lost interest in the event and, as indicated, it became one with almost exclusively religious contestants and of interest only to the religious population. Hebrew University Bible scholar Yair Zakovitch has suggested a number of reasons for the decline in interest in the Bible since the 1960s. Among them are that the Bible has been replaced by a new focus on the Holocaust; the Bible does not resonate with a secular, technological rather than agricultural, individualistic rather than collective society, or with a materialistic, post-Zionist population. The final straw was the growing rift between secular and religious Israelis over such religio-political issues as the sabbath, kosher food, and the IDF draft, especially after the Yom Kippur War of October 1973, when the euphoria following the Six Day War evaporated and a massive chasm opened between messianic religious settlers, for whom the Bible is very contemporary, and the secular public, especially those who emphasized peace and who desired safe borders, not ancient biblical ones.[43] It was only within the world of religious Zionism that serious Bible study developed.

Bar-Ilan University was founded in 1955 by the Mizrahi (religious Zionist) movement, and initially all of its faculty and most of its students were religious. A Bible Department was established, and ultimately it became the largest department for the study of the Hebrew Bible, not only in Israel, but internationally.

One of the most influential teachers of Bible studies was Nehama Leibowitz, who taught at the Mizrahi Women's Teachers' College in Jerusalem

---

circle can be revived and have an impact. See Zakovitch, 'Scripture and Israeli Secular Culture', 314.

[43] Zakovitch, 'Scripture and Israeli Secular Culture', 310–14; id., 'The End of the Century of the Bible' (Heb.), 117–19. In an effort to attract the broad population of Israeli Jews to Tanakh, Rabbi Binyamin Lau initiated a programme, modelled after the Daf Yomi initiative, which aspires to create a broad community of daily study and discussion of one of the 929 chapters of Tanakh (Lau, *Eight Prophets* (Heb.), 13–14). Within a few weeks of its launch in December 2014, the programme had attracted more than 13,000 Facebook followers (Rosenberg, 'Left and Right, Secular and Religious, Brought Together by Bible Study'), and a not insignificant number of religious critics, who argued that the programme's website (www.929.org.il) and Facebook pages (www.facebook.com/929project) were too liberal in the interpretations and commentaries they accepted for posting (see e.g. Ben-Ami, 'Why Provide a Refuge for Provocation?' (Heb.)). Lau steadfastly resists such criticism and argues that Tanakh will be a national treasure and subject of discussion by all only if everyone feels that they can freely express themselves on it (Lau, 'A Home that Includes All' (Heb.)). The extent to which the initial enthusiasm for the programme will continue, or even grow, remains to be seen.

from the early 1930s to 1955. From 1956 to 1971 she taught at Bar-Ilan, but resigned as a result of a strong disagreement with a department head there. Her approach was to focus on a topic in the week's Torah portion, analyse the classic commentators seeking to understand what had led them to offer their commentaries, and evaluate them. Her creativity manifested itself primarily in her extensive and intensive literary analyses rather than in introducing new commentaries of her own. Beginning as stencilled sheets and then appearing as printed pamphlets, Leibowitz's lessons gained in popularity and ultimately became sets of books in Hebrew which were later translated into English and several other languages.[44]

The role of the Bible in religious Zionism significantly intensified after the Six Day War. The Western Wall, the Temple Mount, Judaea, and Samaria were now under Israeli control. Much of the Jewish population of Israel and abroad initially experienced great relief, joy, and pride over Israel's swift victory. Many were struck with a sense of awe by the realization that what they considered the heart of the land of the Bible was once again accessible and under Israel's authority, and some viewed it as a return to history. Amid all this fervour there was a rise in Bible consciousness, particularly among religious and traditional Jews in Israel and abroad.[45]

The Role of Yeshivat Har Etzion in Bible Study

Several months after the war, Yeshivat Har Etzion was founded by Rabbi Yehuda Amital, who in 1971 invited Rabbi Dr Aharon Lichtenstein[46] to join him in its leadership. They were a good team, and Har Etzion came to be known as 'the Harvard of the yeshivot'.[47] One of its unique characteristics was the integration of the intensive study of the Bible into the curriculum. The yeshiva also helped establish Herzog College, which has a centre for Bible research and study and has spurred what many term a revolution in the study of the Bible. Among its pioneers were Rabbi Mordechai Breuer and Rabbi Yoel Bin-Nun.

Rabbi Breuer developed the 'Aspects Theory' (*shitat habehinot*), an approach he viewed as an antidote to the major assertions of biblical criticism concerning the human composition of the Torah, while recognizing that the Torah spoke in several voices. Briefly, he argued that the Torah written by God is not limited by the laws of time, space, or linguistics and that the arguments of the Bible critics, based as they are on human laws, are essentially irrelevant in appli-

---

[44] Unterman, *Nehama Leibowitz*; H. Deutsch, *Nehama* (Heb.).

[45] However, among many secularists who opposed Israel's occupation of the territories, there was an increasing sense of alienation from the Bible.

[46] On Lichtenstein see Chapter 2 n. 32 above.   [47] Chertok, *Stealing Home*, 137.

cation to the Torah. Linguistic differences, for example, are interpreted by him as reflecting different attributes or aspects of God and often include lessons God wishes to us to learn.[48] Breuer's approach enabled Orthodox students of the Bible to feel comfortable, at least initially, studying and even accepting many secular theories and assertions related to biblical criticism with the understanding that they posed no challenge to religious belief in *torah min hashamayim*.[49]

Rabbi Bin-Nun is probably the central figure in the 'revolution' in Bible study that has taken place during the past three to four decades. He is a challenging and creative thinker and writer on a range of topics, especially the role of religious Zionism in Israeli society and world Jewry, but his speciality is the Bible.[50] In that capacity, he heads the centre at Herzog College, is an editorial board member and frequent contributor to *Megadim*, the college's journal, and was one of the initiators of the annual Yemei Iyun Tanakh conference held at the college.[51] Founded initially as two intensive study days which attracted approximately 150 Israeli teachers of Bible studies, the programme has grown to a four-day major conference attracting thousands of participants from around the world, who hear lectures from well-known scholars.[52] In contrast to Breuer, who showed a strong interest in what critical scholars considered sources but interpreted these as original aspects of God's revelation, Bin-Nun developed an approach that places emphasis on the historical, geographical, and linguistic contexts of passages in the Bible. In-depth knowledge of these areas, he strives to demonstrate, both illuminates the Bible and responds to the problems raised by biblical criticism.

---

[48] Ofer (ed.), *The 'Aspects Theory' of Rav Mordechai Breuer*; Breuer, 'The Study of Bible and the Primacy of the Fear of Heaven: Compatibility or Contradiction? (Heb.).'

[49] For many of those seriously interested in Bible study, this was probably a more appealing approach than that of Rabbi Joseph B. Soloveitchik, who declared, 'I have never been seriously troubled by the problem of the Biblical doctrine of creation vis-a-vis the scientific story of evolution at both the cosmic and the organic levels, nor have I been perturbed by the confrontation of the mechanistic interpretation of the human mind with the Biblical spiritual concept of man. I have not been perplexed by the impossibility of fitting the mystery of revelation into the framework of historical empiricism. Moreover, I have not even been troubled by the theories of Biblical criticism which contradict the very foundations upon which the sanctity and integrity of the Scriptures rest' ('The Lonely Man of Faith', 8–9). He did not disclose why he was not troubled by those matters, especially those that he did not reject. See Tamar Ross, 'Orthodoxy and the Challenge of Biblical Criticism'.

[50] A portrait of Bin-Nun which highlights the centrality of Tanakh in his life and his approach to it is found in Halevi, *Like Dreamers*; see esp. 203–4.

[51] H. Angel, '*Torat Hashem Temima*: The Contributions of Rav Yoel Bin-Nun to Religious Tanakh Study'.

[52] 'Thousands in Herzog College Bible Study Days', http://jtec.macam.ac.il/portal/Article Page.aspx?id=1700.

The most profound impact of Yeshivat Har Etzion and Herzog College on the study of the Bible has been in replacing the traditional homiletical approach to exegesis with an approach entitled *tanakh begovah einayim* (literally, 'Bible at eye level'). Other than in medieval northern France, it had always been axiomatic that the Bible could not be understood through the text itself but only via midrash. But Bin-Nun and his colleagues argue that the interpretation of the Bible does not need any middlemen; it can and should be understood through deeper knowledge and understanding of the text itself. This approach has become very popular in the religious Zionist and Modern Orthodox communities in Israel,[53] and also among the traditional, non-religious public there,[54] but there has been some strong reaction against it within the *ḥardal* sector of the religious Zionist community,[55] especially by Rabbi Zvi Israel Tau and Rabbi Shlomo Aviner.[56]

A major work on the Bible which attempts to combine both traditional and modern commentaries and interpretations is the thirty-volume *Da'at mikra* (Knowledge of the Bible), published by Mossad Harav Kook in Jerusalem; each volume is edited by a scholar in the relevant field. An attempt to bolster its 'scientific' status was the publication of a matching atlas, edited by the overall editor of the series, Yehuda Kiel, with Yehuda Elizur, who was a professor of Bible studies and biblical archaeologist at Bar-Ilan University. The entire set has been popular within the religious Zionist and Modern Orthodox communities, many of its volumes were used as textbooks in religious Zionist schools, and Yediot Ahronot published an edition for the traditionally religious sector of the wider public.

The increased interest in the Bible in Israel apparently manifests itself at the university level as well. Bible scholar James Kugel senses that there has been big increase in the number of *kipah*-wearing Bible students at Hebrew University compared to thirty years ago, with a corresponding drop in the number of secular students who choose to do Bible, at least at graduate level. He is not sure about other universities.[57] All of this activity is evidence of a significant increase in interest in the Bible within the religious and traditional communities since the 1960s.

---

[53] See e.g. Bazak, *I Samuel* (Heb.), *II Samuel* (Heb.), and *Until This Day* (Heb.).

[54] See e.g. Lau, *Jeremiah*; id., *Esther* (Heb.); Bin-Nun and Lau, *Isaiah* (Heb.).

[55] The term *ḥardal* is a Hebrew acronym combining haredi and *dati le'umi*, and refers to the more religiously conservative sector of religious Zionism.

[56] See Tau, *The Righteous Person Shall Live by His Faith* (Heb.); Aviner, *Five Videos* (Heb.).

[57] Personal communication, 2 June 2014.

Socio-Political Factors

In addition, some of the popularity of Bible study may be attributed to socio-political factors. The ideological leadership of the settler movement used biblical references to reconstruct locations within Judaea and Samaria as parts of the national homeland in order to create and intensify emotional and ideological connectedness with these territories.[58] Likewise, much of Israeli tourism, especially in these areas, has connected and continues to connect most of the settlements and other sites visited with the Bible. A symbiotic relationship has thus emerged in which the Bible intensifies ties to the land and the land enhances ties to the Bible.

Developments in American Orthodoxy

In American Orthodoxy the relationship to the Bible is much more detached and remote. The language, Hebrew, is difficult enough. In addition, it is a document that relates to distant places, places with which relatively few people have any serious personal connection. It is thus seen as a document that was given in the past but with which one does not connect today.[59] Moreover, there is much less of a gap in America between the Modern and ultra-Orthodox than there is in Israel. As I have argued elsewhere, the overwhelming majority of American Orthodox Jews are neither ultra-Orthodox nor Modern, as those typologies have previously been defined. Rather, increasingly, they are a blend of the two. They are modern in the sense that they are well educated, secularly as well as Jewishly, they interact with the larger society and culture, and they are very pro-Israel. On the other hand, they are increasingly punctilious in matters of religious ritual and practice.[60]

The overwhelming majority of the teachers in American day schools and yeshiva high schools grew up with the traditional approach to teaching the Bible, and that is thus the predominant approach even in yeshivas that project themselves as Modern Orthodox. Under these circumstances, it seems rea-

---

[58] Feige, *Settling in the Hearts*.

[59] I would broadly suggest three distinct types of relationship with Tanakh in different Orthodox communities: (1) For religious Zionists, Tanakh speaks directly to the reader and the reader interprets its words in ways that are contemporarily meaningful. Tanakh is a living document with which one has dialogue. (2) For haredim (ultra-Orthodox), it is a sacred document, 'set apart and forbidden', to use Émile Durkheim's phrase, or 'set apart', as Rashi and numerous others translate it, and 'forbidden' in the sense that no new interpretations are permissible (*ḥadash asur min hatorah*: a play on words to the effect that that which is new is prohibited by the Torah). In this context, communication is one-way—it addresses the reader, but there is no dialogue. It is 'set in stone'; i.e. it does not lend itself to individual interpretation. (3) Diaspora Jews are detached from it. It is written in a foreign language and relates to places, events, and matters that are remote and in the past. [60] Waxman, 'Needed—New Typologies'.

sonable to assume that those who develop a strong interest in the Bible are those who have studied at an Israeli institution which focuses on the modern approaches to biblical research and teaching outlined above, which are radically different from those of their American education.[61] It also seems reasonable to assume that there has been an increase in the number of Orthodox students studying Bible at American universities. Indeed, James Kugel has said that he has seen an increase over the last thirty years in the number of Modern Orthodox undergraduates and graduate Bible students, while the number of Christian or unaffiliated students seems to have remained more or less the same.[62]

It is not only approaches to the Bible that distinguish Israeli religious Zionism/Modern Orthodoxy from American Modern Orthodoxy. American Modern Orthodox Jews who visit Israel for more than a brief week or two may well come into contact with broader intellectual analyses of issues of concern to Modern Orthodoxy than they were aware of in the United States. In Israel, they may find a wide range of books, articles, and lectures in an Orthodox context which give expression to ideas that are not even raised within American Orthodoxy. The greater openness of religious Zionists in Israel may enable and encourage them to 'think out of the box' and express ideas about the Bible that American Orthodox Jews of earlier decades—and most contemporary ones as well—would never have expressed, even if they may have thought them. Some American Orthodox who spend more time in Israel, in programmes such as the year in Israel, are more likely to be exposed to this new approach to the Bible and to retain it when they return to America. Though the attitude found among the religious Zionists in Israel is much less prevalent outside Israel, some of their ideas may be beginning to find expression beyond its borders.

Until recently, those with views and beliefs that did not conform with those of the Orthodox establishment had either to keep their thoughts to themselves or, if they found that too socially isolating, to affiliate with Conservative Judaism and find company with traditionalists there, not because Conservative Judaism was serious about source criticism but simply because it was more accommodating of a much wider range of beliefs and practices than Orthodoxy. Leaving Orthodoxy was not unusual; in fact, the attrition rate of the Orthodox was quite high. Analyses of the 1990 National Jewish Population Survey indicate that it was significantly higher than the Conservative and Reform rates.[63] That has now changed dramatically. Between 1971 and 2013 the

[61] See e.g. S. Z. Berger, 'A Year of Study in an Israeli Yeshiva Program', 17, 90.

[62] Personal communication, 2 June 2014.

[63] Lazerwitz, Winter, Dashefsky, and Tabory, *Jewish Choices*, 78–83; Waxman, *Jewish Baby Boomers*, 77–8.

percentage of American Jews who identify as Conservative declined steadily, from 42 per cent[64] to 18 per cent[65] and, given the age profile of the Conservative population, the indications are that the decline will continue. The retention rate of Orthodoxy, on the other hand, appears to be in an upswing. Culturally, it is no longer a stigma to be Orthodox in contemporary American society; on the contrary, it is 'in' to be Orthodox. And demographically, in contrast to the outlook for Conservative Judaism, the outlook for Orthodoxy is rather positive:[66] in addition to a slowing rate of attrition, the Orthodox fertility rate is significantly higher than that of non-Orthodox American Jews.[67]

A recent magazine article unrelated to the Bible stirred up some heated discussion by highlighting what is seen as a new development in contemporary American Orthodoxy, 'Social Orthodoxy', which entails adherence to Orthodox observance without the 'doxy', the belief system.[68] In fact, the phenomenon is not at all new. In nineteenth-century eastern Europe many Jews maintained traditional religious patterns not so much out of ideological commitment to Orthodox principles, but because it was the cultural behaviour they had internalized. When they emigrated to the United States, they founded synagogues because the synagogue was a central institution in their native communities, and they founded Orthodox synagogues as the only kind of synagogue with which they were familiar. It would be more accurate to describe them as 'Orthoprax', as conforming with Orthodox habit or custom, rather than as ideologically committed Orthodox.[69]

Nor did such orthopraxy begin in nineteenth-century eastern Europe. It has probably been around as long as Judaism itself, though the label that came to be used was 'Orthodoxy', a term first applied pejoratively to traditionalists within Judaism in early nineteenth-century Germany by adherents of Reform.[70] The term focuses on belief because of specific historical circumstances and issues, but it has much more contemporary meaning in terms of practice; that is, 'Orthodox' is understood to mean halakhically observant within a range

[64] Lazerwitz et al., *Jewish Choices*, 40.
[65] Pew Research Center, 'A Portrait of Jewish Americans', 10.
[66] The decline of Conservative Judaism was foreseen by Charles Liebman as early as 1980: see Liebman, 'The Future of Conservative Judaism in the United States'. Evidence from the 2013 Pew study demonstrates the decline. Reasons for it in addition to those suggested by Liebman can be found in Gordis, 'Conservative Judaism: A Requiem', and, from a personal perspective, Gottlieb, 'How Conservative Judaism Lost Me'. The pattern is not unique to Conservative Judaism. See e.g. Kelley, *Why Conservative Churches Are Growing*; D. E. Miller, 'The Future of Liberal Christianity'; Douthat, 'Can Liberal Christianity Be Saved?'
[67] Lazerwitz et al., *Jewish Choices*, 10, 49–50.
[68] Lefkowitz, 'The Rise of Social Orthodoxy'. [69] Waxman, *America's Jews in Transition*, 52.
[70] In the United States the term emerged in the mid-nineteenth century and, likewise, those who adopted it did so in opposition to Reform. See Jacobs, *The Jewish Religion*, 370; Sarna, *American Judaism*, 86–7.

of observances. When one segment of traditional Judaism legitimated a number of practices which the more traditional east European rabbinic leadership in the United States rejected, traditional Judaism in the United States split into two denominations or movements, Conservative and Orthodox.[71]

Be that as it may, it was always assumed that one who identified as and behaved as Orthodox was an Orthodox believer. What has changed is the willingness of individuals who identify as Orthodox to publicly declare that their affiliation is based on a conviction that 'religious practice is an essential component of Jewish continuity', or some other social reason, rather than religious faith. The same factors that contribute to this new openness are probably among those that have contributed to Modern Orthodox thinkers expressing ideas about the Bible that are not in complete harmony with traditional Orthodox approaches and beliefs.

Several, probably interrelated, factors have contributed to this new openness in American Modern Orthodoxy. Before discussing them, however, it should be noted that American Modern Orthodoxy today comprises two distinct sectors. The largest and most established sector is that whose institutional home is Yeshiva University and whose rabbinic organization is the Rabbinical Council of America. Those in this sector now identify themselves as 'Centrist Orthodoxy' and have, in fact, moved to become more demanding both ritually and ideologically.[72] A more recent and considerably smaller sector of Modern Orthodoxy is one which proudly identifies as such and for whom the banner is 'Open Orthodoxy'.[73] Its institutional home is Yeshivat Chovevei Torah. Most of its graduates join the International Rabbinic Fellowship, which is made up of Orthodox rabbis and clergy who gather to discuss issues in an environment which is more amenable to considering a broader range of ideas and issues than is Centrist Orthodoxy.

The Impact of the World Wide Web

In addition to the above, there is the impact of the World Wide Web, which has been influencing the lives of its users in a myriad of ways. In terms of the subject at hand, its major impact has been in making a previously unimaginable amount of information readily available and providing a channel through which to disseminate ideas, often anonymously.[74]

---

[71] Sarna, American Judaism, 165–93.

[72] See pp. 123-5 above.   [73] A. Weiss, 'Open Orthodoxy!'

[74] If, in the early 1980s, Clifford Geertz could suggest that 'The hallmark of modern consciousness . . . is its enormous multiplicity', how much more so is that true for the Internet age? See Geertz, Local Knowledge, 161.

Jews, including the Orthodox, were early users of the Web, and sites catering to a wide range of their interests were soon set up.[75] Although there have
been periodic attempts within the ultra-Orthodox community to ban access-
ing the Internet, these have largely failed. Orthodox Jews have a tradition of
adopting and adapting from the larger culture for the enhancement of Orthodoxy. In the case of the Web, its potential was seen in providing for interaction with Jews around the world, in study and in many other ways. The Web
enhances the 'Orthodox global village'. Traditionalist and Orthodox Jews who
held beliefs and thoughts not sanctioned by the religious establishment could
freely vent their frustrations and express their own positions anonymously
while continuing to express their loyalty to Orthodox Judaism without fear of
being labelled deviants or heretics. As the number of expressions of 'deviant'
notions increased, their appearance became less shocking and less stigmatiz-
ing, and individuals began to express their ideas openly.

Even without the Web, higher education and the publishing industry
have influenced people's readiness to present challenging ideas. In recent years
various works by Orthodox scholars have been published containing ideas
which at one time were considered heretical (and to some still are). Books by
Menachem Kellner and Marc Shapiro, for example, provide a very different
perspective on 'principles of faith' than had previously been current among the
Jewish public, especially the Orthodox public. Likewise, the theory of evolution
was, within Orthodoxy, often categorically labelled 'heresy' until recently, and
still is in much of contemporary Orthodoxy. However, as Rachel Pear has
shown, a number of prominent Modern Orthodox individuals have voiced pro-
evolution positions. In 2005, even the Rabbinical Council of America issued
an, admittedly very guarded, pro-evolution position.[76]

Pluralization without Secularization

Close to half a century ago, Peter Berger argued that the intricately interrelated processes of pluralization, bureaucratization, and secularization,
which are endemic to modernity, have greatly shaken the religious 'plausibility structures'.[77] Several years later, he clarified that, although 'a rumor of
angels' prevailed, it was but a 'rumor' in modern society, and it coexisted with
a 'heretical imperative', that is, the pluralistic character of modern society

---

[75] I know of no studies of Web connectivity among Orthodox Jews in the United States.
However, there are indications of high usage from studies on Internet connectivity and usage
among both religious Zionist youth and haredim in Israel. See Goodman, 'Religious Zionist
Youth on the Internet' (Heb.); Barzilai-Nahon and Barzilai, 'Cultured Technology'.

[76] Pear, '"And It Was Good"?', and 'Differences over Darwinism'.

[77] Berger, *The Sacred Canopy*.

impels us to make choices, including religious choices. We are no longer obliged to follow the beliefs of our forefathers. We choose, even when we choose to be religiously orthodox. From the standpoint of traditional religion, that is heresy.[78] As indicated above, by the end of the century Berger recognized that religion remained as powerful as ever, but that does not mean that there has been no secularization.[79]

There is indeed a secular discourse resulting from modernity, but it can coexist with religious discourses that are not secular at all. What is more, this secular discourse has its roots in the science and technology, which are the driving engine of modernity . . . But this fact has not driven out religion, or even diminished its plausibility among very large numbers of people in most of the world.[80]

The pluralism of society and culture entails several dimensions, and 'to understand the place of religion in the pluralist phenomenon', he argues,

one must note that there are two pluralisms in evidence here. The first is the pluralism of different religious options coexisting in the same society . . . The second is the pluralism of the secular discourse and various religious discourses, also coexisting in the same society. For the faith of individuals the implication of this is simple and exceedingly important. For most religious believers faith and secularity are not mutually exclusive modes of attending to reality; it is not a matter of either/ or, but rather both/and. The ability to handle different discourses . . . is an essential trait of a modern person.[81]

What has developed is that we now have 'a default secular discourse' which 'coexists with a plurality of religious discourses, both in society and in consciousness'.[82]

Berger does not say this, and I am not sure that he would agree, but it seems to me that the pluralized culture and consciousness with which we now live have intra-religious as well as inter-religious dimensions. For many moderns, there has been a weakened sense of transcendence, and what had once been unquestionable *objective* reality is now the individual's decision. That decision may be to become more pious, but it is a personal decision based on the individual's determination of what is more meaningful to him or her.

---

[78] Berger, *The Heretical Imperative*, 27.

[79] Berger, *The Desecularization of the World*, 2; see p. 81 above.

[80] Berger, 'Further Thoughts on Religion and Modernity', 314. This seems similar to an observation made decades earlier by Jacob Katz, namely, 'Secularization has affected the role played by religion generally . . . It did not, however, succeed in ousting religion nor in effacing the particular characteristics of the two religions [Judaism and Christianity] whose interrelation we have been considering' (Katz, *Emancipation and Assimilation*, 125).

[81] Berger, *The Many Altars of Modernity*, 53.

[82] Berger, 'Further Thoughts on Religion and Modernity', 316.

Modernity has brought about numerous social and cultural changes, and these have had an impact on Orthodox Jews. Some staunchly attempt to resist the changes and turn even more inward. This is at the base of much of ultra-Orthodoxy and haredism.[83] For many of the non-haredi Orthodox, the changes have raised serious questions and been a source of inner tension. As Gerald Blidstein points out with respect to the relationship between halakhah and democracy, 'We can admit that we are uncomfortable with some of our materials . . . I think that we ought not be ashamed of the fact of our discomfort and its sources. Such a situation is often just below the surface in the writing of R. Kook, and is probably one of the reasons for the fascination it holds.'[84] It has also been at the heart of many of the challenges presented by the relationship between religion and society in contemporary Israel.

For many, social and cultural changes, especially changes in social values, have led to a reconsideration of traditional interpretations and perspectives. This manifests itself in a variety of ways with respect to attitudes towards women and their place in Orthodox Judaism, and it manifests itself in much more limited but nevertheless significant changes in attitudes towards homosexuals.[85]

Under these circumstances, the traditional notion of *kefirah* (heresy) may no longer be applicable. Indeed, Menachem Kellner argues that there are 'two types of religious faith: one which understands faith as primarily trust in God expressed in concrete behaviour, as against another which understands faith as primarily the acknowledgement of the truth of certain faith claims'.[86] The latter, which is the Maimonidean position, is exclusivist, whereas the former is theologically inclusivist. The exclusivist position may have been appropriate at a time when religion provided a complete and very firm objective reality. Denying or questioning a single item in that objective reality was viewed as threatening the entire system. The situation in modernity appears to be very different. A 2011 survey by the Gallup organization found that more than 90 per cent of Americans continue to profess belief in God and that, 'Despite the many changes that have rippled through American society over the last 6 decades, belief in God as measured in this direct way has remained high and relatively stable.'[87]

---

[83]   J. Katz, 'Orthodoxy in Historical Perspective'; Silber, 'The Emergence of Ultra-Orthodoxy'; Ferziger, *Exclusion and Hierarchy*.   [84]   Blidstein, 'Halakha and Democracy', 29.

[85]   Tamar Ross, 'The Feminist Contribution to Halakhic Discourse'; Borschel-Dan, 'Orthodox, Separate—and Almost Equal'; Bendel, 'Rabbi Avi Gisser' (Heb.), a report of talks by Rabbi Avi Gisser and Rabbanit Esti Rosenberg at a panel sponsored by Bat Kol, a religious lesbian organization, at the Hartman Institute on 14 May 2014. It took place on the evening after Pesach Sheni, a special Pesach for those who were not able to participate in the original (see Num. 9: 6–12).   [86]   Kellner, *Must a Jew Believe Anything?*, 8–9.

[87]   Newport, 'More Than 9 in 10 Americans Continue to Believe in God'.

It seems reasonable to assume that the rate of atheism is higher among young American Jews, since the data in that Gallup survey show that 'Belief in God drops below 90% among younger Americans, liberals, those living in the East, those with postgraduate educations, and political independents.' Even among them, however, there is no evidence of any significant increase in atheism. The available data are inconclusive on the question of agnosticism, and it is possible that there has been an increase in those unsure about the existence of God, although we have no evidence to support that. From all that we have seen of contemporary American Modern Orthodox Jews, they indeed live with and employ a variety of discourses, some religious and some secular. In addition, their religious ideology and social structure facilitate their connections with Israel and their connecting with modern and, to them, meaningful approaches to the Bible. From all appearances, for most of them, their engagement with it is not confrontational and rejecting but, rather, critical and attempting to understand it and oneself more deeply.

CONCLUSION

As HAS BEEN SHOWN throughout this book, American Orthodoxy is anything but static. It has changed and will continue to do so. Demographic studies of the American Orthodox population are snapshots of that population at a particular time. Social scientists can at best project what that group will look like at some future date. Even with increased statistical sophistication, there are limits to predictability.[1] Although we cannot know precisely what the group will be like in the future, one thing is certain: it will not be the same as it is now.

That American Orthodoxy has changed and will continue to do so should be no surprise, for several reasons. The whole notion of Orthodox Judaism as a distinct and separate grouping is, as I suggested in Chapter 7, a Western and a recent one. There has never been such a category among the Sephardim, and even among Ashkenazim it has only existed for a few hundred years. As has been indicated, American Orthodoxy is largely a product of the east European immigration to America in the late nineteenth and early twentieth centuries, followed by the Holocaust-era immigration, deep ties with Israel and, of course degrees of adaptation to American society and culture.

Much of religious behaviour widely viewed as halakhah is actually within the realm of *minhagim*, customs. For example, Haym Soloveitchik points out that,

Strictly speaking, there is no need for separate sinks, for separate dish towels or cupboards. In fact, if the food is served cold, there is no need for separate dishware altogether. The simple fact is that the traditional Jewish kitchen, transmitted from mother to daughter over generations, has been immeasurably and unrecognizably amplified beyond all halakhic requirements. Its classic contours are the product not of legal exegesis, but of the housewife's religious intuition imparted in kitchen apprenticeship.[2]

Religious Jewish women adopted increased and heightened *kashrut* practices, and these became the norm. Likewise, Menachem Elon indicated that

---

[1] Henshel, 'Sociology and Prediction'.   [2] Soloveitchik, 'Rupture and Reconstruction', 66.

customs start with the masses, and go from the bottom up, sometimes to the point where they become actual law.[3]

As with other forms of cultural diffusion, as people move, they bring their religious customs with them and these spread throughout the new culture. That is how Ashkenazi Judaism developed in Erets Yisra'el, and that is how American Orthodoxy developed in the United States.[4] Until relatively recently, international travel was limited to a very small percentage of the population, and cultural change was relatively slow. But during the past 150 years the amount of international travel has increased dramatically, and has introduced fresh customs and ideas to America's Jewish community, particularly from eastern Europe in the years immediately after the Second World War and, in more recent times, from Israel. Developments in technology and communication have also resulted in more rapid change in religious customs.

It is not only customs that change. So do laws—in this context, halakhic rulings, which need to take account of developments in society. The rabbis of the Talmud recognized the need for change under extenuating circumstances, and legitimated it under the banner of a biblical verse: 'It is a time to act for God for they have violated your Torah' (Ps. 119: 126). The rabbis in the Talmud reinterpreted the verse to read not 'It is a time' but 'At a time', i.e. it is appropriate to abrogate a specific Torah injunction when the situation requires it in order to preserve the Torah as a whole. Such cases, however, were specific and for those times alone; they were one-time events and did not entail subsequent changes in religious practice. They may be viewed as similar to the saving of life, which takes precedence over virtually every law in the Torah, and to anything that contributes to saving a life. Rabbi A. I. Kook took it one step further, and argued that saving the Jewish community—even its economy—legitimates introducing temporary permission to overlook the obligation of leaving fields fallow during the Sabbatical Year (*shemitah*).[5]

The temporary permission to plant to during the Sabbatical Year indicates that the legitimacy of change in extenuating circumstances is not limited to one-time events but, rather, applies so long as the circumstances for which the change was introduced persist. Along the same lines, the Talmud states that, although the Oral Law was originally not allowed to be written, the rabbis permitted it, on the basis of the aforementioned verse in Psalms, because the generations no longer recalled the oral tradition.[6] The practice of writing, and now publishing, the Oral Law is so taken for granted in our own times that its publication is celebrated with each new edition, and its religious novelty is not

[3] Elon, *Jewish Law*, ii. 895–944.
[4] On American synagogue customs, see Hacohen, 'Minhag America'.
[5] Kook, *Mishpat kohen*, 358–9. [6] BT *Git.* 60a.

recognized. Nor is transcribing the Oral Law the only instance of such a change: the verse in Psalms quoted above is referred to in a number of other places in the Talmud where the rabbis instituted a practice which contravened the Torah.[7]

Lest it be argued that only the rabbis of the Talmud had the authority to implement such measures, Maimonides, in his introduction to the *Guide of the Perplexed*, legitimates his writing on matters which had previously been carefully concealed: 'I have relied on two premises, the one being [the Sages'] saying in a similar case, *It is time to do something for the Lord, and so on*; the second being their saying, *Let all thy acts be for the sake of Heaven*.'[8]

Of course, this does not mean that all moves towards halakhic change are positive or that anyone can introduce such change. Quite the contrary! Orthodoxy is, by definition, very conservative, and views change as a last resort. The instances when change has been introduced have always been the rare exceptions, prompted by extenuating circumstances and of limited scope.[9] In addition, only changes instituted by those whom the community of Torah scholars recognized as possessing sufficient halakhic expertise have been accepted. As Rabbi Moshe Feinstein stated in the introduction to his published responsa, 'let each Torah scholar and halakhic expert read and decide by himself whether to rule accordingly'.[10] When sufficient numbers of such experts accept a ruling, it becomes the accepted halakhah. However, neither the individual nor the community of Torah scholars and halakhic experts view themselves as innovators. They view themselves as upholders and reinforcers of the tradition, and they sometimes accomplish this by halakhically legitimating a change which has already taken place. David Weiss Halivni puts it this way:

Changes did take place, *but they were not done consciously.* The scholars who legalized them did not perceive themselves as innovators. The changes were integrated into community life long before they sought—and received—legal sanction. They originally came about imperceptibly, unnoticed, the result of a gradual evolutionary process. By the time they demanded legal justification, they were ripe, overgrown, as it were. So much so, that in many an instance, whoever opposed the changes was considered a breaker of tradition, adopting a 'holier than thou' attitude.[11]

The challenge for those who wish to introduce changes is to convince the community of recognized Torah scholars and halakhic experts that those

---

[7] For special cases where it was deemed proper not to follow a Torah dictate, see BT *Yev.* 79a. On that instance, see also Levinas, *Nine Talmudic Readings*, 25–9.
[8] *Guide of the Perplexed*, i. 9b (trans. Pines, p. 16).
[9] See Zoldan, 'It Is a Time to Act for God for They Have Violated Your Torah' (Heb.).
[10] Introduction to *Igerot mosheh, Oraḥ ḥayim*, pt. 1.
[11] Halivni, *The Book and the Sword*, 112.

changes are warranted. This requires demonstrating one's halakhic expertise to that community. Moreover, the evidence indicates that not only halakhic expertise is involved but tact and diplomacy as well. As Aviad Hollander suggests in his comparison of two rabbis who disagreed with the community of recognized Torah scholars and halakhic experts, paying homage to the accepted authorities is a much more beneficial approach than challenging them.[12]

Sometimes change may occur as a two-step process in which a sufficient number of observant Jews who are not necessarily halakhic experts are convinced of the legitimacy of the change and act accordingly. That, in turn, may be viewed as an extenuating circumstance requiring the introduction of some change by the community of halakhic experts. There is no clear formula by which one can predict what the consequences of overt attempts to introduce change will be. History has seen instances both where such measures led to a break in the Jewish community and where the change became part of the halakhic tradition.

A major development that has taken place in modernity is in the perception of identity, and the nature of the individual's identification with and within the community. In a traditional society, a Jew derived his or her identity from the community; one needed the community and it had strong social control. That is why excommunication was the strongest sanction—it meant stripping the individual of their identity. In modern societies, the individual creates his or her own identity and chooses which groups with which to identify. The Jewish community thus became a voluntary group. It needed members rather than the members needing it. Traditional societies did not need to engage in religious outreach; that is a consequence of the voluntary nature of Jewish identity and identification. The first half of the twentieth century in America witnessed a significant rate of defection from Orthodoxy, but around mid-century several developments began to slow that down. The Chabad movement was still relatively new as a factor in the United States, and its impact did not fully emerge until the final quarter of the century. As discussed above, the growth of day schools and yeshivas created a new environment for American Orthodox Jewry which noticeably increased its rate of retention. In addition, a number of outreach efforts, most notably Yeshiva University's Torah Leadership Seminar under the direction of Rabbi Abraham Stern, and its Jewish Studies Program under the direction of Rabbi Morris J. Besdin, managed to further slow the rate of defection,[13] but it still remained significant. The 1990 National Jewish Population Survey indicated that, 'among those raised Orthodox, just 24% are still Orthodox'. Most switched to the Conservative movement, a smaller number to

---

[12] Hollander, 'The Relationship between Halakhic Decisors and Their Peers', 106.
[13] Geller, *Orthodoxy Awakens*, 234–8.

Reform, and 8 per cent had no denominational preference.[14] Although part of that perceived Orthodox decline may have been due to a very loose definition of what 'raised Orthodox' actually meant—it may have meant nothing more than that, when one went to synagogue, it was to an Orthodox one—there was evidence that defection from Orthodoxy persisted. Towards the end of the century however, as evidence of rates of 50 per cent and more of intermarriage among the non-Orthodox emerged, there was an increased sense of optimism, if not triumphalism, among many Orthodox Jews. Once again, there were calls for establishing firm boundaries to keep out those deemed to be deviant from Orthodoxy.

However, although the Orthodox thought that they were essentially immune to the changes in identity and identification in the surrounding society, there in fact seem to be few options readily available for avoiding the consequences of postmodernity. Increasingly, the notion that it is the individual who creates his or her Orthodox identity has taken hold. As Yael Steimetz suggests, today Orthodoxy is no longer defined by adherence to a group of religious norms. Individuals who are not observant of halakhah nevertheless identify as Orthodox and feel that no one can take that identity from them.[15] Under these conditions, calls for the establishment of Orthodox boundaries appear to be increasingly irrelevant. Rather than trying to keep people out, it would appear to be more meaningful and productive to be welcoming them in, while making efforts to enhance the Orthodox identity of all who view themselves as part of Orthodoxy. Such enhancement is not only in terms of what is popularly perceived as stricter halakhic observance—both of rituals pertaining to the relationship between the individual and God (*bein adam lamakom*) and of those pertaining to the relationship between individuals (*bein adam leḥavero*)—but also requires greater sensitivity to general morality.[16] Contrary to what many believe, there are strong arguments for the superiority of the latter, what Daniel Sperber calls 'social *mitzvot*'.[17]

Yet there are those who do decide to leave Orthodoxy. Indeed, there has recently been a spate of books and articles about, and also by, individuals who, for different reasons and with different consequences, have done so. Some had been hasidic, others ultra-Orthodox, and still others Modern Orthodox.[18] Of course, these are not necessarily representative of anything but a growing readiness to 'go public' with one's religious conflicts and the existence of an

---

[14] Lazerwitz et al., *Jewish Choices*, 80.   [15] Steimetz, 'Let's Talk About It'.

[16] A. Lichtenstein, 'Does Judaism Recognize an Ethic Independent of Halakhah?', in id., *Leaves of Faith*, ii. 33–56.   [17] Sperber, *On the Relationship of Mitzvot*, 13–31.

[18] See e.g. Davidman, *Becoming Un-Orthodox*; Deen, *All Who Go Do Not Return*; Deitsch, *Here and There*; Lavin, 'Off the Path of Orthodoxy'; Margolies, 'Taking Off My Tefillin'; Tova Ross, 'How Ex-Frum Memoirs Became New York Publishing's Hottest New Trend'.

increasingly responsive public. The 2007 Pew Religious Landscape Survey suggested that religious switching among Americans in general, including Jews, is much more prevalent than it had been. Among those raised as Jews, 8.4 per cent currently identify with another religion, and many others do not identify with any religion. Among non-Jewish Americans the rates of switching are generally higher.[19] That survey did not allow for denominational analysis, so we have no evidence of the rates among Orthodox Jews. There are data on religious switching in Israel, and there we do have evidence of a considerably lower rate of switching among ultra-Orthodox Jews than among others.

Israel's Central Bureau of Statistics carries out an annual social survey, and the 2012 survey indicated that almost 90 per cent of those who, at the age of 15, were in ultra-Orthodox ('haredi') families currently identified as ultra-Orthodox, and 4.4 per cent identified as 'religious' (but not ultra-Orthodox). Among those who, at 15, were in a 'religious' family, less than half (46.1%) currently identified as 'religious' and 5.3 per cent identified as ultra-Orthodox. Also in the group of those in a 'religious' family, 48.6 per cent currently identified as less religiously observant than their families were when they were 15. However, among those who said that when they were 15 their families were 'traditional but religious'—presumably more Modern Orthodox than those who identified simply as 'religious'—44.1 per cent currently identified as 'traditional but religious', 8.3 per cent now identified as 'religious', and 4.3 per cent identified as ultra-Orthodox. It thus appears that there is a small growth in religious observance and identification among the 'traditional but religious' and a significant decline among the 'religious'.[20]

Israeli Orthodoxy is different from American Orthodoxy, and one can only speculate about similar patterns in the United States. On the one hand, it might be suggested that rates of attrition among Israeli 'religious' Jews are higher because, unlike the ultra-Orthodox, they are willing to enlist in the Israel Defense Forces (IDF), and military service is known to have a significant impact on one's religiosity.[21] This may also be one of the reasons for the higher rate of retention among the ultra-Orthodox: although the overwhelm-

[19] Rebhun, *Jews and the American Religious Landscape*.

[20] I thank Nadia Beider for providing me with these data analyses.

[21] Despite the long-standing and staunch opposition of the ultra-Orthodox rabbinic elite to military service for ultra-Orthodox men (and, even more, for women), the rates of ultra-Orthodox enlistment have been rising noticeably in recent years, both because of the IDF's increased attention to their special needs and because there is a growing number of ultra-Orthodox young men who refuse to resign themselves to a life of poverty, which is frequently the fate of those who do not serve in the IDF. Many jobs are limited to those who have served and, in addition, ultra-Orthodox enlistees frequently gain knowledge and skills which greatly enhance their career prospects after their service. See Bior, 'For Some Haredim, the IDF Serves as Gateway to Successful Career'.

ing majority of Sephardi and hasidic ultra-Orthodox Israelis are not opposed to the state—they are actually the most nationalist sector of Israel's Jewish population[22]—they oppose compulsory military service because of its potential impact on the religiosity of the recruits. Some Israeli Jews may also have fewer concerns about leaving Orthodoxy, because Judaism is the state religion and they do not feel they need the Orthodox structure to keep them within the Jewish fold. In the United States, by contrast, there is no compulsory military service and few Orthodox Jews volunteer for the armed forces. In addition, there are those who continue to identify as Orthodox for social reasons, because they view it as a way of keeping themselves, and especially their children, within the Jewish fold with norms and values that they view as positive.[23] On the other hand, although they do not enlist in the military, the vast majority of Modern Orthodox youth and an apparently increasing number of ultra-Orthodox youth in the United States do go to colleges and universities that are not exclusively Jewish, where their chances of socializing with non-Jews increase significantly, and thus their chances of disengaging from an Orthodox lifestyle. A recent survey of those who had left Orthodoxy suggests that a significant number of respondents, especially among the Modern Orthodox, left as a result of exposure to new ideas through lectures, discussions, and reading material which contradicted, or at least indicated that there is no proof for, some of what they were taught in their Orthodox upbringing.[24] Much more research is needed to be able to estimate the number who leave Orthodoxy and the extent to which exposure to new ideas is actually a major factor in their decision. If it is, it suggests that day school and yeshiva high school education need to be re-evaluated to meet contemporary challenges. This is all speculation because we have no empirical data on the situation in the United States and probably won't have any for the foreseeable future because of the financial and structural difficulties involved. Although we have no reliable evidence on rates of leaving Orthodoxy, insights from social psychology do suggest a considerably lower rate of defection from ultra-Orthodoxy than from Modern Orthodoxy in the United States.

A pioneer in the study of socialization, that is, how people become social beings, was an early American sociologist, Charles Horton Cooley, who developed the concept of 'the looking-glass self'.[25] By this he meant that the self is actually a reflection because we see ourselves through the eyes of others. How do I know if I am good at what I do? Through how others respond to it, personally, in reports, reviews, and other formal or informal

[22] Leon, *The Mitre and the Flag* (Heb.).   [23] Lefkowitz, 'The Rise of Social Orthodoxy'.
[24] Nishma Research, 'Starting a Conversation', 24.
[25] Cooley, *Human Nature and the Social Order*, 152.

feedback. How do I know whether I am a good parent, worker, boss? Through the feedback I receive from my colleagues, subordinates, and superiors. If all of them give negative feedback, it will be difficult to maintain a positive self-image; in fact, someone who does so under those circumstances is said to be 'out of touch with reality'. A contemporary of Cooley who also helped pioneer our understanding of socialization was the American philosopher and social psychologist George Herbert Mead. He emphasized language as the most important organization of human symbols. Through language, the individual who contemplates himself or herself becomes both subject and object simultaneously. Language also permits us to 'take the role of the other', that is, to fit ourselves into roles as they have been portrayed for us. Mead argues that we develop as social beings by taking on roles that are out there and 'playing' them. The more we 'play' the roles, the more they become a part of us and the more we identify ourselves by them. For example, when a new parent is confronted for the first time with a situation involving their baby calling for action, they may not know what to do, and they may ask someone for advice or consult a guide on childcare. At the time, they may think of themselves as 'acting like a parent'. After playing the role for a while, they will view themselves 'as a parent' rather than as acting like one. They have internalized the role of parent. And so it goes with all of the roles we play. As adults, of course, people are much more capable of establishing what Erving Goffman called 'role distance', that is, maintaining some distance between themselves and the roles they play when they are required to act in ways with which they don't agree.[26] Other than that, the more one plays a role, the more it becomes a part of one's identity.[27] That is, perhaps, the basis for what Paul Ritterband and Steven Cohen have called the 'more the more' theory, that is, the more Jews take one aspect of Jewish life seriously the more they will take other aspects of Jewish life seriously.[28] Ritterband and Cohen focused on Jewish philanthropy, but we find the same principle operating in other Jewish behaviour, such as mate selection. Perhaps this can explain the higher retention rate of the ultra-Orthodox, namely, that they are more self-consciously engaged in Orthodox Jewish behaviour and act in an Orthodox fashion more frequently than other denominations. They therefore internalize their role as Orthodox to a greater degree and are less likely to change their Jewish denomination than others.

In addition, as discussed in Chapter 3 above, ultra-Orthodox Jews in

[26] Goffman, *Encounters*, 85–132.

[27] Perhaps this is the underlying rationale for R. Judah's view that individuals should always involve themselves with Torah and *mitsvot*: even if they begin by doing it with an ulterior motive, they will eventually come to do it for its own sake (BT *San.* 105*b*).

[28] Ritterband and Cohen, 'Will the Well Run Dry?'

Responses to 'How many of your close friends are Jewish?' (%)

	Ultra-Orthodox	Modern Orthodox	Conservative	Reform
All of them	33.4	13.1	3.6	1.3
Most of them	51.4	53.2	37.3	29.0
Some of them	12.5	30.9	43.2	51.4
Hardly any of them	0.8	1.3	15.1	16.9
None of them	1.8	1.6	0.7	1.4
Total	99.9	100.1	99.9	100

America are the most likely to live in strongly Jewish neighbourhoods.[29] They do so for religious as well as ethnic reasons. It is in those neighbourhoods that they are most likely to be able to satisfy their religious needs, including synagogues for prayer, Orthodox schools for their children, groups of people with whom to study on a regular basis, ritual baths, and shops carrying the goods that they need and want.[30]

As the table above indicates, ultra-Orthodox Jews are most likely to have Jews as their closest friends. In other words, ultra-Orthodox Jews are more intimately connected with each other than with Jews of other denominations. Two American social scientists, Nicholas Christakis and James Fowler, studied the subject of human connections extensively and found that our connections affect every aspect of our daily lives:

How we feel, what we know, whom we marry, whether we fall ill, how much money we make, and whether we vote all depend on the ties that bind us. Social networks spread happiness, generosity, and love. They are always there, exerting both subtle and dramatic influence over our choices, actions, thoughts, feelings, even our desires.

[29] Although we do not have data specifically on the neighbourhood choices of ultra-Orthodox Jews, the 1990 National Jewish Population Survey found that a significantly higher percentage of Orthodox—including ultra-Orthodox and Modern Orthodox—Jews than other Jews say that living in a Jewish neighbourhood is very important to them, and a significantly higher percentage of these Jews actually live in all-Jewish neighbourhoods. In both cases, the percentages vary denominationally, and we can assume that they would be highest for the ultra-Orthodox.

[30] Support for this pattern is found in the Talmud: 'Rabbi Jose ben Kisma said: Once I was walking on the road and someone greeted me, and I returned the greeting. He said to me, "My master, where are you from?" I said to him, "I am from a great city of sages and scribes." He said to me, "My master, would you like to live with us in our place, and I would give you millions of golden dinars [a unit of money], precious stones and pearls?" I replied, "Even if you gave me all the silver, gold, precious stones, and pearls in the world, I would not live anywhere but in a place of Torah"' (Mishnah *Avot* 6: 9).

And our connections do not end with the people we know. Beyond our own social horizons, friends of friends of friends can start chain reactions that eventually reach us, like waves from distant lands that wash up on our shores.[31]

Christakis and Fowler provide strong evidence indicating that we are influenced by our friends and the friends of our friends, and the stronger the ties, the greater the reinforcement. Religion plays a major role in social networks and connections, because 'God can actually be seen as a part of the social network. This involves not just the personification of a deity but the addition of a deity into the social fabric.'[32] It seems reasonable to assume that ultra-Orthodox Jews have the most personified conception of, as well as the most intense relationship with, God. God is most obviously 'present' within ultra-Orthodox communities. This reinforces the social networks within those communities, resulting in greater social solidarity and relatively low defection rates. Networking and socialization, as well as higher birth rates, mean that the ultra-Orthodox will be an increasing majority of American Orthodox Jews.

This does not mean that Modern Orthodoxy will disappear or even weaken significantly. Demographically, although it loses from members switching out, it also gains from switching in from among the non-Orthodox who are traditionally inclined and are increasingly dissatisfied with developments in non-Orthodox Judaism in America. The more traditional sector of Conservative Judaism, for example, has reportedly provided not insignificant numbers to Modern Orthodoxy in the past twenty or thirty years, and there are probably others in the wider Jewish population who will decide to switch in. There are also potential switchers from ultra-Orthodoxy who, for one reason or another, are searching for something different. How much they will gain from switching depends on how theologically, philosophically, and practically attractive they find Modern Orthodoxy to be. Some recent developments, such as the production of traditional and modern Jewish books in a style and a language to which moderns can relate, will probably contribute. Modern Orthodoxy might also need to re-examine its institutional framework in an effort to be more inclusive, for example, of those who feel they cannot afford the high cost of Modern Orthodox living.

However, for all of the reasons discussed, Modern Orthodoxy will inevitably continue to be a minority within American Orthodoxy, and one of the consequences of that is, for example, that kashrut-certifying agencies will cater to the needs and demands of the ultra-Orthodox. Some Modern Orthodox find this restrictive because it suggests to them that they are less than truly Orthodox and that the products they use are not sufficiently kosher.

---

[31] Christakis and Fowler, Connected, 7.   [32] Ibid. 242.

It also requires them to purchase items that receive extra supervision and which are therefore more expensive. This situation is a challenge to the Modern Orthodox to learn more and to think independently—but that is indeed what philosophical Modern Orthodoxy is all about. Perhaps a more enthusiastic acceptance of this and of the other challenges of Modern Orthodoxy might foster a more positive and confident sense of its role.

Another factor complicating our ability to predict future trends in American Orthodoxy is connected with a recent development in ultra-Orthodoxy in the United States. As indicated above and as Adam Ferziger has demonstrated,[33] there has been a dramatic shift in ultra-Orthodoxy's approach to outreach, from a stance of disdain if not outright opposition to one of active engagement. An unexplored question is the extent to which this was sparked by economic need. I and several colleagues have been debating for decades whether economic realities will result in a crash of the ultra-Orthodox lifestyle. With several generations of ultra-Orthodox Jews with large families, who have little or no secular education or desire to leave the walls of the yeshiva, some of my colleagues argue, there are no longer working parents who can support the *kolel* lifestyle on which ultra-Orthodoxy is based. They are convinced that it must soon collapse under the weight of economic necessity. I have argued that I see growth rather than potential collapse. Ultra-Orthodox communities have grown in terms of both population size and economic viability. Alongside the poverty without a 'culture of poverty',[34] there is apparently increasing wealth, and there is significant involvement of the well-to-do with their less financially well-off fellows. The biblical pact between Issachar and Zebulun[35] reflects a real religious obligation. It may well be that the proportion of Issachars, those devoted to full-time Torah learning, will decline somewhat under financial pressure, and more of them will enter the labour market, but they will probably still remain identified with and committed to the ultra-Orthodox community. Although economic constraints do not appear to be having a negative effect on ultra-Orthodoxy, it remains to be seen how the new outreach efforts will affect it.

A further unknown factor is the influence of the hasidim, the largest and most rapidly growing sector within American Orthodoxy, on American Orthodoxy as a whole. In the eight-county New York area consisting of New York City's five boroughs plus Nassau, Suffolk, and Westchester, the Orthodox grew from 13 per cent of the Jewish population in 1991 to 20 per cent in 2011.[36] Hasidim

---

[33] Ferziger, *Beyond Sectarianism*, esp. 175–94.   [34] Lewis, 'The Culture of Poverty'.

[35] *Bereshit rabah* 99: 9 relates that two sons of Jacob made an arrangement whereby Zebulun, who was blessed with business acumen, supported his brother Issachar, who was a Torah scholar, and the latter studied Torah for the families of both.

[36] S. M. Cohen, Ukeles, and Miller, *Jewish Community Study of New York*, 121.

comprise 48.5 per cent of the Orthodox population in this area, with the largest Orthodox population in the United States, followed by the Modern Orthodox (31.8%) and the 'yeshivish' (19.7%).[37] Although it is true that New York is not the United States, the core of Orthodox Jews in the country live in and around it. It is therefore difficult to imagine that the growing hasidic segment of Orthodoxy there will not have a significant impact on the rest of American Orthodox Judaism.

Finally, it is difficult to predict what the impact of ultra-Orthodox demographic growth will be on relations between them and the broader organized Jewish communal structure as well as between the American Jewish community and the larger society. As I have discussed, the ultra-Orthodox have historically tended to remain apart from the organized Jewish communal structure. In light of their low status in terms of formal education, it is possible that, as their numbers increase, so will their social welfare needs. Given what appears to be the growing involvement of traditional, that is, Orthodox and Conservative, Jews in communal leadership,[38] there may be an inclination among some in the ultra-Orthodox community to move closer to the broader organized community, especially if this will help ease some of the financial pressures in their own community.

Although we cannot predict the direction, we can predict that American Orthodoxy will change, and it will probably change even more rapidly than it has in the past. Much as many might deny it, Orthodoxy is affected by and does respond to its social environment. That is why American Orthodoxy today is different from what it was a century ago, and is different from Orthodoxy in the United Kingdom, Europe, and even Israel.

[37] S. M. Cohen, Ukeles, and Miller, *Jewish Community Study of New York*, 213.
[38] Jick, 'The Transformation of Jewish Social Work'; S. M. Cohen, 'Profiling the Professionals', 23. On the appointment, for the first time, of an Orthodox Jew as the chief executive officer and executive vice president of UJA-Federation of New York, see Guttman, 'Eric Goldstein, New York Federation Chief, Is Not Outsider'; Rosenblatt, 'UJA-Fed.'s New Exec Calls for Broader "Kehillah"'.

BIBLIOGRAPHY

AHREN, RAPHAEL, 'Efrat Rabbi Tilts against Passover Food Restrictions for Ashkenazi Jews', *Haaretz* (15 Apr. 2011), http://www.haaretz.com/israel-news/efrat-rabbi-tilts-against-passover-food-restrictions-for-ashkenazi-jews-1.356076.

ALMOND, GABRIEL A., R. SCOTT APPLEBY, and EMMANUEL SIVAN, *Strong Religion: The Rise of Fundamentalisms around the World* (Chicago: University of Chicago Press, 2003).

AMIT, YAIRAH, 'Has the Status of Scripture Declined?' (Heb.), *Zemanim*, 95 (Summer 2006), 111–15.

ANGEL, HAYYIM, '*Torat Hashem Temima*: The Contributions of Rav Yoel Bin-Nun to Religious Tanakh Study', *Tradition*, 40/3 (Fall 2007), 5–18.

ANGEL, MARC D., *Foundations of Sephardic Spirituality: The Inner Life of Jews of the Ottoman Empire* (Woodstock, Vt.: Jewish Lights, 2006).

ANON., 'Brief Biography of the Author' (Heb.), in Yaakov Willowsky [Ridvaz], *Sefer nimukei ridvaz al hatorah*] (Chicago: privately published, 1904); rev. edn. (Benei Berak: Hamerkaz Le'idud Meḥkarim Toraniyim Beyisra'el, 1992), 7–8.

ARIAN, ASHER, and AYALA KEISSAR-SUGARMEN, *A Portrait of Israeli Jews: Beliefs, Observance, and Values of Israeli Jews, 2009* (Jerusalem: Guttman Center for Surveys of the Israel Democracy Institute/Avi Chai-Israel Foundation, 2012).

ARIEL, SHMUEL, 'Concubinage is Not Friendship' (Heb.), *Akdamot*, 17 (2006), 41–66.

AVINER, SHLOMO, *Five Videos of Lectures on 'Tanakh at Eye Height'* (Heb.), http://shlomo-aviner.net/.

BACHRACH, SUSAN, ANITA KASSOF, and EDWARD PHILLIPS (eds.), *Flight and Rescue* (Washington, DC: United States Holocaust Memorial Museum, 2001).

BACON, GERSHON C., *The Politics of Tradition: Agudat Yisrael in Poland, 1916–1939* (Jerusalem: Magnes Press, 1996).

BARZILAI-NAHON, KARINE, and GAD BARZILAI, 'Cultured Technology: The Internet and Religious Fundamentalism', *The Information Society*, 21/1 (Jan.–Mar. 2005), 25–40.

BAZAK, AMNON, *I Samuel: A King in Israel* [Shemuel I: melekh beyisra'el] (Jerusalem: Maggid, 2013).

—— *II Samuel: David the King* [Shemuel II: malkhut david] (Jerusalem: Maggid, 2013).

—— *Until This Day: Fundamental Questions in Bible Teaching* [Ad hayom hazeh] (Tel Aviv: Miskal-Yediot Ahronot/Sifrei Hemed, 2013).

BECHHOFER, YOSEF GAVRIEL, 'An Analysis of *Darchei HaLimud* (Methodologies of Talmud Study) Centering on a Cup of Tea', http://www.aishdas.org/rygb/derachim.htm.

—— 'Telshe: 120 Years since the Founding of the Yeshiva', http://www.aishdas.org/rygb/telshe.htm.

BECKER, AVI, 'Chabad, a Success Story', *Haaretz* (7 Dec. 2005), http://www.haaretz.com/chabad-a-success-story-1.176056.

BELCOVE-SHALIN, JANET S. (ed.), *New World Hasidim: Ethnographic Studies of Hasidic Jews in America* (Albany: State University of New York Press, 1995).

BELKIN, SAMUEL, *Essays in Traditional Jewish Thought* (New York: Philosophical Library, 1956).

BEN-AMI, ARIEL, 'Why Provide a Refuge for Provocation?' (Heb.), *Makor Rishon* (1 July 2016), Shabbat Literary Supplement, 4–5.

BEN-RAFAEL, ELIEZER, *Jewish Identities: Fifty Intellectuals Answer Ben-Gurion* (Leiden: Brill, 2002).

BENDEL, NETANEL, 'Rabbi Avi Gisser: "I Will Permit a Lesbian Family to Live in Ofra"' (Heb.) (18 Aug. 2014), http://m.kipa.co.il/now/56906.html.

BERGER, DAVID, *Cultures in Collision and Conversation: Essays in the Intellectual History of the Jews* (Boston: Academic Studies Press, 2011).

—— *The Rebbe, the Messiah, and the Scandal of Orthodox Indifference* (London: Littman Library of Jewish Civilization, 2001).

—— Review of Samuel C. Heilman and Steven M. Cohen, *Cosmopolitans and Parochials: Modern Orthodox Jews in America, Modern Judaism*, 11/2 (May 1991), 261–72.

BERGER, JOSEPH, *The Pious Ones: The World of Hasidim and Their Battles with America* (New York: HarperPerennial, 2014).

—— 'Rabbis Who Were Sages, Not Saints', *New York Times* (26 Apr. 2003), p. B7.

BERGER, MICHA, 'Brisk and Telz', *Kol Hamevaser* ('The Jewish Thought Magazine of the Yeshiva University Student Body') (23 Dec. 2010), 24–5.

BERGER, PETER L., 'A Bleak Outlook Is Seen for Religion', *New York Times* (25 Feb. 1968), 3.

—— (ed.), *The Desecularization of the World: Resurgent Religion and World Politics* (Washington, DC: Ethics and Public Policy Center; Grand Rapids, Mich.: Eerdmans, 1999).

—— 'Further Thoughts on Religion and Modernity', *Society*, 49/4 (July/Aug. 2012), 313–16.

—— *The Heretical Imperative: Contemporary Possibilities of Religious Affirmation* (Garden City, NY: Anchor Doubleday, 1979).

—— *The Many Altars of Modernity: Toward a Paradigm for Religion in a Pluralist Age* (Boston: De Gruyter, 2014).

—— *A Rumor of Angels: Modern Society and the Rediscovery of the Supernatural* (Garden City, NY: Doubleday, 1969).

—— *The Sacred Canopy: Elements of a Sociological Theory of Religion* (Garden City, NY: Doubleday, 1967).

BERGER, SHALOM Z., 'A Year of Study in an Israeli Yeshiva Program: Before and After', Ph.D. diss., Azrieli Graduate Institute for Jewish Education and Administration, Yeshiva University, 1997.

—— DANIEL JACOBSON, and CHAIM I. WAXMAN, *Flipping Out? Myth or Fact: The Impact of the 'Year in Israel'* (New York: Yashar Books, 2007).

BERGER, SHULAMITH Z., The Early History of the Young Israel Movement', unpublished YIVO seminar paper (Fall 1982).

BERKOVITZ, ELIEZER, *Not in Heaven: The Nature and Function of Halakha* (New York: Ktav, 1983).

—— *Stipulation in Marriage and Divorce* [Tenai benisu'in uveget: berurei halakhah] (Jerusalem: Mossad Harav Kook, 1967).

BERMAN, ELI, 'Sect, Subsidy, and Sacrifice: An Economist's View of Ultra-Orthodox Jews', *Quarterly Journal of Economics*, 115/3 (Aug. 2000), 905–53.

BIN-NUN, YOEL, 'On the Study of Tanakh in Yeshivas' (Heb.), in Yehoshua Reis (ed.), *My Constant Delight: Contemporary Religious Zionist Perspectives on Tanakh Study* [Hi siḥati: al derekh limud hatanakh] (Jerusalem: Maggid; Alon Shvut: Yeshivat Har Etzion/Herzog College, 2013), 157–80.

—— and BINYAMIN LAU, *Isaiah* [Yeshayahu] (Tel Aviv: Miskal-Yediot Ahronot/ Sifrei Hemed, 2013).

BIOR, HAIM, 'For Some Haredim, the IDF Serves as Gateway to Successful Career', *Haaretz* (18 Apr. 2015), http://www.haaretz.com/israel-news/business/premium-1.652326.

BIRGER, JON, 'What Two Religions Tell Us about the Dating Crisis', *Time* (24 Aug. 2015), http://time.com/dateonomics/.

BLAU, YITZCHAK, ALAN JOTKOWITZ, and REUVEN ZIEGLER (eds.), 'Studies in the Thought and Scholarship of Rabbi Aharon Lichtenstein zt"l', *Tradition*, 47/4 (Winter 2015), special issue.

BLAU, YOSEF (ed.), *The Conceptual Approach to Jewish Learning* (New York: Yeshiva University Press, 2006).

BLEICH, J. DAVID, *Contemporary Halakhic Problems*, vol. iv (New York: Ktav/Yeshiva University Press, 2011).

—— '"Lomdut" and "Pesak": Theoretical Analysis and Halakhic Decision-Making', in Yosef Blau (ed.), *The Conceptual Approach to Jewish Learning* (New York: Yeshiva University Press, 2006), 87–114.

—— 'Of Cerebral, Respiratory and Cardiac Death', *Tradition*, 24/3 (Spring 1989), 44–66.

BLEICH, J. DAVID, *Time of Death in Jewish Law* (Brooklyn: Z. Berman, 1991).

BLIDSTEIN, GERALD J., 'Halakha and Democracy', *Tradition*, 32/1 (Fall 1997), 6–39.

BLONDHEIM, MENAHEM, 'The Orthodox Rabbinate Discovers America: The Geography of the Mind in a Communication Matrix' (Heb.), in Miriam Eliav-Feldon (ed.), *Following Columbus: America 1492–1992* [Harabanut ha'ortodoksit megalah et amerikah] (Jerusalem: Zalman Shazar Center for Jewish History, 1996), 483–510.

BLUM, BRIAN, 'This Normal Life: Pick and Choose-daism', *Jerusalem Post Magazine* (19 June 2015), 33.

BLUMBERG, ANTONIO, 'The Hasidic Hipsters of Zusha Are Here to Rock the World of Jewish Music', *Huffington Post* (26 Oct. 2014), http://www.huffington post.com/2014/10/26/zusha-band_n_6043368.html.

BOBKER, JOE, 'To Flee or to Stay?', *Ḥakirah*, 9 (Winter 2010), 81–118.

BOCK, JANE D., 'Doing the Right Thing? Single Mothers by Choice and the Struggle for Legitimacy', *Gender & Society*, 14/1 (Feb. 2000), 62–86.

BOMZER, HERBERT W., *The Kollel in America* (New York: Sheingold, 1985).

BOROWITZ, EUGENE B., *A New Jewish Theology in the Making* (Philadelphia: Westminster Press, 1968).

BORSCHEL-DAN, AMANDA, 'Orthodox, Separate—and Almost Equal', *Times of Israel* (21 Nov. 2013), http://www.timesofisrael.com/orthodox-separate-and-almost-equal/.

BREGER, SARAH, 'Do 1 Rabba, 2 Rabbis and 1 Yeshiva = a New Denomination?', *Moment*, 35/6 (Nov./Dec. 2010), 38.

BREITOWITZ, IRVING A., *Between Civil and Religious Law: The Plight of the Agunah in American Society* (Westport, Conn.: Greenwood Press, 1993).

BRETTLER, MARC ZVI, and EDWARD BREUER, 'Jewish Readings of the Bible', in John Riches (ed.), *The New Cambridge History of the Bible: From 1750 to the Present*, vol. iv (Cambridge: Cambridge University Press, 2015), 285–313.

BREUER, MORDECHAI, *Modernity Within Tradition: The Social History of Orthodox Jewry in Imperial Germany*, trans. Elizabeth Petuchowski (New York: Columbia University Press, 1992).

—— 'The Study of Bible and the Primacy of the Fear of Heaven: Compatibility or Contradiction?', in Shalom Carmy (ed.), *Modern Scholarship in the Study of Torah: Contributions and Limitations*, Orthodox Forum series (Northvale, NJ: Jason Aronson, 1996), 159–80.

BRODBAR-NEMZER, JAY, 'Divorce and the Jewish Community: The Impact of Jewish Commitment', *Journal of Jewish Communal Service*, 61/2 (1984), 150–9.

BRODIE, ISRAEL, *The Strength of My Heart: Sermons and Addresses, 1948–1965* (London: G. George, 1969).

BRONNER, SIMON J., 'The Lieberman Syndrome: Public and Private Jewishness in American Political Culture', *Journal of Modern Jewish Studies*, 2/1 (Apr. 2003), 35–58.

BRONSPIEGEL, ABBA, 'Separate Prayer Quorums for Women' (Heb.), *Hadarom*, 54 (1985), 51–3.

BRONSTEIN, AVRAHAM, 'On Leaders and Followers in the Age of Big Torah', *Jerusalem Post* (28 Sept. 2015), http://www.jpost.com/landedpages/printarticle.aspx?id=419336.

BROWN, BENJAMIN, 'From Political Fortification to Cultural Fortification: The Hazon Ish and the Establishment of the Path of Haredi Jewry in Erets Yisra'el' (Heb.), in Mordechai Bar-On and Zvi Zameret (eds.), *Two Sides of the Bridge: Religion and State at the Beginning of Israel* [Shenei evrei hagesher: dat umedinah bereshit darkah shel yisra'el] (Jerusalem: Yad Izhak Ben-Zvi, 2002), 364–413.

—— 'The Hafets Hayim on the Halakhic Status of the Non-Observant' (Heb.), in Benjamin Brown, Menachem Lorberbaum, Avinoam Rosenak, and Yedidia Z. Stern (eds.), *Religion and Politics in Jewish Thought* [Al da'at hakahal: dat vepolitikah behagut hayehudit], vol. ii (Jerusalem: Israel Democracy Center and Zalman Shazar Center for Jewish History, 2012), 787–831.

—— *The Lithuanian Musar Movement: Personalities and Ideas* [Tenuat hamusar halita'it: ishim vera'ayonot] (Moshav Ben Shemen: Modan; Tel Aviv: Department of Defense Printing Office, 2014).

—— 'The Polemic of Da'at Torah in Religious Zionism: The Background, Positions, and Consequences' (Heb.), in Asher Cohen (ed.), *Religious Zionism: Era of Changes* [Hatsiyonut hadatit: idan hatemurot] (Jerusalem: Mosad Bialik, 2004), 422–74.

—— 'Stringency: Five Types from the Modern Era' (Heb.), *Dinei Yisrael*, 20–21 (2000/1), 123–237.

BROYDE, MICHAEL J., 'Hair Covering and Jewish Law: Biblical and Objective (*Dat Moshe*) or Rabbinic and Subjective (*Dat Yehudit*)?', *Tradition*, 42/3 (Fall 2009), 97–179.

—— 'The 1992 New York Get Law', *Tradition*, 29/4 (Summer 1995), 5–13.

—— and IRA BEDZOW, *The Codification of Jewish Law and an Introduction to the Jurisprudence of the 'Mishna Berura'* (Boston: Academic Studies Press, 2014).

—— and SHLOMO M. BRODY, 'Orthodox Women Rabbis? Tentative Thoughts That Distinguish Between the Timely and the Timeless', *Ḥakirah*, 11 (Spring 2011), 25–58.

—— and AVI WAGNER, 'Halachic Responses to Sociological and Technological Change', *Journal of Halacha and Contemporary Society*, 39 (2000), 95–122.

BRUNI, FRANK, 'Thousands Celebrate Completion of Talmud Study', *New York Times* (29 Sept. 1997), p. B1.

BULKA, REUVEN P. (ed.), *Dimensions of Orthodox Judaism* (New York: Ktav, 1983).

CAPLAN, KIMMY, 'The Beginning of "Hamizrahi" in America' (Heb.), *Contemporary Jewry*, 13 (1999), 173–206.

CAPLAN, KIMMY, 'Haredim and Western Culture: A View from Both Sides of the Ocean', in Meir Litvak (ed.), *Middle Eastern Societies and the West: Accommodation or Clash of Civilizations* (Tel Aviv: Moshe Dayan Center for Middle Eastern and African Studies, 2006), 269–88.

—— *Orthodoxy in the New World: Immigrant Rabbis and Preaching in America (1881–1924)* [Ortodoksiyah ba'olam heḥadash: rabanim vedarshanut be'amerikah] (Jerusalem: Zalman Shazar Center for Jewish History, 2002).

CATTAN, NACHA, 'Conservative Head Calls Sabbath-Driving Rule a "Mistake"', *Forward* (7 Nov. 2003), 1.

—— 'Judaic Studies Classes See Enrollment Boom', *Forward* (23 Jan. 2004), http://forward.com/culture/6176/judaic-studies-classes-see-enrollment-boom/.

CENTRAL CONFERENCE OF AMERICAN RABBIS, 'Resolution on Same Gender Officiation', 111th Convention (Mar. 2000), http://ccarnet.org/rabbis-speak/resolutions/all/same-gender-officiation/.

CHERLOW, YUVAL, 'Birth Without Marriage' (Heb.), pt. 1 (2007), http://ypt.co.il/beit-hamidrash/view.asp?id=4442; pt. 2, http://ypt.co.il/beit-hamidrash/view.asp?id=4452.

—— *The Private Sphere: Responsa Dealing with Modesty, Marriage and Family Given Over the Internet* [Reshut hayaḥid: teshuvot shenitnu ba'internet be'inyanei tseniyut, zugiyut umishpaḥah] (Petah Tikvah: Yeshivat Hesder Petah Tikvah, 2003).

CHERTOK, HAIM, *Stealing Home: Israel Bound and Rebound* (New York: Fordham University Press, 1988).

CHISWICK, CARMEL U., *Judaism in Transition: How Economic Choices Shape Religious Tradition* (Stanford: Stanford University Press, 2014).

CHRISTAKIS, NICHOLAS A., and JAMES H. FOWLER, *Connected: The Surprising Power of Our Social Networks and How They Shape Our Lives* (New York: Little, Brown, 2009).

COHEN, NAOMI W., *American Jews and the Zionist Idea* (Hoboken, NJ: Ktav, 1975).

—— *Encounter with Emancipation: The German Jews in the United States, 1830–1914* (Philadelphia: Jewish Publication Society of America, 1984).

COHEN, STEVEN M., 'Non-Denominational and Post-Denominational: Two Tendencies in American Jewry', *Contact*, 7/4 (Summer 2005), 7–8.

—— 'Profiling the Jewish Studies Profession in North America: Highlights from the Survey of AJS Members', http://www.ajsnet.org/surveys/AJS-2014–Full-Survey-Report.pdf.

—— 'Profiling the Professionals: Who's Serving Our Communities?', Berman Jewish Policy Archive (2010), http://www.bjpa.org/Publications/details.cfm?PublicationID=7471.

—— *Ties and Tensions: The 1986 Survey of American Jewish Attitudes Toward Israel and Israelis* (New York: American Jewish Committee, 1987).

——JACOB B. UKELES, and RON MILLER, *Jewish Community Study of New York: 2011 Comprehensive Report* (New York: UJA-Federation of New York, 2012).

——and JUDITH VEINSTEIN, 'The 2008 Association for Jewish Studies Membership Survey' (27 Apr. 2008), http://www.ajsnet.org/survey.pdf.

COHN, WERNER, 'The Politics of American Jews', in Marshall Sklare (ed.), *The Jews: Social Patterns of an American Group* (New York: The Free Press, 1958), 614–26.

COOLEY, CHARLES HORTON, *Human Nature and the Social Order* (New York: Scribner's, 1902).

CRABTREE, STEVE, 'Religiosity Highest in World's Poorest Nations' (31 Aug. 2010), http://www.gallup.com/poll/142727/religiosity-highest-world-poorest-nations. aspx.

DAUM, MENACHEM, and OREN RUDAVSKY (dir.), *A Life Apart: Hasidim in America* (1997).

DAVIDMAN, LYNN, *Becoming Un-Orthodox: Stories of Ex-Hasidic Jews* (New York: Oxford University Press, 2014).

DAVIS, MOSHE, *The Emergence of Conservative Judaism: The Historical School in 19th Century America* (Philadelphia: Jewish Publication Society of America, 1963).

DAVIS, NANCY J., and ROBERT V. ROBINSON, 'Religious Orthodoxy in American Society: The Myth of a Monolithic Camp', *Journal for the Scientific Study of Religion*, 35/3 (Sept. 1996), 229–45.

DEEN, SHULEM, *All Who Go Do Not Return: A Memoir* (Minneapolis: Graywolf Press, 2015).

DEITSCH, CHAYA, *Here and There: Leaving Hasidism, Keeping My Family* (New York: Schocken, 2015).

DELLAPERGOLA, SERGIO, 'World Jewish Population, 2015', in Arnold Dashefsky and Ira M. Sheskin (eds.), *American Jewish Year Book 2015* (Dordrecht: Springer, 2015), 273–364.

——AMOS GILBOA, and RAMI TAL (eds.), *The Jewish People Policy Planning Institute Planning Assessment, 2004–2005: The Jewish People between Thriving and Decline* (Jerusalem: Jewish People Policy Planning Institute, 2005).

——and UZI REBHUN, 'Sociodemographic and Identification Aspects of Sephardi and Ashkenazi Jews in the United States, 1990' (Heb.), in Michel Abitbol, Galit Hazan-Rokem, and Yom Tov Assis (eds.), *Hispano-Jewish Civilization after 1492* [Moreshet yahadut sefarad vehamizraḥ] (Jerusalem: Misgav Yeru-shalayim, 1997), 105–35.

DESSLER, ELIYAHU ELIEZER, 'Letters of Rabbi Eliyahu Eliezer Dessler, author of *Mikhtav me'eliyahu*' (Heb.), *Oraita* [Netanya], 15 (Apr. 1986), 310–15.

DEUTSCH, HAYUTA, *Neḥama: The Life of Nehama Leibowitz* [Neḥamah: sipur ḥayeha shel neḥamah leibowitz] (Tel Aviv: Miskal-Yediot Ahronot, 2008).

DEUTSCH, SHAUL SHIMON, *Larger Than Life: The Life and Times of the Lubavitcher Rebbe Rabbi Menachem Mendel Schneerson*, 2 vols. (New York: Chasidic Historical Productions, 1995, 1997).

DIAMOND, ETAN, *And I Will Dwell in Their Midst: Orthodox Jews in Suburbia* (Chapel Hill: University of North Carolina Press, 2000).

DINARI, YEDIDYA ALTER, *The Rabbis of Germany and Austria at the Close of the Middle Ages: Their Conceptions and Halakhic Writings* [Ḥakhmei ashkenaz beshilhei yemei habeinayim: darkheihem vekitveihem behalakhah] (Jerusalem: Bialik Institute, 1984).

DOUGLAS, MARY, *Purity and Danger: An Analysis of the Concepts of Pollution and Taboo* (London: Ark Paperbacks, 1984).

DOUTHAT, ROSS, 'Can Liberal Christianity Be Saved?', *New York Times* (15 July 2012), p. SR11.

DUBOWSKI, SANDI SIMCHA (dir.), *Trembling Before G-d* (San Marino, Calif.: Cinephil; Tel Aviv: Keshet Broadcasting, 2001).

DUGAN, GEORGE, 'Orthodox Rabbis to Meet Upstate', *New York Times* (25 June 1966), 16.

DURKHEIM, ÉMILE, *The Elementary Forms of Religious Life* (New York: The Free Press, 1968).

—— *The Rules of the Sociological Method* (New York: Free Press of Glencoe, 1964).

DÜWELL, MARCUS, *Bioethics: Methods, Theories, Domains* (London: Routledge, 2012).

EHRLICH, YIFAT, 'A Full Stomach' (Heb.), *Makor Rishon* (8 May 2009), Dyokan Magazine, 10–14.

EIDENSOHN, DANIEL, *Child and Domestic Abuse*, 2 vols. (Jerusalem: Emunah Press, 2010).

—— 'Child and Domestic Abuse: Compact Practical Guide' (CreateSpace, 2011), http://chabadinfo.com/crown_heights/tomorrow-crown-heights-asifa-to-combat-child-abuse/.

EISEN, ROBERT, 'Jewish Studies and the Academic Teaching of Religion', *Liberal Education*, 87/4 (Fall 2001), 14–17.

EISENSTADT, BEN-ZION, *Rabbis and Writers of the Generation*, v: *Jewish Sages in America* [Dor rabanav vesofrav, v: ḥakhmei yisra'el be'amerikah] (New York: A. H. Rosenberg, 1902).

ELAZAR, DANIEL J., *The Other Jews: The Sephardim Today* (New York: Basic Books, 1989).

ELBERG, RABBI SIMCHA, 'Benai Berakism' (Heb.), *Hapardes*, 38/3 (Nov./Dec. 1963), 5.

ELEFF, ZEV, and MENACHEM BUTLER, 'How Bat Mitzvah Became Orthodox', *Torah Musings* (26 May 2016), http://www.torahmusings.com/2016/05/bat-mitzvah-became-orthodox/.

ELLENSON, DAVID, *Rabbi Esriel Hildesheimer and the Creation of a Modern Jewish Orthodoxy* (Tuscaloosa: University of Alabama Press, 1990).

—— *Tradition in Transition: Orthodoxy, Halakhah, and the Boundaries of Modern Jewish Identity* (Lanham, Md.: University Press of America, 1989).

ELLIS, CHRISTOPHER, and JAMES A. STIMSON, *Ideology in America* (Cambridge: Cambridge University Press, 2012), 115–48.

ELON, MENACHEM, *Jewish Law: History, Sources, Principles*, vol. ii, trans. Bernard Auerbach and Melvin J. Sykes (Philadelphia: Jewish Publication Society of America, 1994).

ENGELBERG, ARI, 'Religious Zionist Singles and Late-Modern Youth Culture', *Israel Studies Review*, 28/2 (Winter 2013), 1–17.

—— 'Seeking a "Pure Relationship"? Israeli Religious-Zionist Singles Looking for Love and Marriage', *Religion*, 41/3 (2011), 431–48.

ENGELMAN, URIAH ZVI, 'Jewish Statistics in the US Census of Religious Bodies (1850–1936)', *Jewish Social Studies*, 9/2 (Apr. 1947), 127–74.

ETKES, IMMANUEL, *Rabbi Israel Salanter and the Mussar Movement: Seeking the Torah of Truth*, trans. Jonathan Chipman (Philadelphia: Jewish Publication Society of America, 1993).

ETTINGER, YAIR, 'Of Pride and Prayer', *Haaretz* (26 Feb. 2009), http://www.haaretz.com/of-pride-and-prayer-1.271022.

FARBER, ROBERTA ROSENBERG, 'The Programmatic Response of the Ultra-Orthodox American Jewish Community to Wife Abuse: Social Change within a Traditional Religious Community', *Contemporary Jewry*, 26 (2006), 114–57.

FARBER, SETH, *An American Orthodox Dreamer: Rabbi Joseph B. Soloveitchik and Boston's Maimonides School* (Waltham, Mass.: Brandeis University Press, 2004).

FARBER, ZEV (ed.), *Halakhic Realities: Collected Essays on Brain Death* (Jerusalem: Maggid, 2015).

FEIGE, MICHAEL, *Settling in the Hearts: Jewish Fundamentalism in the Occupied Territories* (Detroit: Wayne State University Press, 2009).

FEINSTEIN, RABBI MOSHE, *Igerot mosheh, Even ha'ezer*: pt. 1 (New York, 1961); pt. 2 (New York, 1964); pt. 4 (New York, 1964).

—— *Igerot mosheh, Ḥoshen mishpat* (New York, 1964).

—— *Igerot mosheh, Oraḥ ḥayim*: pt. 1 (New York, 1959); pt. 2 (New York, 1964); pt. 3 (New York, 1973); pt. 4 (Jerusalem, 1982); pt. 5 (Jerusalem, 1996).

—— *Igerot mosheh, Yoreh de'ah*: pt. 1 (New York, 1959); pt. 2 (New York, 1973); pt. 3 (Brooklyn, 1982); pt. 4 (Jerusalem, 1996).

FELDMAN, AHARON, 'Halakhic Feminism or Feminist Halakha?', *Tradition*, 33/2 (Winter 1999), 61–79.

FERST, DEVRA, and JANE EISNER, 'Jewish Women Lag Behind Men in Promotion and Pay', *Forward* (17 Dec. 2010), 1, 6.

FERZIGER, ADAM S., *Beyond Sectarianism: The Realignment of American Orthodox Judaism* (Detroit: Wayne State University Press, 2015).

—— *Centered on Study: Typologies of the American Community Kollel*, Research and Position Papers 18 (Bar-Ilan: Rappaport Center for Assimilation Research and Strengthening Jewish Vitality, 2009).

—— *Exclusion and Hierarchy: Orthodoxy, Nonobservance, and the Emergence of Modern Jewish Identity* (Philadelphia: University of Pennsylvania Press, 2005).

—— *Training American Orthodox Rabbis to Play a Role in Confronting Assimilation: Programs, Methodologies and Directions*, Research and Position Papers 4 (Bar-Ilan: Rappaport Center for Assimilation Research and Strengthening Jewish Vitality, 2003).

FINKE, ROGER, 'Demographics of Religious Participation: An Ecological Approach, 1850–1980', *Journal for the Scientific Study of Religion*, 28/1 (Mar. 1989), 45–58.

FINKELMAN, YOEL, 'Haredi Isolation in Changing Environments: A Case Study in Yeshiva Immigration', *Modern Judaism*, 22/1 (Feb. 2002), 61–82.

—— 'An Ideology for American Yeshiva Students: The Sermons of R. Aharon Kotler', *Journal of Jewish Studies*, 58/2 (Autumn 2007), 314–32.

—— 'A Prayer Book of One's Own', *First Things*, 196 (Oct. 2009), 11–12.

—— *Strictly Kosher Reading: Popular Literature and the Condition of Contemporary Orthodoxy* (Boston: Academic Studies Press, 2011).

FINKELSTEIN, BARUCH, 'Characteristics and Patterns in Rabbi Moshe Feinstein's Rulings Regarding Questions of Fertility, Contraception and Abortion' [Me'afyanei pesikah shel harav mosheh feinshtein le'or pesakav bishe'elot legabei poriyut, meniyat herayon, vehapalah], MA diss., Talmud Department, Bar-Ilan University, Ramat Gan, 2006.

FISCHLER, MARCELLE S., 'Hofstra's Law Dean Stands Out, But Still Fits In', *New York Times* (18 Sept. 2005), p. LI4.

FISHKOFF, SUE, *The Rebbe's Army: Inside the World of Chabad-Lubavitch* (New York: Schocken, 2003).

FISKE, EDWARD, 'Rabbi's Rabbi Keeps the Law Up to Date', *New York Times* (23 June 1972), 39.

FRANCES, YAAKOV (KOBY), 'A Qualitative Study of Sexual-Religious Conflict in Single Orthodox Jewish Men', Ph.D. diss., Graduate Faculty in Psychology, City University of New York, 2008.

FREEDMAN, SAMUEL G., *Jew vs. Jew: The Struggle for the Soul of American Jewry* (New York: Simon & Schuster, 2000).

FREEZE, CHAERAN, *Jewish Marriage and Divorce in Imperial Russia* (Hanover, NH: University Press of New England/Brandeis University Press, 2001).

FREUD-KANDEL, MIRI J., *Orthodox Judaism in Britain since 1913: An Ideology Forsaken* (London: Vallentine Mitchell, 2006).

FRIEDMAN, MENACHEM, 'Life Tradition and Book Tradition', in Harvey E. Goldberg (ed.), *Judaism Viewed from Within and from Without: Anthropological Studies* (Albany: State University of New York Press, 1987), 235–55.

FRIEDMAN, MICHELLE, 'On Intimacy, Love, *Kedushah* and Sexuality: Reflections on the 5th Annual YCT Rabbinical School/Community Yom Iyyun in Conjunction with Congregation Ohab Zedek', *Milin Havivin*, 2 (2006), 185–8.

FRIESEL, EVYATAR, 'The Meaning of Zionism and Its Influence among the American Jewish Religious Movements', in Shmuel Almog, Jehuda Reinharz, and Anita Shapira (eds.), *Zionism and Religion* (Hanover, NH: University Press of New England/Brandeis University Press, 1998), 175–86.

FRIMER, ARYEH A., and DOV I. FRIMER, 'Women's Prayer Services—Theory and Practice', *Tradition*, 32/2 (Winter 1998), 5–118.

FUCHS, LAWRENCE H., *The Political Behavior of American Jews* (Glencoe, Ill.: The Free Press, 1956).

GALINSKY, JUDAH D., 'On Popular Halakhic Literature and the Jewish Reading Audience in Fourteenth-Century Spain', *Jewish Quarterly Review*, 98/3 (Summer 2008), 305–27.

GEERTZ, CLIFFORD, *Local Knowledge: Further Essays in Interpretive Anthropology* (New York: Basic Books, 1983).

GELLER, VICTOR B., *Orthodoxy Awakens: The Belkin Era and Yeshiva University* (Jerusalem: Urim Publications, 2003).

GELLMAN, YEHUDA JEROME, *This Was From God: A Contemporary Theology of Torah and History* (Boston: Academic Studies Press, 2016).

GLOCK, CHARLES Y., and RODNEY STARK, *Religion and Society in Tension* (Chicago: Rand McNally, 1965).

GOFFMAN, ERVING, *Encounters: Two Studies in the Sociology of Interaction* (Indianapolis: Bobbs-Merrill, 1961).

GOLDBERG, HAROLD, 'Dr. Greenberg Discusses Orthodoxy, YU, Viet Nam & Sex', *The Commentator* (28 Apr. 1966), 6 ff.

GOLDBERG, HILLEL, *Israel Salanter, Text, Structure, Idea: The Ethics and Theology of an Early Psychologist of the Unconscious* (New York: Ktav, 1982).

GOLDBERG, NATHAN, JACOB LESTCHINSKY, and MAX WEINREICH, *The Classification of Jewish Immigrants and Its Implications, a Survey of Opinion: 140 Replies to a Questionnaire and Papers* (New York: YIVO Institute for Jewish Research, 1945).

GOLDMAN, ARI L., 'The Jewish "Newsroom"', *Jewish Week* (6 Jan. 2016), http://www.thejewishweek.com/news/new-york/jewish-newsroom.

GOLDSCHEIDER, CALVIN, 'Childlessness and Religiosity: An Exploratory Analysis' (1969), repr. in Uziel O. Schmelz, Paul Glickson, and Sergio DellaPergola (eds.), *Papers in Jewish Demography* (Jerusalem: Hebrew University Institute of Contemporary Jewry, 1973).

GOLDSCHEIDER, CALVIN, 'Family Changes and the Challenge to American Orthodoxy: The Implications of Recent Social Science Data', *Tradition*, 23/1 (Summer
1987), 71–81.

GOLDSTEIN, SIDNEY, and CALVIN GOLDSCHEIDER, *Jewish Americans: Three
Generations in a Jewish Community* (Englewood Cliffs, NJ: Prentice Hall,
1968).

GOODMAN, YONA, 'Religious Zionist Youth on the Internet: Extent of the Situation
and Dealing with It Educationally' (Heb.), *Tsohar*, 33 (Summer 2008), 85–94.

GORDIS, DANIEL, 'Conservative Judaism: A Requiem', *Jewish Review of Books*
(Winter 2014), http://jewishreviewofbooks.com/articles/566/requiem-for-a-
movement/.

GOREN, SHLOMO, *Medical Torah: Halakhic Studies in Medicine* [Torat harefuah:
meḥkarim hilkhatiyim benosei refuah] (Jerusalem: Ha-idra Raba and Mesora
La-am, 2001).

GOTTLIEB, MICHAH, 'How Conservative Judaism Lost Me—the Reason I Drifted
Away: I Wasn't Wanted', *Forward* (8 Nov. 2013), 9; http://forward.com/articles/
186693/how-conservative-judaism-lost-me/.

GRAHAM, DAVID, 'Enumerating Britain's Jewish Population: Reassessing the
2001 Census in the Context of One Hundred Years of Indirect Estimates',
Jewish Journal of Sociology, 53 (2011), 7–28.

GRAZI, RICHARD V., *Overcoming Infertility: A Guide for Jewish Couples* (New Milford,
Conn.: Toby Press, 2005).

GREENBERG, IRVING, 'Greenberg Clarifies and Defends His Views', *The
Commentator* (12 May 1966), 8–9.

GREENBERG, STEVEN, 'The Orthodox Bookshelf: A Response to Asher Lopatin',
Edah Journal, 5/2 (2006), 2–5.

——*Wrestling with God and Men: Homosexuality in the Jewish Tradition* (Madison:
University of Wisconsin Press, 2004).

GRINSTEIN, HYMAN B., 'The Efforts of East European Jewry to Organize Its Own
Community in the United States', *Publications of the American Jewish Historical
Society*, 49/2 (Dec. 1959), 73–89.

—— *The Rise of the Jewish Community of New York, 1654–1860* (Philadelphia: Jewish
Publication Society of America, 1945).

GROSS, MAX, 'Exercising to a Rabbinic Beat', *Forward* (7 May 2004), 15.

GROSSMAN, AVRAHAM, 'The Origins of Martyrdom in Early Ashkenaz' (Heb.), in
Isaiah M. Gafni and Aviezer Ravitzky (eds.), *Sanctity of Life and Martyrdom:
Studies in Memory of Amir Yekutiel* [Kedushat haḥayim veḥeruf hanefesh]
(Jerusalem: Zalman Shazar Center for Jewish History, 1992), 99–130.

GROSSMAN, LAWRENCE, 'In What Sense Did Orthodoxy Believe the Torah To Be
Divine?', http://thetorah.com/in-what-sense-did-orthodoxy-believe-the-torah-
to-be-divine/.

GUROCK, JEFFREY S., *American Jewish Orthodoxy in Historical Perspective* (Hoboken, NJ: Ktav, 1996).

—— 'American Orthodox Organizations in Support of Zionism, 1880–1930', in Shmuel Almog, Jehuda Reinharz, and Anita Shapira (eds.), *Zionism and Religion* (Hanover, NH: Brandeis University Press, 1998), 219–34.

—— *Judaism's Encounter with American Sports* (Bloomington: Indiana University Press, 2005).

—— *The Men and Women of Yeshiva: Higher Education, Orthodoxy, and American Judaism* (New York: Columbia University Press, 1988).

—— (ed.), *Ramaz: School, Community, Scholarship, and Orthodoxy* (Hoboken, NJ: Ktav, 1989).

—— 'Twentieth-Century American Orthodoxy's Era of Non-Observance 1900–1960', *Torah U-Madda Journal*, 9 (2000), 87–107.

GUTEL, NERIA MOSHE, *Natural Changes in Halakhah* [Sefer hishtanut tiviyim behalakhah] (Jerusalem: Yahdav, 1995).

GUTTMAN, NATHAN, 'Eric Goldstein, New York Federation Chief, Is Not Outsider His Profile Suggests', *Forward* (31 Jan. 2014), http://forward.com/news/191917/eric-goldstein-new-york-federation-chief-is-not-ou/.

—— 'Jack Lew's Life Shaped by Faith and Service', *Forward* (25 Jan. 2013), 1, 7.

HACOHEN, AVIAD, 'Minhag America', in Simcha Goldin, Naomi Feuchtwanger-Sarig, Joseph Isaac Lifshitz, Jean Baumgarten, and Hasia Diner (eds.), *Minhagim: Custom and Practice in Jewish Life* (Berlin: Walter de Gruyter, forthcoming).

HACOHEN, ISRAEL MEIR, 'Kuntres nefutsot yisra'el', in id., *Shem olam*, vol. ii (Warsaw: Unterhendler, 1897), 31–46.

—— *Mishnah berurah*, 5 vols. (New York: Rabbi Mendel Zaks, 1952).

—— *Nidḥei yisra'el* (Warsaw: Halter & Eisenstadt, 1894).

HACOHEN, SHMUEL AVIDOR, *Unique in His Generation: A Biography of Chief Rabbi Isaac Halevi Herzog* [Yaḥid bedoro: harav yitsḥak halevi hertsog] (Jerusalem: Keter, 1980), 161–4.

HALEVI, YOSSI KLEIN, *Like Dreamers: The Story of the Israeli Paratroopers Who Reunited Jerusalem and Divided a Nation* (New York: HarperCollins, 2013).

HALIVNI, DAVID WEISS, *The Book and the Sword: A Life of Learning in the Shadow of Destruction* (New York: Farrar, Straus & Giroux, 1996).

HALLAMISH, MOSHE, and DOV SCHWARTZ, 'Edut le'aharon: Jubilee Volume in Honor of Rabbi Dr. Aharon Lichtenstein' (Heb.), *Da'at*, 76 (2014), special issue.

HARRIS, LIS, *Holy Days: The World of a Hasidic Family* (New York: Summit, 1985).

HARRIS, MICHAEL J., *Faith Without Fear* (London: Vallentine Mitchell, 2016).

HARTMAN, HARRIET, and MOSHE HARTMAN, *Gender and American Jews: Patterns in Work, Education, and Family in Contemporary Life* (Hanover, NH: Brandeis University Press/University Press of New England, 2009).

HEFTER, HERZL, '"In God's Hands": The Religious Phenomenology of R. Mordechai Yosef of Izbica', *Tradition*, 46/1 (Spring 2013), 43–65.

—— 'Why I Ordained Women', *Times of Israel* (19 July 2015), http:// blogs.timesof israel.com/why-i-ordained-women/.

HEHASID, JUDAH, *Sefer haḥasidim*, ed. Reuven Margoliot, expanded edn. (Jerusalem: Mossad Harav Kook, 2004).

HEILMAN, SAMUEL C., *Defenders of the Faith: Inside Ultra-Orthodox Jewry* (New York: Schocken, 1992).

—— *The People of the Book: Drama, Fellowship, and Religion* (Chicago: University of Chicago Press, 1983).

—— and STEVEN M. COHEN, *Cosmopolitans and Parochials: Modern Orthodox Jews in America* (Chicago: University of Chicago Press, 1989).

—— and MENACHEM FRIEDMAN, *The Rebbe: The Life and Afterlife of Menachem Mendel Schneerson* (Princeton, NJ: Princeton University Press, 2010).

HEILMAN, URIEL, 'Is Kosher Switch Really Kosher for Shabbat?', Jewish Telegraphic Agency (16 Apr. 2015), http://www.jta.org/2015/04/16/news-opinion/ united-states/is-kosher-switch-really-kosher-for-shabbat/.

HELFGOT, NATHANIEL (ed.), *Community, Covenant, and Commitment: Selected Letters and Communications of Rabbi Joseph B. Soloveitchik* (Jersey City, NJ: Ktav/Toras HoRav Foundation, 2005).

—— (comp.), 'Statement of Principles', http://statementofprinciplesnya.blogspot. co.il/.

HELMREICH, WILLIAM B., *Against All Odds: Holocaust Survivors and the Successful Lives They Made in America* (New York: Simon & Schuster, 1992).

—— *The World of the Yeshiva: An Intimate Portrait of Orthodox Jewry* (New York: The Free Press, 1982).

HENKIN, YEHUDA HERZL, 'Beware of What May Develop' (Heb.), *Akdamot*, 17 (2006), 33–40.

HENSHEL, RICHARD L., 'Sociology and Prediction', *The American Sociologist*, 6/3 (Aug. 1971), 213–20.

HERMANN, TAMAR, GILAD BE'ERY, ELLA HELLER, CHANAN COHEN, YUVAL LEBEL, HANAN MOZES, and KALMAN NEUMAN, *The National-Religious Sector in Israel 2014* [Datiyim? Le'umiyim! Hamaḥaneh hadati-le'umi beyisra'el 2014] (Jerusalem: Israel Democracy Institute, 2014).

HERRING, BASIL, and KENNETH AUMAN (eds.), *The Prenuptial Agreement: Halakhic and Pastoral Considerations* (Northvale, NJ: Jason Aronson, 1996).

HERRMANN, MICHELE, 'Behind the News: Yeshiva Hit Hard by Madoff Scam; Other Higher Ed Institutions Affected', *University Business*, 12/2 (Feb. 2009), 12.

HERTZ, JOSEPH H. (trans. and commentary), *The Pentateuch and Haftorahs*, 2nd edn. (London: Soncino Press, 1963).

HERTZ, ROSANNA, *Single by Chance, Mothers by Choice* (New York: Oxford University Press, 2008).

HERTZBERG, ARTHUR, '"Treifene Medina": Learned Opposition to Emigration to the United States', in *Proceedings of the Eighth World Congress of Jewish Studies* (Jerusalem: World Union of Jewish Studies, 1984).

HERZL, THEODOR, *Old-New Land*, trans. Lotta Levensohn (New York: Bloch, 1960).

IIESCIIEL, ABRAHAM JOSHUA, *Israel: An Echo of Eternity* (New York, Farrar, Straus & Giroux, 1969).

HIMMELFARB, MILTON, 'The Jewish Vote (Again)', *Commentary*, 55/6 (June 1973), 81–5.

HIRSCH, SAMSON RAPHAEL, *Collected Writings*, vol. vi (New York: Feldheim, 1990).

HOCHBAUM, MARTIN, *The Jewish Vote in the 1984 Presidential Election* (New York: American Jewish Congress, Commission on National Affairs, 1985).

HOLLANDER, AVIAD YEHIEL, 'The Relationship between Halakhic Decisors and Their Peers as a Determining Factor in the Acceptance of Their Decisions: A Step in Understanding Interpeer Effects in Halakhic Discourse', *Jewish Law Association Studies*, 20 (2010), 96–108.

HOROWITZ, ISAIAH, *Shenei luḥot haberit* (Jerusalem, 1972).

HUNTER, JAMES DAVISON, *Culture Wars: The Struggle to Define America* (New York: HarperCollins, 1991).

—— *Evangelicalism: The Coming Generation* (Chicago: University of Chicago Press, 1987).

IRSHAI, RONIT, 'Dignity, Honor, and Equality in Contemporary Halachic Thinking: The Case of Torah Reading by Women in Israeli Modern Orthodoxy', *Modern Judaism*, 33/3 (Oct. 2013), 332–56.

IRWIN, MICHAEL D., CHARLES M. TOLBERT, and THOMAS LYSON, 'There's No Place Like Home: Nonmigration and Civic Engagement', *Environment and Planning A*, 31/12 (Dec. 1999), 2223–38.

JACOBS, LOUIS, *Beyond Reasonable Doubt* (Oxford: Littman Library of Jewish Civilization, 2004).

—— *God, Torah, Israel: Traditionalism without Fundamentalism* (Cincinnati: Hebrew Union College Press, 1990).

—— *Helping with Inquiries: An Autobiography* (London: Vallentine Mitchell, 1989).

—— *The Jewish Religion: A Companion* (Oxford: Oxford University Press, 1995).

—— *A Tree of Life: Diversity, Flexibility, and Creativity in Jewish Law*, 2nd edn. (Oxford: Littman Library of Jewish Civilization, 2000).

—— *We Have Reason to Believe*, 1st edn. (London: Vallentine Mitchell, 1957).

JAKOBOVITS, IMMANUEL, 'Deans and Rabbis, Part 2: Survey of Recent Periodical Halakhic Literature', *Tradition*, 8/2 (Summer 1966), 74–9.

JAPHET, SARA, 'The Establishment and Early History of the Bible Department' (Heb.), in Hagit Lavski (ed.), *History of the Hebrew University of Jerusalem: Realization and Growth* [Toledot ha'universitah ha'ivrit biyerushalayim: hitbosesut utsemiḥah] (Jerusalem: Magnes Press, 2005), 283–303.

—— 'Major Trends in the Study of Medieval Jewish Exegesis in Northern France', *Terumah*, 9 (2000), 43–61.

JEWISH TELEGRAPHIC AGENCY, 'In Protest, Rabbi Avi Weiss Quits Rabbinical Council of America' (29 June 2015), http://www.jta.org/2015/06/29/news-opinion/united-states/in-protest-rabbi-avi-weiss-quits-rabbinical-council-of-america/.

JICK, LEON A., *The Americanization of the Synagogue, 1820–1870* (Hanover, NH: University Press of New England/Brandeis University Press, 1976).

—— 'The Transformation of Jewish Social Work', *Journal of Jewish Communal Service*, 75/2 (Winter 1998), 114–20.

JOHNSTON, WM. ROBERT, 'Worldwide Abortions by Region and Year, 1922–2014', http://www.johnstonsarchive.net/policy/abortion/worldabortiontally.html/.

JOSELIT, JENNA WEISSMAN, *New York's Jewish Jews: The Orthodox Community in the Interwar Years* (Bloomington: Indiana University Press, 1990).

JOSEPH, NORMA BAUMEL, 'Ritual, Law, and Praxis: An American Response to Bat Mitsva Celebrations', *Modern Judaism*, 22/3 (Oct. 2002), 234–60.

JUERGENSMEYER, MARK, *Global Rebellion: Religious Challenges to the Secular State, from Christian Militias to Al Qaeda* (Berkeley: University of California Press, 2008).

—— *The New Cold War? Religious Nationalism Confronts the Secular State* (Berkeley: University of California Press, 1993).

KAHANA, MAOZ, 'The Hatam Sofer: The Decisor in His Own Eyes' (Heb.), *Tarbiz*, 76/3–4 (2007), 519–56.

KAMENETSKY, NATHAN, *Making of a Godol: A Study of Episodes in the Lives of Great Torah Personalities*, 2 vols. (Jerusalem: Hamesorah, 2002).

KAMENETSKY, YAAKOV, *Emet leya'akov: iyunim bemikra al nevi'im ukhetuvim*, ed. Yosef Kamenetsky, 2 vols. (Jerusalem, 2015).

KAPLAN, ARTHUR L., and ROBERT ARP (eds.), *Contemporary Debates in Bioethics* (Oxford: Wiley Blackwell, 2014).

KAPLAN, LAWRENCE, '*Daas Torah*: A Modern Conception of Rabbinic Authority', in Moshe Sokol (ed.), *Rabbinic Authority and Personal Autonomy*, Orthodox Forum series (Northvale, NJ: Jason Aronson, 1992), 1–60.

—— 'From Cooperation to Conflict: Rabbi Professor Emanuel Rackman, Rav Joseph B. Soloveitchik, and the Evolution of American Modern Orthodoxy', *Modern Judaism*, 30/1 (Feb. 2010), 46–68.

KAPLAN, SARAH, 'When Are You Dead? It May Depend on Which Hospital Makes the Call', *Washington Post* (29 Dec. 2015), https://www.washingtonpost.com/news/morning-mix/wp/2015/12/29/when-are-you-dead-it-may-depend-on-which-hospital-makes-the-call/.

KARP, ABRAHAM J., 'The Ridwas, Rabbi Jacob David Wilowsky, 1845–1913', in Arthur A. Chiel (ed.), *Perspectives on Jews and Judaism: Essays in Honor of Wolfe Kelman* (New York: Rabbinical Assembly, 1978), 215–37.

KATZ, DOVID, *Lithuanian Jewish Culture* (Budapest: Central European University Press, 2010).

KATZ, JACOB, *Divine Law in Human Hands: Case Studies in Halakhic Flexibility* (Jerusalem: Magnes Press, 1998).

——*Emancipation and Assimilation: Studies in Modern Jewish History* (Farnborough: Gregg International, 1972).

——'Orthodoxy in Historical Perspective', in Peter Y. Medding (ed.), *The Challenge of Modernity and Jewish Orthodoxy*, Studies in Contemporary Jewry 2 (Bloomington: Indiana University Press, 1986), 3–17.

—— The *'Shabbes Goy': A Study in Halakhic Flexibility*, trans. Yoel Lerner (Philadelphia: Jewish Publication Society of America, 1989).

—— *Tradition and Crisis: Jewish Society at the End of the Middle Ages*, trans. Bernard Dov Cooperman (New York: New York University Press, 1993).

—— *With My Own Eyes: The Autobiography of an Historian*, trans. Ann Brenner and Ziporah Brody (Waltham, Mass.: Brandeis University Press, 1995).

KATZ, STEVEN T., and STEVEN BAYME (eds.), *Continuity and Change: A Festschrift in Honor of Irving Greenberg's 75th Birthday* (Lanham, Md.: University Press of America, 2010).

KELEMEN, LAWRENCE, *To Kindle a Soul* (Southfield, Mich.: Targum Press, 2001).

KELLEY, DEAN M., *Why Conservative Churches Are Growing* (New York: Harper & Row, 1972).

KELLNER, MENACHEM, 'Louis Jacobs' Doctrine of Revelation', *Tradition*, 14/4 (Fall 1974), 143–7.

—— *Maimonides' Confrontation with Mysticism* (Oxford: Littman Library of Jewish Civilization, 2006).

—— *Maimonides on the 'Decline of the Generations' and the Nature of Rabbinic Authority* (Albany: State University of New York Press, 1996).

—— *Must a Jew Believe Anything?* (London: Littman Library of Jewish Civilization, 1999).

KELMAN, ARI Y., *The Reality of the Virtual: Looking for Jewish Leadership Online* (New York: Avi Chai Foundation, 2010).

KEREN-KRATZ, MENACHEM, 'Rabbi Joel Teitelbaum—the Satmar Rebbe (1887–1979): Biography' [R' yo'el teitelbaum—harabi mesatmar], Ph.D. diss., Department of Jewish History, Tel Aviv University, 2013.

KLAPERMAN, GILBERT, *The Story of Yeshiva University: The First Jewish University in America* (New York: Macmillan, 1969).

KLIGMAN, MARK, 'Contemporary Jewish Music in America', in David Singer (ed.), *American Jewish Year Book*, 101 (Dordrecht: Springer, 2001), 88–141.

——'On the Creators and Consumers of Orthodox Popular Music in Brooklyn', *YIVO Annual*, 23 (1996), 259–93.

——'Recent Trends in New American Jewish Music', in Dana Evan Kaplan (ed.), *The Cambridge Companion to American Judaism* (New York: Cambridge University Press, 2005), 363–80.

KOOK, ABRAHAM ISAAC HAKOHEN, *Mishpat kohen*, 2nd, corrected and expanded, edn. (Jerusalem: Mossad Harav Kook, 1966).

KORN, EUGENE, 'The Man of Faith and Religious Dialogue: Revisiting "Confrontation" after Forty Years', revised version of a paper presented at the conference, 'Rabbi Joseph Soloveitchik on Interreligious Dialogue: Forty Years Later', Boston College, Center for Christian-Jewish Learning, 23 Nov. 2003.

KOTLER, AHARON, 'On the Maintenance of Torah in Israel' (Heb.), in *Va'ad leharamat keren hatorah, kuntres keter torah* (New York, 1944), 31–2.

KRAUS, YITSHAK, *The Seventh: Messianism in the Last Generation of Habad* [Hashevi'i: Meshiḥiyut bedor hashevi'i shel ḥabad] (Tel Aviv: Miskal-Yediot Ahronot/Sifrei Hemed, 2007).

KUSTANOWITZ, ESTHER D., 'Morateinu Alissa Thomas-Newborn Joins the Clergy', *Jewish Journal* (5 May 2015), http://www.jewishjournal.com/los_angeles/article/morateinu_alissa_thomas_newborn_joins_the_clergy/.

KUZNETS, SIMON, 'Immigration of Russian Jews to the United States: Background and Structure', *Perspectives in American History*, 9 (1975), 35–124.

LAMM, NORMAN, 'Some Comments on Centrist Orthodoxy', *Tradition*, 22/3 (Fall 1986), 1–12.

—— *Torah Umadda: The Encounter of Religious Learning and Worldly Knowledge in the Jewish Tradition* (Northvale, NJ: Jason Aronson, 1990).

LANDES, DAVID, 'How Lakewood, N.J., is Redefining What It Means To Be Orthodox in America', *Tablet Magazine* (5 June 2013), http://www.tabletmag.com/jewish-life-and-religion/133643/lakewood-redefining-orthodoxy/.

LAOR, IZHAK, 'Samson Was Lame in Both Legs' (Heb.), *Haaretz* (17 Jan. 2006), 'Culture and Literature' section.

LAU, BINYAMIN ('BENI'), *Eight Prophets: In the Bonds of Love* [Shemonah nevi'im: be'avutot ahavah] (Yediot Ahronot/Sifrei Hemed, 2016).

—— *Esther: Reading the Megillah* [Ester: keriat hamegilah] (Tel Aviv: Miskal-Yediot Ahronot/Sifrei Hemed, 2011).

——'A Home that Includes All: Only Recognition that the Torah Belongs to All of Her Sons and Daughters Creates an Invitation for a Real Meeting' (Heb.), *Makor Rishon* (1 July 2016), Shabbat Literary Supplement, 4.

——*Jeremiah: The Fate of a Prophet*, trans. Sara Daniel (Jerusalem: Maggid, 2013).

LAVIE, ALIZA (ed.), *Women's Prayer* [Tefilat nashim: pesifas nashi shel tefilot vesipurim] (Tel Aviv: Yediot Aharonot-Mishkal, 2005); English edn.: *A Jewish Woman's Prayer Book* (New York: Spiegel & Grau/Random House, 2008).

LAVIN, TALIA, 'For Many Agunot, Halachic Prenups Won't Break Their Chains', *Times of Israel* (30 Nov. 2013), http://www.timesofisrael.com/for-many-agunot-halachic-prenups-wont-break-their-chains/.

——'Off the Path of Orthodoxy', *New Yorker* (31 July 2015), http://www.newyorker.com/news/news-desk/off-the-path-of-orthodoxy/.

LAZERWITZ, BERNARD, 'Contrasting the Effects of Generation, Class, Sex, and Age on Group Identification in the Jewish and Protestant Communities', *Social Forces*, 49/1 (Sept. 1970), 50–9.

——J. ALAN WINTER, ARNOLD DASHEFSKY, and EPHRAIM TABORY, *Jewish Choices: American Jewish Denominationalism* (Albany: State University of New York Press, 1998).

LEFKOWITZ, JAY P., 'The Rise of Social Orthodoxy: A Personal Account', *Commentary* (Apr. 2014), 37–42.

LEHRER, EVELYN L., and CARMEL U. CHISWICK, 'Religion as a Determinant of Marital Stability', *Demography*, 30/3 (1993), 385–404.

LEIBOVITZ, LIEL, 'Orthodox Boom Reshaping West Side', *Jewish Week* (2 July 2004), 1.

LENSKI, GERHARD E., *Power and Privilege: A Theory of Social Stratification* (Chapel Hill: University of North Carolina Press, 1984).

LEON, NISSIM, *Gentle Ultra-Orthodoxy: Religious Renewal in Oriental Jewry in Israel* [Harediyut rakah] (Jerusalem: Yad Izhak Ben-Zvi, 2010).

——*The Mitre and the Flag: Oppositional Nationalism within Mizrahi Haredism* [Hamitsnefet vehadegel: le'umiut shekeneged baharediut hamizrahit] (Tel Aviv: Hakibuts Hame'uhad and Van Leer Jerusalem Institute, 2016).

——and BENJAMIN BROWN (eds.), *The Gdoilim: Leaders Who Shaped the Israeli Haredi Jewry* [Hagedolim: ishim she'itsevu et penei hayahadut haharedit] (Jerusalem: Magnes Press/Van Leer Jerusalem Institute, 2017).

LEVINAS, EMMANUEL, *Nine Talmudic Readings*, trans. Annette Aronowicz (Bloomington: Indiana University Press, 1990).

LEVINE, HILLEL, *In Search of Sugihara: The Elusive Japanese Diplomat Who Risked His Life to Rescue 10,000 Jews from the Holocaust* (New York: The Free Press, 1996).

LEVY, SHLOMIT, HANNA LEVINSOHN, AND ELIHU KATZ, *A Portrait of Israeli Jewry: Beliefs, Observances and Values among Israeli Jews 2000* (Jerusalem: Guttman Center of the Israel Democracy Institute/Avi Chai, 2002).

LEWIS, OSCAR, 'The Culture of Poverty', *Trans-action*, 1/1 (Nov. 1963), 17–19.

LEWITTES, MENDELL, *Principles and Development of Jewish Law: The Concepts and History of Rabbinic Jurisprudence from Its Inception to Modern Times* (New York: Bloch, 1987).

LICHTENSTEIN, AHARON, *By His Light: Character and Values in the Service of God*, based on addresses by Rabbi Aharon Lichtenstein, adapted by Reuven Ziegler (Jersey City, NJ: Ktav; Alon Shvut: Yeshivat Har Etzion, 2002).

—— *Leaves of Faith: The World of Jewish Learning*, 2 vols. (Jersey City, NJ: Ktav, 2003, 2004).

LICHTENSTEIN, TOVAH, 'Reflections on the Influence of the Rov on the American Jewish Religious Community', *Tradition*, 44/4 (Winter 2011), 7–22.

LIEBMAN, CHARLES S., *The Ambivalent American Jew: Politics, Religion and Family in American Jewish Life* (Philadelphia: Jewish Publication Society of America, 1973).

—— *Aspects of the Religious Behavior of American Jews* (New York: Ktav, 1974).

—— 'Changing Social Characteristics of Orthodox, Conservative and Reform Jews', *Sociological Analysis*, 27/4 (Winter 1966), 210–22.

—— 'Emanuel Rackman and Modern Orthodoxy: Some Personal Recollections', in Moshe Beer (ed.), *Studies in Halakhah and Jewish Thought: Presented to Rabbi Prof. Menachem Emanuel Rackman on His 80th Anniversary* [Meḥkarim behalakhah ubemaḥshevet yisra'el], Hebrew and English (Ramat Gan: Bar-Ilan University Press, 1994), 23–31.

—— 'Extremism as a Religious Norm', *Journal for the Scientific Study of Religion*, 22/1 (Mar. 1983), 75–86.

—— 'The Future of Conservative Judaism in the United States', *Jerusalem Letters: Viewpoints*, 11 (31 Mar. 1980).

—— 'Modern Orthodoxy in Israel', *Judaism*, 47/4 (1998), 405–11.

—— 'Orthodoxy in American Jewish Life', *American Jewish Year Book*, 66 (Philadelphia: Jewish Publication Society of America, 1965), 21–97.

LIPKA, MICHAEL, '5 Facts about Prayer', Pew Research Center (6 May 2015), http://www.pewresearch.org/fact-tank/2015/05/06/5-facts-about-prayer/.

—— 'What Surveys Say about Worship Attendance—and Why Some Stay Home', Pew Research Center (13 Sept. 2013), http://www.pewresearch.org/fact-tank/2013/09/13/what-surveys-say-about-worship-attendance-and-why-some-stay-home/.

LIPMAN, STEVE, 'For Many Orthodox Teens, "Half Shabbos" Is a Way of Life', *Jewish Week* (22 June 2011), http://www.thejewishweek.com/news/national/many-orthodox-teens-half-shabbos-way-life.

—— 'Gay YU Panel Broadens Discussion, Debate', *The Jewish Week* (29 Dec. 2009), http://www.thejewishweek.com/news/new_york/gay_yu_panel_broadens_discussion_debate_0.

LITVIN, BARUCH, and SIDNEY HOENIG, *Jewish Identity: Modern Responsa and Opinions on the Registration of Children of Mixed Marriages* (New York: Phillip Feldheim, 1965).

LOCKSHIN, MARTIN, 'Get Ready for Duelling Prayerbooks', *Canadian Jewish News* (7 May 2009), 9.

LOPATIN, ASHER, 'How to Rejuvenate Modern Orthodoxy', *Mosaic* (19 Aug. 2015), http://mosaicmagazine.com/response/2014/08/how-to-rejuvenate-modern-orthodoxy/.

—— 'Non-Heart-Beating Donation from Brain Dead Patients: Rav Ahron Solo-veichik's Solution', in Zev Farber (ed.), *Halakhic Realities: Collected Essays on Brain Death* (Jerusalem: Maggid, 2015), 255–61.

—— 'What Makes a Book Orthodox?', *Edah Journal*, 4/2 (2004), 2–11.

LUKES, STEVEN, *Emile Durkheim: His Life and Work. A Historical and Critical Study* (Stanford: Stanford University Press, 1985).

MAGID, SHAUL, *Hasidism on the Margin* (Madison: University of Wisconsin Press, 2003).

MAIMONIDES, MOSES, *The Guide of the Perplexed*, trans. Shlomo Pines (Chicago: University of Chicago Press, 1963).

—— *Hakdamot leperush hamishnah*, ed. Mordechai Dov Rabinowitz (Jerusalem: Mossad Harav Kook, 1960).

—— *Mishneh torah* (New York: Hotzoas Rambam, 1956).

MALAKH, DANIEL, 'Changes in Nature as a Resolution of Contradictions between Religion and Science' (Heb.), *Teḥumin*, 18 (1998), 371–83.

MALINOWITZ, CHAIM Z., and MICHAEL J. BROYDE, 'The 1992 New York Get Law: An Exchange', *Tradition*, 31/3 (Spring 1997), 23–41.

MARGOLIES, ARI, 'Taking Off My Tefillin', *Tablet Magazine* (30 Aug. 2012), http://www.tabletmag.com/jewish-life-and-religion/110594/taking-off-my-tefillin/.

MARSDEN, GEORGE M., *The Twilight of the American Enlightenment: The 1950s and the Crisis of Liberal Belief* (New York: Basic Books, 2014).

—— *Understanding Fundamentalism and Evangelicalism* (Grand Rapids, Mich.: W. B. Eerdmans, 1991).

MAY, DARREN, 'YU Roshei Yeshiva Address the Topic of Women Rabbis', *The Commentator* (30 Nov. 2015), 8.

MAYER, EGON, and CHAIM I. WAXMAN, 'Modern Jewish Orthodoxy in America—Toward the Year 2000', *Tradition*, 16/3 (Spring 1977), 98–112.

MEDAN, YAACOV, 'Anyone Who Says David Sinned is Mistaken' (Heb.), in Yehoshua Reis (ed.), *My Constant Delight: Contemporary Religious Zionist Perspectives on Tanakh Study* [Hi siḥati: al derekh limud hatanakh] (Jerusalem: Maggid; Alon Shvut: Yeshivat Har Etzion/Herzog College, 2013), 83–96.

MEDOFF, RAFAEL, *Did the Jewish Vote Cost Truman New York? A New Look at the 1948 Presidential Race* (Washington, DC: David S. Wyman Institute for Holo-caust Studies, 2012).

MEISELMAN, MOSHE, *Jewish Woman in Jewish Law* (New York: Ktav/Yeshiva University Press, 1978).

MEISELMAN, SHULAMIT SOLOVEITCHIK, *The Soloveitchik Heritage: A Daughter's Memoir* (Hoboken, NJ: Ktav, 1995).

MEYER, MICHAEL A., *Response to Modernity: A History of the Reform Movement in Judaism* (New York: Oxford University Press, 1988).

MICHELS, ROBERT, *Political Parties: A Sociological Study of the Oligarchical Tendencies of Modern Democracy* (New York: The Free Press, 1962).

MILLER, CHAIM, *Turning Judaism Outwards: A Biography of the Rebbe, Menachem Mendel Schneerson* (Brooklyn: Kol Menachem, 2014).

MILLER, DONALD E., 'The Future of Liberal Christianity', *Christian Century* (10 Mar. 1982), 266.

MILLER, MARGARET A., 'The Meaning of the Baccalaureate', *About Campus* (Sept./Oct. 2003), 2–8.

MINTZ, ADAM, 'A Chapter in American Orthodoxy: The Eruvin in Brooklyn', *Ḥakirah*, 14 (Winter 2012), 21–59.

—— 'Halakhah in America: The History of City Eruvin, 1894–1962', Ph.D. diss., New York University, 2011.

MINTZ, JEROME, *Hasidic People: A Place in the New World* (Cambridge, Mass.: Harvard University Press, 1998).

MIRSKY, SAMUEL K. (ed.), *Jewish Institutions of Higher Learning in Europe: Their Development and Destruction* [Mosedot torah be'eiropah bevinyanam uveḥurbanam] (New York: Ogen Publishing House of Histadruth Ivrith of America, 1956).

MIRSKY, YEHUDAH, 'Musar Movement', in Gershon David Hundert (ed.), *YIVO Encyclopedia of Jews in Eastern Europe*, vol. ii (New Haven: Yale University Press, 2008), 1214–16.

—— *Rav Kook : Mystic in a Time of Revolution* (New Haven, Conn.: Yale University Press, 2014).

MOORE, DEBORAH DASH, *At Home in America: Second Generation New York Jews* (New York: Columbia University Press, 1981).

NARDI, NOAH, 'A Survey of Jewish Day Schools in America', *Jewish Education*, 15/2 (Sept. 1944), 12–26.

NEWMAN, ANDY, 'Orthodox Jews Celebrate End of a True Sabbatical', *New York Times* (2 Mar. 2005), p. B3.

NEWPORT, FRANK, 'Americans' Church Attendance Inches Up in 2010', Gallup (25 June 2010), http://www.gallup.com/poll/141044/americans-church-attendance-inches-2010.aspx/.

—— 'More than 9 in 10 Americans Continue to Believe in God', Gallup (3 June 2011), http://www.gallup.com/poll/147887/americans-continue-believe-god. aspx/.

Nishma Research, 'Starting a Conversation: A Pioneering Survey of Those Who Have Left the Orthodox Community' (19 June 2016), www.nishmaresearch. com/assets/pdf/Report_Survey_of_Those_Who_Left_Orthodoxy_Nishma_ Research_June_2016.pdf.

NUSBACHER, AILENE COHEN, 'Efforts at Change in a Traditional Denomination: The Case of Orthodox Women's Prayer Groups', *Nashim*, 2 (1999), 95–112.

OFER, YOSEF (ed.), *The 'Aspects Theory' of Rav Mordechai Breuer: Articles and Responses* [Shitat habeḥinot shel harav mordechai breuer: kovets ma'amarim uteguvot] (Alon Shvut: Tevunot Hegyonot, 2005).

OPPENHEIMER, MARK, 'Beggarville', *New York Times Magazine* (19 Oct. 2014), 40(L) ff.

ORBACH, MICHAEL, 'Homosexuality Panel Draws Hundreds; Rosh Yeshiva Rabbi Mayer Twersky Sharply Critical in Beis Medrash Remarks', *Jewish Star* (1 Jan. 2010), http://thejewishstar.com/stories/Dont-ask-dont-tell-at-YU-Dont-ask, 1385.

OTTERMAN, SHARON, 'Orthodox Jews Celebrate Cycle of Talmudic Study', *New York Times* (2 Aug. 2012), p. A17.

PACHTER, IDO, 'Head-Covering for Women', pts. 1 and 2 (Heb.), *Shabaton*, 729 (11 July 2015), 18; 730 (18 July 2015), 18–19.

PEAR, RACHEL S. A., '"And It Was Good"? American Modern Orthodox Engagement with Darwinism from 1925 to the Present (2012)', Ph.D. diss., Science, Technology and Society Program, Bar-Ilan University, 2012.

—— 'Differences over Darwinism: American Orthodox Jewish Responses to Evolution in the 1920s', *Aleph*, 15/22 (2015), 9–61.

PELCOVITZ, RALPH, 'The Teshuva Phenomenon: The Other Side of the Coin', *Jewish Life*, 4/3 (1980), 16 ff.

PENSAK, MARGIE, 'Keeping the Bar Out of Bas Mitzvahs', *Where What When* (May 2004), 102.

PERLMANN, JOEL, *The Local Geographic Origins of Russian-Jewish Immigrants, circa 1900*, Working Paper 465 (Annandale-on-Hudson, NY: Levy Economics Institute of Bard College, 2006).

Pew Forum on Religion & Public Life, 'U.S. Religious Landscape Survey: Religious Affiliation: Diverse and Dynamic' (Feb. 2008), http://www.pewforum.org/ files/2013/05/report-religious-landscape-study-full.pdf/.

Pew Research Center, 'Is There a Culture War?' (23 May 2006), http://www. pewforum.org/2006/05/23/is-there-a-culture-war/.

—— 'A Portrait of American Orthodox Jews: A Further Analysis of the 2013 Survey of U.S. Jews' (26 Aug. 2015), http://www.pewforum.org/2015/08/26/a-portrait-of-american-orthodox-jews/.

—— 'A Portrait of Jewish Americans' (1 Oct. 2013), http://www.pewforum.org/ 2013/10/01/jewish-american-beliefs-attitudes-culture-survey/.

Pew Research Center, 'Prayer in America' (7 May 2009), http://www.pewresearch. org/2009/05/07/prayer-in-america/.

POGREBIN, ABIGAIL, 'America's 50 Most Influential Rabbis', *The Daily Beast* (16 Apr. 2011), http://www.thedailybeast.com/articles/2011/04/16/50-most-influential-rabbis-in-america.html.

POPE, LISTON, 'Religion and the Class Structure', *Annals of the American Academy of Political and Social Science*, 256 (Mar. 1948), 84–91.

POPENOE, DAVID, *Life Without Father: Compelling New Evidence that Fatherhood and Marriage are Indispensable for the Good of Children and Society* (Cambridge, Mass.: Harvard University Press, 1999).

Proceedings of the Rabbinical Assembly, vol. xiv (New York: Rabbinical Assembly, 1950).

Rabbinical Council of America, Halakha Committee, 'Halachic Issues in the Determination of Death and in Organ Transplantation: Including an Evaluation of the Neurological "Brain Death" Standard', http://www.rabbis.org/pdfs/ Halachi_%20Issues_the_Determination.pdf.

—— '2015 Resolution: RCA Policy Concerning Women Rabbis', http://www.rabbis. org/news/article.cfm?id=105835.

RABINOVITCH, NACHUM L., *Studies in Maimonides* [Iyunim bemishnato shel harambam], 2nd edn., ed. Gad Cohen and Avihai Gamdani (Maale Adumim: Maaliot, 2010).

RAKEFFET-ROTHKOFF, AARON, *Bernard Revel: Builder of American Jewish Orthodoxy* (Philadelphia: Jewish Publication Society of America, 1972).

—— *The Rav: The World of Rabbi Joseph B. Soloveitchik*, 2 vols. (Hoboken, NJ: Ktav, 1999).

—— *The Silver Era: Rabbi Eliezer Silver and His Generation*, rev. edn. (Jerusalem: Yeshiva University Press/Feldheim, 1988).

RAPOPORT, CHAIM, *Judaism and Homosexuality: An Authentic Orthodox View* (London: Vallentine Mitchell, 2004).

RAUB, DEBORAH FINEBLUM, 'For American Expats, a Home Away From Home', *Jerusalem Post* (21 Dec. 2012), 25–6 ('In Jerusalem').

REBHUN, UZI, *Jews and the American Religious Landscape* (New York: Columbia University Press, 2016).

—— and LILACH LEV ARI, *American Israelis: Migration, Transnationalism, and Diasporic Identity* (Leiden: Brill, 2010).

REGUER, SARA, *My Father's Journey: A Memoir of Lost Worlds of Jewish Lithuania* (Boston: Academic Studies Press, 2015).

RISKIN, SHLOMO, *Listening to God: Inspirational Stories for my Grandchildren* (Jerusalem: Maggid, 2010).

—— 'Women's *Aliyah* to the Torah' (Heb.), *Teḥumin*, 28 (2008), 258–70.

RITTERBAND, PAUL, and STEVEN M. COHEN, 'Will the Well Run Dry? The Future of Jewish Giving in America', *Response*, 12/1 (Summer 1979), 9–17.

ROOF, WADE CLARK, and WILLIAM MCKINNEY, *American Mainline Religion* (New Brunswick, NJ: Rutgers University Press, 1988).

ROSENAK, AVINOAM, *Rabbi A. I. Kook* (Heb.) (Jerusalem: Zalman Shazar Center, 2006).

ROSENBERG, YAIR, 'Left and Right, Secular and Religious, Brought Together by Bible Study', *Tablet Magazine* (9 Jan. 2015), http://www.tabletmag.com/jewish-life-and-religion/188150/israeli-bible-study-929.

ROSENBLATT, GARY, 'UJA-Fed.'s New Exec Calls for Broader "Kehillah"', *Jewish Week* (28 Jan. 2014), http://www.thejewishweek.com/news/new-york/uja-feds-new-exec-calls-broader-kehillah.

ROSENBLUM, YONOSON, *Rav Dessler: The Life and Impact of Rabbi Eliyahu Eliezer Dessler, the Michtav M'Eliyahu* (Brooklyn: Mesorah, 2000).

ROSENSWEIG, MICHAEL, 'The Study of the Talmud in Contemporary Yeshivot', in Sharon Liberman Mintz and Gabriel M. Goldstein (eds.), *Printing the Talmud: From Bomberg to Schottenstein* (New York: Yeshiva University Museum, 2005), 111–20.

ROSENWAIKE, IRA, 'A Synthetic Estimate of American Jewish Population Movement Over the Last Three Decades', in Uziel O. Schmelz and Sergio Della-Pergola (eds.), *Papers in Jewish Demography 1977* (Jerusalem: Hebrew University, 1980), 83–102.

ROSNER, FRED, and MOSHE DAVID TENDLER, 'Definition of Death in Judaism', *Journal of Halacha and Contemporary Society*, 17 (1989), 14–31.

ROSNER, SHMUEL, 'How Israel's Modern-Orthodox Jews Came Out of the Closet', *New York Times* (4 Aug. 2016), http://www.nytimes.com/2016/08/05/opinion/how-israels-modern-orthodox-jews-came-out-of-the-closet.html?_r=1.

ROSS, DVORA, 'Artificial Insemination in Single Women' (Heb.), in Micah D. Halpern and Chana Safrai (eds.), *Jewish Legal Writings by Women* (Jerusalem: Urim Publications, 1998), 45–72 (Hebrew section).

ROSS, TAMAR, 'The Cognitive Value of Religious Truth Statements: Rabbi A. I. Kook and Postmodernism', in Yaakov Elman and Jeffrey S. Gurock (eds.), *Hazon Nahum: Studies in Jewish Law, Thought and History Presented to Dr. Norman Lamm on the Occasion of his Seventieth Birthday* (New York: Yeshiva University Press, 1997), 479–529; published in Hebrew as 'Rabbi A. I. Kook and Postmodernism', *Akdamot*, 10 (2000), 185–224.

—— *Expanding the Palace of Torah: Orthodoxy and Feminism* (Hanover, NH: Brandeis University Press/University Press of New England, 2004).

—— 'The Feminist Contribution to Halakhic Discourse: *Kol Be-isha Erva* as a Test Case', *Emor*, 1 (2010), 37–69.

ROSS, TAMAR, 'Orthodoxy and the Challenge of Biblical Criticism: Reflections on the Importance of Asking the Right Question' (2015), http://thetorah.com/the-challenge-of-biblical-criticism/.

ROSS, TOVA, 'How Ex-Frum Memoirs Became New York Publishing's Hottest New Trend', http://www.tabletmag.com/jewish-arts-and-culture/books/158130/ex-frum-memoirs/.

ROTEM, TAMAR, 'That's How They Want It', Haaretz (9 June 2004), http://www.haaretz.co.il/misc/1.973250.

ROTH, JOEL, 'Homosexuality', Rabbinical Assembly, Council on Jewish Law and Standards, EH 24.1992b (25 Mar. 1992), https://www.rabbinicalassembly.org/sites/default/files/public/halakhah/teshuvot/19912000/roth_homosexual.pdf.

ROTH, SOL, The Jewish Idea of Community (New York: Yeshiva University Press, 1977).

ROTHKOFF, AARON, see Rakeffet-Rothkoff

ROTHSTEIN, GIDON, 'Women's Aliyyot in Contemporary Synagogues', Tradition, 39/2 (Summer 2005), 36–58.

SACKS, JONATHAN, 'The Man Who Turned Judaism Outward', http://www.chabad.org/therebbe/article_cdo/aid/933172/jewish/the-man-who-turned-judaism-outward.htm/.

—— Traditional Alternatives: Orthodoxy and the Future of the Jewish People (London: Jews' College, 1989).

'Sacred Texts: App Aims to Solve Sms-during-Sabbath Problem', Haaretz (1 Oct. 2014), http://www.haaretz.com/jewish/news/ 1.618622/.

SALAMON, MICHAEL J. The Shidduch Crisis: Causes and Cures (Jerusalem: Urim Publications, 2008).

SAMET, MOSHE, Chapters in the History of Orthodoxy [Heḥadash asur min hatorah: perakim betoledot ha'ortodoksiyah] (Jerusalem: Hebrew University/Dinur Center for Research in Jewish History/Carmel, 2005).

SANDERS, ALAN R., EDEN R. MARTIN, GARY W. BEECHAM, SHENGRU GUO, KHYTAM DAWOOD, GERULF RIEGER, JUDITH A. BADNER, ELLIOT S. GERSHON, RITESHA S. KRISHNAPPA, ALANA B. KOLUNDZIJA, JUBAO DUAN, PABLO V. GEJMAN, and J. MICHAEL BAILEY, 'Genome-Wide Scan Demonstrates Significant Linkage for Male Sexual Orientation', Psychological Medicine, 45/7 (May 2015), 1379–88.

SANGHAVI, DARSHAK, 'The Last Decision', New York Times Magazine (16 Dec. 2009), pp. SM38 ff.

SARNA, JONATHAN, American Judaism: A History (New Haven: Yale University Press, 2004).

—— 'How Matzah Became Square: Manischewitz and the Development of Machine-Made Matzah in the United States' (Victor J. Selmanowitz Lecture, Touro College, 2005).

SCHACHTER, ZVI (HERSCHEL), 'Go Out and Walk in the Footsteps of the Flock' (Heb.), *Beit yitzḥak* (1984/5), 118–34.

SCHACTER, JACOB J., 'Haskalah, Secular Studies and the Closing of the Yeshiva in Volozhin', *Torah U-Madda Journal*, 2 (1990), 76–133.

—— 'Torah U-Madda Revisited: The Editor's Introduction', *Torah U-Madda Journal*, 1 (1989), 1–22.

SCHICK, MARVIN, *A Census of Jewish Day Schools in the United States 2013–2014* (New York: Avi Chai Foundation, 2014).

SCHIFF, ALVIN I., *The Jewish Day School in America* (New York: Jewish Education Committee, 1966).

SHAFRAN, AVI, 'Dissembling Before G-d', *Jewish Journal of Greater Los Angeles* (21 Feb. 2002), http://www.jewishjournal.com/arts/article/dissembling_before_gd_20020222.

—— 'I Have a Dream' (29 Dec. 2003), http://www.jlaw.com/Commentary/ihaveadream.html/.

—— 'Swearing Off the "U" Word', *Ami Magazine* (30 Jan. 2011), http://www.cross-currents.com/archives/2011/01/30/swearing-off-the-u-word/.

SHAPIRA, ANITA, 'Ben-Gurion and the Bible: The Forging of an Historical Narrative?', *Middle Eastern Studies*, 33/4 (Oct. 1997), 645–74.

—— 'The Bible and Israeli Identity', *AJS Review*, 28/1 (2004), 11–42.

—— *The Bible and Israeli Identity* [Hatanakh vehazehut hayisra'elit] (Jerusalem: Magnes Press, 2005).

SHAPIRO, MARC B., 'The Brisker Method Reconsidered: Review Essay', *Tradition*, 31/33 (Spring 1997), 78–102.

—— *Changing the Immutable: How Orthodox Judaism Rewrites Its History* (Oxford: Littman Library of Jewish Civilization, 2015).

—— *The Limits of Orthodox Theology: Maimonides' Thirteen Principles Reappraised* (Oxford: Littman Library of Jewish Civilization, 2004).

SHAPIRO, MENDEL, '*Qeri'at ha-Torah* by Women: A Halakhic Analysis', *Edah Journal*, 1/2 (2001), 2–52.

SHATZ, DAVID, 'Rav Kook and Modern Orthodoxy: The Ambiguities of "Openness"', in Moshe Z. Sokol (ed.), *Engaging Modernity: Rabbinic Leaders and the Challenges of the Twentieth Century*, Orthodox Forum series (Northvale, NJ: Jason Aronson, 1997), 91–115.

SHERAMY, RONA, 'From the Executive Director', *AJS Perspectives* (Fall 2010), 4.

—— 'From the Executive Director', *AJS Perspectives* (Spring 2011), 4, 56.

SHERMAN, MOSHE D., 'Bernard Illowy and Nineteenth-Century American Orthodoxy', Ph.D. diss., Yeshiva University, 1991.

—— *Orthodox Judaism in America: A Biographical Dictionary and Sourcebook* (Westport, Conn.: Greenwood Press, 1996).

SHTERNBUCH, MOSHE, *Teshuvot vehanhagot hashalem*, 2 vols. (Jerusalem, 1994).

SHULMAN, ELI BARUCH, and MICHAEL J. BROYDE, 'Hair Covering and Jewish Law: A Response', *Tradition*, 43/2 (Summer 2010), 73–108.

SHWAYDER, MAYA, 'More Than 5,000 Chabad Emissaries Convene in Crown Heights for Night of Dancing', *Jerusalem Post* (11 May 2013), 4.

SILBER, MICHAEL K., 'The Emergence of Ultra-Orthodoxy: The Invention of a Tradition', in Jack Wertheimer (ed.), *The Uses of Tradition: Jewish Continuity in the Modern Era* (New York: Jewish Theological Seminary of America, 1992), 23–84.

SILVERSTEIN, ALAN, *Alternatives to Assimilation: The Response of Reform Judaism to American Culture, 1840–1930* (Hanover, NH: University Press of New England/Brandeis University Press, 1994).

SIMON, URIEL, *Seek Peace and Pursue It: Topical Issue in Light of the Bible / The Bible in Light of Topical Issues* [Bakesh shalom veradfehu: she'elot hasha'ah be'or hamikra / hamikra be'or she'elot hasha'ah], 2nd, expanded, edn. (Tel Aviv: Yediot Ahronot/Sifrei Hemed, 2004), 23–46.

SINGER, DAVID, 'Debating Modern Orthodoxy at Yeshiva College: The Greenberg–Lichtenstein Exchange of 1966', *Modern Judaism*, 26/2 (May 2006), 113–26.

—— 'Emanuel Rackman: Gadfly of Modern Orthodoxy', *Modern Judaism*, 28/2 (May 2008), 134–48.

—— 'Thumbs and Eggs', *Moment*, 3/9 (Sept. 1978), 36–7.

—— 'The Yeshivah World', *Commentary* (Oct. 1976), 70–2.

SKLARE, MARSHALL, *Conservative Judaism: An American Religious Movement* (New York: Schocken Books, 1972).

SLIFKIN, NATAN, *Mysterious Creatures: Intriguing Torah Enigmas of Natural and Unnatural History* (Southfield, Mich.: Zoo Torah and Targum Press, 2003).

—— *The Science of Torah* (Southfield, Mich.: Targum Press, 2001).

SOFER, MOSES, *Teshuvot haḥatam sofer* (Jerusalem: Machon Hatam Sofer, 1973).

SOLOMON, NORMAN, *The Analytic Movement: Hayyim Soloveitchik and His Circle* (Atlanta, Ga.: Scholars' Press, 1993).

—— *Torah from Heaven: The Reconstruction of Faith* (Oxford: Littman Library of Jewish Civilization, 2012).

SOLOVEICHIK, AHRON, 'Death According to the Halacha', *Journal of Halacha and Contemporary Society*, 17 (1989), 41–8.

SOLOVEITCHIK, HAYM, 'Clarifications and Reply', *Torah U-Madda Journal*, 7 (1997), 137–49.

—— *Collected Essays*, vol. i (Oxford: Littman Library of Jewish Civilization, 2013).

—— *Halakhah, Economy, and Self-Perception: Mortgaging in the Middle Ages* [Halakhah, kalkalah, vedimui-atsmi: hamashkona'ut biyemei habeina'im] (Jerusalem: Magnes Press, 1985).

—— *Principles and Pressures: Jewish Trade in Gentile Wine in the Middle Ages* [Yeinam: saḥar beyeinam shel goyim] (Tel Aviv: Alma and Am Oved, 2003).

—— 'Rupture and Reconstruction: The Transformation of Contemporary Orthodoxy', *Tradition*, 28/4 (Fall 1994), 64–130.

—— *Wine in Ashkenaz in the Middle Ages: Yeyn Nesekh—A Study in the History of Halakhah* [Hayayin biyemei habeinayim: yein nesekh—perek betoledot hahalakhah be'ashkenaz] (Jerusalem: Zalman Shazar Center for Jewish History, 2008).

SOLOVEITCHIK, JOSEPH B., 'Confrontation', *Tradition*, 6/2 (Spring/Summer 1964), 5–29.

—— *Five Lectures* [Ḥamesh derashot] (Jerusalem: World Mizrachi Organization, 1973); English edn.: *The Rav Speaks: Five Addresses Delivered to Conventions of the Mizrachi Religious Zionist Movement during the Period 1962–1967* (Jerusalem: Tal Orot Institute, 1983).

—— *Halakhic Man*, trans. Lawrence Kaplan (Philadelphia: Jewish Publication Society of America, 1983).

—— *In Aloneness, in Togetherness* [Besod hayaḥid vehayaḥad: mivḥar ketavim ivriyim], ed. Pinchas Peli (Jerusalem: Orot, 1976).

—— 'The Lonely Man of Faith', *Tradition*, 7/2 (Summer 1965), 5–67.

—— *The Lonely Man of Faith* (New York: Doubleday, 1992).

—— *Matters of Contemplation and Appreciation* [Divrei hagut veha'arakhah] (Jerusalem: Elinor Library of the Torah Education Department of the World Zionist Organization, 1982).

—— *On Repentance* [Al hateshuvah] (Jerusalem: World Zionist Organization, 1975); 1st English edn. 1980; rev. edn., *Soloveitchik on Repentance*, trans. and ed. Pinchas Peli (Mahwah, NJ: Paulist Press, 1984).

SOYER, DANIEL, *Jewish Immigrant Associations and American Identity in New York, 1880–1939* (Detroit: Wayne State University Press, 2001).

SPERBER, DANIEL, 'Congregational Dignity and Human Dignity: Women and Public Torah Reading', *Edah Journal*, 3/2 (2002), 2–14.

—— *Jewish Customs* [Minhagei yisra'el], vol. ii (Jerusalem: Mossad Harav Kook, 1991).

—— *On the Relationship of Mitzvot between Man and His Neighbor and Man and His Maker* (Jerusalem: Urim Publications, 2014).

—— *The Path of Halakhah: Women Reading the Torah. A Case of Pesika Policy* [Darkah shel halakhah: keriyat nashim batorah. Perakim bimediniyut pesikah] (Jerusalem: Rubin Mass, 2007).

—— *The Ways of Pesikah: Methods and Approaches for Halakhic Decision-Making* [Netivot shel pesikah: kelim vegishah leposek hahalakhah] (Jerusalem: Rubin Mass, 2008).

SPITZER, YANNAY, 'Pogroms, Networks, and Migration: The Jewish Migration from the Russian Empire to the United States 1881–1914'. Paper presented at the Brown University Population Studies and Training Center, 28 Sept. 2014.

STAETSKY, L. DANIEL, and JONATHAN BOYD, Strictly Orthodox Rising: What the Demography of British Jews Tells Us about the Future of the Community (London: Institute for Jewish Policy Research, 2015).

STAMPFER, SHAUL, Families, Rabbis, and Education: Traditional Jewish Society in Nineteenth-Century Eastern Europe (Oxford: Littman Library of Jewish Civilization, 2010).

—— 'The Geographic Background of East European Jewish Migration to the United States before World War I', in Ira A. Glazier and Luigi de Rosa (eds.), Migration across Time and Nations: Population Mobility in Historical Contexts (New York: Holmes & Meier, 1986), 220–30.

—— 'How Jewish Society Adapted to Change in Male/Female Relationships in 19th/Early 20th Century Eastern Europe', in Rivkah Blau (ed.), Gender Relationships in Marriage and Out, Orthodox Forum series (New York: Yeshiva University Press, 2007), 65–84.

—— Lithuanian Yeshivas of the Nineteenth Century: Creating a Tradition of Learning (Oxford: Littman Library of Jewish Civilization, 2012).

—— 'Marital Patterns in Interwar Poland', in Yisrael Gutman (ed.), The Jews of Poland between Two World Wars (Hanover, NH: University Press of New England/Brandeis University Press, 1989), 173–97.

STEINMETZ, YAEL, 'Let's Talk About It: Identity Conflicts in the Discourse of American Modern Orthodox Jews as Portrayed in the Social Media' [Bo'u nedaber al zeh: sugyot zehut basiaḥ ha'ortodoksi-moderni be'amerikah bire'i merḥav hamedyah haḥevratit], Ph.D. diss., Bar-Ilan University, Faculty of Jewish Studies, Department of Jewish History and Contemporary Jewry, 2015.

STEINSALTZ, ADIN EVEN-ISRAEL, My Rebbe (Jerusalem: Maggid, 2014).

STOLOW, JEREMY, Orthodox by Design: Judaism, Print Politics, and the ArtScroll Revolution (Berkeley: University of California Press, 2010).

STUMP, ROGER W., 'Regional Migration and Religious Commitment in the United States', Journal for the Scientific Study of Religion, 23/3 (Sept. 1984), 292–303.

SUSSMAN, LANCE J., Isaac Leeser and the Making of American Judaism (Detroit: Wayne State University Press, 1995).

—— 'Isaac Leeser and the Protestantization of American Judaism', American Jewish Archives, 38 (Apr. 1986), 1–21.

TABAK, ISRAEL, 'Rabbi Abraham Rice of Baltimore: Pioneer of Orthodox Judaism in America', Tradition, 7/2 (Summer 1965), 100–20.

TARAGIN, REUVEN, 'Limud torah she-ba'al peh: The Goals and Methodology of the Brisker Derekh', Alei Etzion, 7 (1997/8), 83–93.

TA-SHMA, ISRAEL M., Early Franco-German Ritual and Custom [Minhag ashkenaz hakadmon] (Jerusalem: Magnes Press, 1992).

TATZ, AKIVA, *Anatomy of a Search: Personal Drama in the Teshuva Revolution* (Brooklyn: Mesorah, 1987).

TAU, ZVI ISRAEL, *The Righteous Person Shall Live by His Faith: On the Way to Teach Torah* [Tsadik be'emunato yiḥyeh: al hagishah lelimud torah] (Jerusalem, 2002).

TEITELBAUM, JOEL, 'A Responsum on the Prohibition of Artificial Insemination from the Sperm of a Different Man', *Hamaor*, 15/9 [Hebrew cover]; 14/7 [English cover] (Aug. 1964), 3–13.

TELUSHKIN, JOSEPH, *Rebbe: The Life and Teachings of Menachem M. Schneerson, the Most Influential Rabbi in Modern History* (New York: Harper Wave, 2014).

TEMKIN, SEFTON D., *Creating American Reform Judaism: The Life and Times of Isaac Mayer Wise* (Oxford: Littman Library of Jewish Civilization, 1998).

TENDLER, MOSHE D., and FRED ROSNER, 'Communications: Brain Death', *Tradition*, 28/3 (Summer 1994), 94–6.

TENE, ELAD, 'Efrat's Rabbi: Same-Sex Couple Can Raise a Family' (1 Jan. 2009), http://www.ynetnews.com/articles/0,7340,L-3647929,00.html/.

THOMAS, WILLIAM I., and DOROTHY SWAINE THOMAS, *The Child in America: Behavior Problems and Programs* (New York: Knopf, 1928).

TIKOCHINSKI, SHLOMO, *Torah Scholarship, Musar, and Elitism: The Slobodka Yeshiva from Lithuania to Mandate Palestine* [Lamdanut musar ve'elitizm: yeshivat slabodka melita le'erets yisra'el] (Jerusalem: Zalman Shazar Center for Jewish History, 2016).

TIKOCHINSKY, MIKHAL, and RACHEL SHPRECHER FRANKEL, 'Warn Them about the Concubine' (Heb.), *Akdamot*, 17 (2006), 67–76.

TURETSKY, YEHUDA, and CHAIM I. WAXMAN, 'Sliding to the Left? Contemporary American Modern Orthodoxy', *Modern Judaism*, 31/2 (May 2011), 119–41.

TWERSKI, ABRAHAM J., *Getting Up When You're Down: A Mature Discussion of an Adult Malady—Depression and Related Conditions* (Brooklyn: Shaar Press/Mesorah, 1995).

—— *The Shame Borne in Silence: Spouse Abuse in the Jewish Community* (Jerusalem: Urim Publications, 2015).

—— *Successful Relationships: At Home, at Work, and with Friends: Bringing Control Issues Under Control* (Brooklyn: Shaar Press/Mesorah, 2003).

TWERSKY, ISADORE, 'Some Aspects of the Jewish Attitude toward the Welfare State', *Tradition*, 5/2 (Spring 1963), 137–58.

Ukeles Associates, *Young Jewish Adults in the United States Today* (New York: American Jewish Committee, 2006).

UNGER-SARGON, BATYA, 'Orthodox Yeshiva Set to Ordain Three Women: Just Don't Call Them "Rabbi"', *Tablet* (10 June 2013), http://www.tabletmag.com/jewish-life-and-religion/134369/orthodox-women-ordained/.

'Union of Orthodox Congregations', *American Hebrew*, 68/7 (4 Jan. 1901), 236.

Union of Orthodox Rabbis of the United States and Canada, *Jubilee Book of the Union of Orthodox Rabbis of the United States and Canada* [Sefer hayovel shel agudat harabanim ha'ortodoksim de'artsot haberit vekanadah] (New York: Arium Press, 1927/8).

UNTERMAN, YAEL, *Nehama Leibowitz: Teacher and Bible Scholar* (Jerusalem: Urim Publications, 2009).

URBACH, EPHRAIM E., *The Halakhah: Its Sources and Development* [Hahalakhah: mekoroteiha vehitpaṭhutah] (Tel Aviv: Massada, 1984).

VEBLEN, THORSTEIN, *The Higher Learning in America: A Memorandum on the Conduct of Universities by Business Men* (New York: B. W. Huebsch, 1918).

WAITE, LINDA J., 'The American Jewish Family: What We Know. What We Need To Know', *Contemporary Jewry*, 23/1 (Dec. 2002), 35–63.

WALDENBERG, ELIEZER YEHUDA, *She'elot uteshuvot tsits eli'ezer*, vol. ix (Jerusalem, 1967).

WANG, WENDY, and KIM PARKER, 'Record Share of Americans Have Never Married, as Values, Economics and Gender Patterns Change', Pew Research Center, Social and Demographic Trends project (Sept. 2014), http://www.pewsocialtrends.org/2014/09/24/record-share-of-americans-have-never-married/.

WARNER, W. LLOYD, and LEO SROLE, *The Social Systems of American Ethnic Groups*, Yankee City series 3 (New Haven: Yale University Press, 1945).

WAXMAN, CHAIM I., *American Aliya: Portrait of an Innovative Migration Movement* (Detroit: Wayne State University Press, 1989).

—— 'American Modern Orthodoxy: Confronting Cultural Challenges', *Edah Journal*, 4/1 (May 2004), 1–13.

—— *America's Jews in Transition* (Philadelphia: Temple University Press, 1983).

—— 'Defensive in the Center', *Conversations*, 20 (Autumn 2014), 1–9.

—— '*Giyur* in the Context of National Identity', in Adam Mintz and Marc D. Stern (eds.), *Conversion, Intermarriage, and Jewish Identity*, Orthodox Forum series (New York: Yeshiva University Press/Ktav; Jerusalem: Urim Publications, 2015), 151–85.

—— 'The Haredization of American Orthodox Jewry', *Jerusalem Letters: Viewpoints* (Jerusalem Center for Public Affairs), 376 (15 Feb. 1998).

—— 'If I Forget Thee, O Jerusalem...: The Impact of Israel on American Orthodox Jewry', in id. (ed.), *Religious Zionism Post Disengagement: Future Directions* (New York: Yeshiva University Press; Jersey City, NJ: Ktav, 2008), 415–32.

—— 'Is It All in the Name?', *Ami Magazine* (16 Feb. 2011), 20.

—— *Jewish Baby Boomers: A Communal Perspective* (Albany: State University of New York Press, 2001).

—— 'Modern Orthodox Jewry in the United States and Religious Zionist Jewry in

Israel' [Hayahadut ha'ortodoksit modernit be'artsot haberit vehayahadut hatsiyonit datit beyisra'el], paper delivered at the conference on 'New Religious Zionism', Bar-Ilan University, 26 Mar. 2014.

—— 'Multiculturalism, Conversion, and the Future of Israel', *Israel Studies Review*, 28/1 (Summer 2013), 33–53.

—— 'Needed—New Typologies: The Complexity of American Orthodoxy in the 21st Century', in Stuart Cohen and Bernard Susser (eds.), *Ambivalent Jew: Charles Liebman in Memoriam* (New York: Jewish Theological Seminary of America, 2007), 135–53.

—— 'Reb David—Ha-Rav David Lifshitz, z"l: An Intimate Portrait', in Menachem Butler and Zev Nagel (eds.), *My Yeshiva College: 75 Years of Memories* (New York: Yashar Books, 2006), 294–7.

—— 'The Role and Authority of the Rabbi in American Society', in Susan Last Stone (ed.), *Rabbinic and Lay Communal Authority*, Orthodox Forum series (New York: Yeshiva University Press, 2006), 93–112, 165–70.

—— 'The Sabbath as Dialectic: The Meaning and Role', *Judaism*, 31/1 (Winter 1982), 37–44.

—— *The Stigma of Poverty: A Critique of Poverty Theories and Policies* (New York: Pergamon Press, 1977; 2nd edn., 1983).

—— 'Toward a Sociology of *Pesak*', in Moshe Z. Sokol (ed.), *Rabbinic Authority and Personal Autonomy* Orthodox Forum series (Northvale, NJ: Jason Aronson, 1992), 217–38.

—— 'What We Don't Know about the Judaism of America's Jews', *Contemporary Jewry* 23/1 (2002), 72–95.

WEBER, MAX, *Economy and Society*, 2 vols. (New York: Bedminster, 1968).

—— *The Methodology of the Social Sciences*, trans and ed. Edward A. Shils and Henry A. Finch (Glencoe, Ill.: The Free Press, 1949).

WEINBERGER, MOSES, *People Walk on Their Heads: Jews and Judaism in New York*, trans. and ed. Jonathan D. Sarna (New York: Holmes & Meier, 1982).

WEINER, JULIE, 'Todah "Rabba"?', *Jewish Week* (26 Jan. 2010), http://www.the jewishweek.com/news/short_takes/todah_%E2%80%98rabba%E2%80%99.

WEISBERG, HERBERT F., 'Reconsidering Jewish Presidential Voting Statistics', *Contemporary Jewry*, 32/3 (Oct. 2012), 215–36.

WEISS, AVRAHAM [AVI], 'Defining "Open Orthodoxy"', *Tablet Magazine*, http://www.tabletmag.com/jewish-life-and-religion/191907/defining-open-orthodoxy.

—— 'Open Orthodoxy! A Modern Orthodox Rabbi's Creed', *Judaism*, 46/4 (Fall 1997), 409–21.

—— *Women at Prayer: A Halakhic Analysis of Women's Prayer Groups*, 3rd, expanded, edn. (Hoboken, NJ: Ktav, 2001).

WEISS, STEVEN I., 'Orthodox Rabbis Launch Book Ban', *Forward* (21 Jan. 2005), 1.

WEISSER, MICHAEL R., *A Brotherhood of Memory: Jewish Landsmanshaftn in the New World* (Ithaca, NY: Cornell University Press, 1989).

WEISSMAN, DEBORAH, and LAUREN B. GRANITE, 'Bais Ya'akov Schools', http:// jwa.org/encyclopedia/article/bais-yaakov-schools.

WEITZMAN, GIDON, 'Technology in the Service of the First Mitzvah', *Ḥakirah*, 6 (Summer 2008), 259–67.

WELCH, MICHAEL R., and JOHN BALTZELL, 'Geographic Mobility, Social Integration, and Church Attendance', *Journal for the Scientific Study of Religion*, 23/1 (Mar. 1984), 75–91.

WERDIGER, ESTHER, 'Lipa Schmeltzer, the Hasidic Jew who Makes Hilarious, Magic Music Videos', *The Awl* (9 Feb. 9 2013), https://theawl.com/lipa-schmeltzer-the-hasidic-jew-who-makes-hilarious-magic-music-videos-7acec48f6585#.fb8g132ms.

WILLIG, MORDECHAI, 'Trampled Laws', http://torahweb.org/torah/2015/parsha/rwil_ekev.html.

WILSON, SCOTT, 'Ultra-Orthodox Jews Find Gym to Call Their Own', *Seattle Times* (29 Apr. 2007), p. A16.

WISCHNITZER, MARK, *To Dwell in Safety: The Story of Jewish Migration Since 1880* (Philadelphia: Jewish Publication Society of America, 1948).

WODZIŃSKI, MARCIN, *Haskalah and Hasidism in the Kingdom of Poland: A History of Conflict* (Oxford: Littman Library of Jewish Civilization, 2005).

WOLOWELSKY, JOEL B., 'Conscientious Consciousness', *JOFA Journal*, 5/2 (Summer 2004), 7–8.

WOUK, HERMAN, *Inside, Outside* (Boston: Little, Brown, 1985).

WUTHNOW, ROBERT, and KEVIN CHRISTIANO, 'The Effects of Residential Migration on Church Attendance in the United States', in Robert Wuthnow (ed.), *The Religious Dimension: New Directions in Quantitative Research* (New York: Academic Press, 1979), 257–75.

YAARI, *Emissaries from Erets Yisra'el* [Sheluḥei erets yisra'el] (Jerusalem: Mossad Harav Kook, 1951).

ZAKOVITCH, YAIR, 'Scripture and Israeli Secular Culture', in Benjamin D. Sommer (ed.), *Jewish Concepts of Scripture: A Comparative Introduction* (New York: New York University Press, 2012), 299–316.

—— 'The End of the Century of the Bible' (Heb.), in Israel Bartal (ed.), *The Full Cart: One Hundred and Twenty Years of Israeli Culture* [Ha'agalah hamele'ah] (Jerusalem: Magnes Press, 2002), 110–20.

ZALKIN, MORDECHAI, *From Ḥeder to School: Modernization Processes in East European Jewish Education* [El heikhal hahaskalah: tahalikhei modernizatsyah beḥinukh hayehudi bemizraḥ eiropah bame'ah hatesha-esrei] (Tel Aviv: Hakibuts Hame'uhad, 2008).

—— 'Leading Local Rabbi'? *Rabbi and Community in Eastern Europe in the Nineteenth*

Century [Mara d'atra? Rav ukehilah bemizraḥ eiropah bame'ah hatesha-esrei] (Jerusalem: Magnes Press, forthcoming).

—— 'Lithuanian Jewry and the Concept of "East European Jewry"', in ar nas Liekis, Antony Polonsky, and Chaeran Freeze (eds.), *Jews in the Former Grand Duchy of Lithuania since 1772*, Polin: Studies in Polish Jewry 25 (Oxford: Littman Library of Jewish Civilization, 2013), 57–70.

—— *A New Dawn: The Jewish Enlightenment in the Russian Empire—Social Aspects* [Be'alot hashaḥar: hahaskalah hayehudit ba'emperiyah harusit bame'ah hatesha-esrei] (Jerusalem: Magnes Press, 2000).

ZERUBAVEL, YAEL, 'A Secular Return to the Bible? Reflections on Israeli Society, National Memory, and the Politics of the Past', *AJS Perspectives* (Spring 2011), 30–1.

ZOHAR, ZVI, 'Intimacy within Halakhah without a Marriage Ceremony' (Heb.), *Akdamot*, 17 (2006), 11–33.

ZOLA, GARY PHILLIP, *Isaac Harby of Charleston, 1788–1828: Jewish Reformer and Intellectual* (Tuscaloosa: University of Alabama Press, 1994).

ZOLDAN, YEHUDA, 'It Is a Time to Act for God for They Have Violated Your Torah' (Heb.), *Peri ha'arets*, 6 (1983), 9–26.

INDEX

Page numbers in italic refer to tables

Printed and bound by CPI Group (UK) Ltd, Croydon, CR0 4YY

15/05/2024

14502622-0001